For Queen and Country

BYRON FARWELL

ALLEN LANE

ALLEN LANE
Penguin Books Ltd
536 King's Road
London sw10 ouH

First published in the U.S.A. as *Mr. Kipling's Army*
by W. W. Norton & Company 1981
First published in Great Britain 1981
Copyright © Byron Farwell, 1981

ISBN 0 7139 1241 3

Set in Electra

Printed in the United States of America

For Ruth Saxby:
Of mothers-in-law, the best

CONTENTS

ILLUSTRATIONS

NINETEENTH·CENTURY CHANGES
IN THE TITLES OF REGIMENTS OF INFANTRY

This table gives the old, pre-Cardwell numbers of infantry regiments of the line, numbers which give their order of precedence in the army, together with the names used after 1881.

REGT.	NEW TITLE.
1st	The Royal Scots (Lothian Regiment)
2nd	Queen's (Royal West Surrey Regiment)
3rd	The Buffs (East Kent Regiment)
4th	King's Own (Royal Lancaster Regiment)
5th	Northumberland Fusiliers
6th	Royal Warwickshire Regiment
7th	Royal Fusiliers (City of London Regiment)
8th	The King's (Liverpool Regiment)
9th	Norfolk Regiment
10th	Lincolnshire Regiment
11th	Devonshire Regiment
12th	Suffolk Regiment
13th	Prince Albert's (Somersetshire Light Inf.)
14th	Prince of Wales' Own (W. Yorkshire Regt.)
15th	East Yorkshire Regiment
16th	Bedfordshire Regiment
17th	Leicestershire Regiment
18th	Royal Irish Regiment
19th	Princess of Wales' Own (Yorkshire Regt.)
20th	Lancashire Fusiliers
21st	Royal Scots Fusiliers
22nd	Cheshire Regiment
23rd	Royal Welsh Fusiliers
24th	South Wales Borderers
25th	King's Own Borderers
26th	1 Bn. The Cameronians (Scottish Rifles)
27th	1 Bn. Royal Inniskilling Fusiliers
28th	1 Bn. Gloucestershire Regiment
29th	1 Bn. Worcestershire Regiment
30th	1 Bn. East Lancashire Regiment
31st	1 Bn. East Surrey Regiment
32nd	1 Bn. Duke of Cornwall's Light Infantry
33rd	1 Bn. Duke of Wellington's (W. Riding Regt.)
34th	1 Bn. The Border Regiment
35th	1 Bn. Royal Sussex Regiment
36th	2 Bn. Worcestershire Regiment
37th	1 Bn. Hampshire Regiment
38th	1 Bn. South Staffordshire Regiment
39th	1 Bn. Dorsetshire Regiment
40th	1 Bn. Prince of Wales' Volunteers (South Lancashire Regiment)
41st	1 Bn. Welsh Regiment
42nd	1 Bn. The Black Watch (Royal Highlanders)
43rd	1 Bn. Oxfordshire Light Infantry
44th	1 Bn. Essex Regiment
45th	1 Bn. Sherwood Foresters (Derbyshire Regiment)
46th	2 Bn. Duke of Cornwall's Light Infantry
47th	1 Bn. The Loyal North Lancashire Regt.
48th	1 Bn. Northamptonshire Regiment
49th	1 Bn. Princess Charlotte of Wales' (Berkshire Regiment)
50th	1 Bn. Queen's Own (Royal W. Kent Regt.)
51st	1 Bn. King's Own Light Infanty (South Yorkshire Regiment)
52nd	2 Bn. Oxfordshire Light Infantry
53rd	1 Bn. King's (Shropshire Light Infantry)
54th	2 Bn. Dorsetshire Regiment
55th	2 Bn. The Border Regiment
56th	2 Bn. Essex Regiment
57th	1 Bn. Duke of Cambridge's Own (Middlesex Regiment)
58th	2 Bn. Northamptonshire Regiment
59th	2 Bn. East Lancashire Regiment
60th	King's Royal Rifle Corps
61st	2 Bn. Gloucestershire Regiment
62nd	1 Bn. Duke of Edinburgh's (Wiltshire Regiment)
63rd	1 Bn. Manchester Regiment
64th	1 Bn. Prince of Wales' (North Staffordshire Regiment)
65th	1 Bn. York and Lancaster Regiment
66th	2 Bn. Princess Charlotte of Wales' (Berkshire Regiment)
67th	2 Bn. Hampshire Regiment
68th	1 Bn. Durham Light Infantry
69th	2 Bn. Welsh Regiment
70th	2 Bn. East Surrey Regiment
71st	1 Bn. Highland Light Infantry
72nd	1 Bn. Seaforth Highlanders (Ross-shire Buffs, The Duke of Albany's)
73rd	2 Bn. The Black Watch (Royal Highlanders)
74th	2 Bn. Highland Light Infantry
75th	1 Bn. Gordon Highlanders
76th	2 Bn. Duke of Wellington's West Riding Regiment
77th	2 Bn. Duke of Cambridge's Own (Middlesex Regiment)
78th	2 Bn. Seaforth Highlanders (Ross-shire Buffs, The Duke of Albany's)
79th	2 Bn. Queen's Own Cameron Highlanders
80th	2 Bn. South Staffordshire Regiment
81st	2 Bn. Loyal North Lancashire Regiment
82nd	2 Bn. Prince of Wales' Volunteers (South Lancashire Regiment)
83rd	1 Bn. Royal Irish Rifles
84th	2 Bn. York and Lancaster Regiment
85th	2 Bn. King's (Shropshire Light Infantry)
86th	2 Bn. Royal Irish Rifles
87th	1 Bn. Princess Victoria's (Royal Irish Fusiliers)
88th	1 Bn. Connaught Rangers
89th	2 Bn. Princess Victoria's (Royal Irish Fusiliers)
90th	2 Bn. Cameronians (Scottish Rifles)
91st	1 Bn. Princess Louise's (Argyll and Sutherland Highlanders)
92nd	2 Bn. Gordon Highlanders
93rd	2 Bn. Princess Louise's (Argyll and Sutherland Highlanders)
94th	2 Bn. Connaught Rangers
95th	2 Bn. Sherwood Foresters (Derbyshire Regiment)
96th	2 Bn. Manchester Regiment
97th	2 Bn. The Queen's Own (Royal W. Kent Regiment)
98th	2 Bn. Prince of Wales' (North Staffordshire Regiment)
99th	2 Bn. Duke of Edinburgh's (Wiltshire Regiment)
100th	1 Bn. The Prince of Wales' Leinster Regiment (Royal Canadians)
101st	1 Bn. Royal Munster Fusiliers
102nd	1 Bn. Royal Dublin Fusiliers
103rd	2 Bn. Royal Dublin Fusiliers
104th	2 Bn. Royal Munster Fusiliers
105th	2 Bn. The King's Own Light Infantry (South Yorkshire Regiment)
106th	2 Bn. Durham Light Infantry
107th	2 Bn. Royal Sussex Regiment
108th	2 Bn. Royal Inniskilling Fusiliers
109th	2 Bn. The Prince of Wales' Leinster Regiment (Royal Canadians)

FOREWORD

One day in London about ten years ago, I was walking to the Guards Club with a friend, a retired colonel. He was talking to me about a distinguished military writer whom we both knew, and he said, 'He was not a real soldier, you know; he was only in the war'.

I must at once confess that although I have spent seven years as a soldier in two wars, I am not a 'real soldier' either. However, this is a book about real soldiers, professional officers and other ranks, in the British army as it was in the days of Queen Victoria and Edward VII.

This is not a history of the British army, but a look at it as it was in its pre-World War I days, in its day-to-day existence; it is an Upstairs, Downstairs view of a remarkable institution which in the past has been more often remarked upon than studied. J. B. Priestley once spoke of 'this small, odd, rather absurd British Army', and H. D. Arnold-Forster, somewhat unfairly perhaps, referred to it as 'a social institution prepared for every emergency except that of war'. I have here drawn a profile of that army as it existed prior to the Great War of 1914–18: its attitudes, customs, pleasures, way of life; its character and its mannerisms, its opinions and prejudices. In spite of reforms and fashions and technological changes, it remained extraordinarily homologous for an incredibly long time, for generations, in fact, until its last remnants disappeared in mud and blood in Flanders.

11

Occasionally – about every thirty or fifty years – the British army has rumbled, heaved, groaned, and slowly made changes. There have been few as radical as those which took place in the 1960s, when some famous old regiments disappeared, others were amalgamated, and new methods of administration and organization were tried. Even so, the army has not yet accommodated itself to Britain's diminished place in the world: not only do a number of the old regiments still exist, but many of the Victorian customs and attitudes are alive and well. To avoid tiresome repetition of sentences containing 'was and is' or 'did and still do', I have confined myself, except in a few instances, to describing the army's habits and ways in the past tense. The story of the peculiarities of the present British army is left to others.

It was my original intention to focus on the army as it existed about 1900, or at least the years bracketed by Cardwell's reforms in the 1870s and early 1880s and the virtual destruction of the old regiments at the first battle of Ypres; in other words, the time when Rudyard Kipling (1865–1936) wrote his stories and poems about the army and its soldiers. But customs, traditions, habits, the heavy weight of history, played such an important part in the life of the regiments that much of the behaviour of officers and their men would not be understandable without going further back.

The names and numbers of regiments changed over the years, frequently half a dozen times. Some of these changes were minor – the official name of the Royal Scots from July 1881 until July of the following year was 'The Lothian Regiment (Royal Scots)', and then from 1882 until 1920 'The Royal Scots (The Lothian Regiment)' – but others were more radical: the regiment prior to 1881 officially called 'The 14th (Buckinghamshire – The Prince of Wales Own) Regiment of Foot' became 'The Prince of Wales Own (West Yorkshire Regiment)', but was in practice called (as it later became officially) 'The West Yorkshire Regiment', or, colloquially, 'The West Yorks'. To reduce the confusion, I have, usually, when making reference to a regiment before 1881, adopted the common usage – e.g., 14th Foot – and followed it with the name generally used after 1881 in parenthesis.

It was common for British soldiers to refer to their battalion as a regiment (as it indeed was in one-battalion regiments) and to refer to the battalion's commanding officer (usually a lieutenant-colonel) as colonel of the regiment. The word 'corps' is sometimes loosely used to mean a unit of almost any size larger than a company. It is also used to designate an entire arm or service (as Corps of Royal Engineers); but in the strict organizational sense, an army corps consists of two or more divisions plus some supporting units.

It is often said that an army is a reflection of the state it serves. There is some truth in this; it is equally true that a nation sometimes becomes a reflection of its army. This was noticeably so in Sparta and Prussia. Less obvious perhaps was the relationship between the British army and the Empire. The army was designed for and was the product of imperial needs, needs which it had itself largely created. Unlike the French, German and Russian armies, the British land forces after Waterloo were not expected to fight on the European continent. The British army, therefore, was not much influenced by other armies and was more inclined to cling to the past and to develop its own peculiarities. Emory Upton, the American soldier, writing in the 1870s, commented: 'The adherence of England to a military system, inherited from the last century, can only be explained by her insular position, and the security from invasion afforded by a powerful navy'.

The army of which Kipling wrote lived by a system now despised, adhered to a set of attitudes and beliefs now mocked, and entertained a view of the world now thought to be amusing. Yet, one wonders if a second look is not called for in this age of guided missiles and superior electronics, where the most technologically superior army the world has ever known has been put to flight by Asian peasants in black pyjamas. The British regimental system was eccentric and, viewed through accountants' eyes, expensive; but it did create that spirit in its combatant services which won wars. The attitudes, beliefs and prejudices of the officer corps appear arrogant and ridiculous; yet these British officers were among the bravest of the brave, and they won wars.

FOR QUEEN AND COUNTRY

The Duke of Cambridge addressing the 42nd Highlanders (*Photo: Graham Brandon*)

A PECULIAR
LITTLE ARMY

It was a peculiar army, the Victorian–Edwardian army about which Rudyard Kipling wrote so many of his stories and poems; indeed, it was perhaps the most peculiar in modern history. It was not, however, without its charm: it tolerated its eccentrics and regarded its own eccentricities as normal. Not the least of its oddities was that no one commanded it: that is, no one person controlled the land forces which created and maintained the British Empire.

There existed, in addition to the regular army, the Indian army, which was in fact until 1895 three armies; for each of the three presidencies – Madras, Bombay and Bengal – had its own, with its own commander-in-chief. Before the Indian Mutiny of 1857–9 they were the private property of a chartered commercial company, the Honourable East India Company, and were not part of the forces of the Crown. Even after the Mutiny, the Indian army was financed by the Indian taxpayers, and its size and composition were determined by the Government of India; Parliament had no say, and it was not subject to the Annual Mutiny Act, that peculiar Act of Parliament, renewed yearly, which, among other things, provides legal justification for the existence of a standing army. In addition to the Indian army, there was also what was called 'the army in India', which consisted of regiments of regulars that were, in effect, rented from the Crown by the East India Company or the Government of India.

In a building that was once the Horse Guards barracks in London there presided another commander-in-chief, but his authority was limited. He was in theory under the Secretary of State for War, but in practice, until near the end of the nineteenth century, he reported to no one. He did not control the soldiers scattered about in the colonies, for these came under the Colonial Office. He did not command the Yeomanry or Militia, for these were the responsibility of the Home Office, which also clothed all the troops. He did not command the artillery or the engineers, for these, as well as all fortifications, came under the Master General of the Ordnance, a separate entity who reported, in effect, to no one. He had nothing to say about transport or supply, for these functions were the responsibility of the Treasury and did not come into the army's hands until 1888.

Prior to the Crimean War (1854–6) the army was administered by a total of thirteen departments, and any cooperation between them was largely dependent upon such customs and traditions as had developed over the years and upon the whims and caprices of the departmental heads and their clerks. In the sixty years between the Crimean War and the First World War there was a gradual drift towards centralization of command, but with the exception of a couple of convulsions, reform came with glacial slowness.

By 1890 every other European nation had formed a general staff. But not Britain. Henry Campbell-Bannerman, when Secretary for War in the 1890s, declared that a general staff would be 'absolutely mischievous and dangerous to the state'. There had never been much planning. In 1856 Lord Panmure, Secretary for War, said that 'the system by which an army should be provisioned, moved, and brought to act in the field and trenches is non-existent'. In spite of numerous commissions looking into army affairs and the attempts at reform, this situation changed little. Thirty-six years later, in 1892, Ralph Knox, Permanent Under-Secretary of State for War, said: 'No plan that I know of has been worked out with a view to meeting any emergency'. In 1904, only ten years before the First World War, the Duke of Connaught, the army's first inspector-general, pronounced in his first report that 'the British Army at home is far from being ready and efficient for war'. In the Victorian era generals sent to fight a campaign usually selected their staffs from among pleasant aristocrats: 'The young bloods of Mayfair were chosen because of their lineage, cash and ability to ride a hunter at a five-barred gate'. Not until 1906 was the British army given the support and direction of a general staff. Even then, as Lord Chandos once pointed out, strategy had to be devised while keeping clearly in mind the idiosyncrasies of the British character and of the British army.

There was almost no cooperation between army and navy. The War Office and the Admiralty each seemed to pretend that the other did not exist. A commission presided over by Lord Hartington in 1899 discovered that admirals and generals never corresponded with each other and that all official communication was carried on by two civilians: the Under-Secretary for War and the Secretary to the Admiralty. It was also stated in evidence that 'no combined plan of operation for the defence of the Empire in any given contingency has ever been worked out by the two departments'. It did seem extraordinarily difficult for the army and navy to agree on anything. When the War Office, which was responsible for minefields used for the defence of ports, asked the navy to provide vessels for their protection, the Admiralty refused. The file on this subject passed back and forth between Pall Mall and Whitehall for seven years: the Admiralty never did agree.

General Sir William Butler, referring to the period about 1880, remarked: 'An army, the officers of which are dressed for the benefit of the London tailor, and the soldiers of which are administered largely in the interests of the War Office clerk, must of necessity afford situations replete with humour'. Amidst the tangled lines of control there was red tape in abundance and it certainly required a sense of humour to deal with some of it.

Colonel Henry Hallam Parr was once approached by an officer who said he was in need of proof of his existence in order to draw his pay. Parr duly wrote a certificate, dated it and signed it. But nothing so simple would do. The officer explained that he had already proved that he was alive in the current month; he needed to prove that he had been alive the previous month. Would Parr back-date the certificate?

General Evelyn Wood once had a similar problem. A lengthy correspondence over several months proved futile. At length he appealed directly to the Secretary of State for War: 'As a personal request, could you persuade your Department that I was alive from the 22nd December last to the 14th February, which has hitherto been denied, and I have been refused Half-Pay for that period'.

An artillery officer in the Crimea received a notice from England stating that Gunner Brown, whom he had reported dead, had appeared alive and well at Woolwich. An explanation was demanded. The officer replied that he had known Gunner Brown well, had visited him in hospital, and had attended his funeral. He was not, he added, responsible for his subsequent movements.

Colonel (later General) F.I. Maxse once wrote: 'During the years which intervened between Waterloo and Colenso [i.e. from 1815 to 1900], we perfected in peace a system of minimising a commander's power and, by means of elaborate regulations, promoted the art of evading personal censure into an exact science'.

Throughout the Victorian era there was a continuing debate as to whether the army belonged to the Crown or to Parliament. Firmly believing that the army was the Queen's, the Duke of Cambridge, the Queen's cousin and for nearly forty years the commander-in-chief at the Horse Guards, resented all interference from politicians. Firm believers that the army was an instrument of Parliament were the succession of Secretaries of State for War who struggled to bring it under their control. The politicians won in the end, but the arguments over the degree of civilian interference or influence on army affairs continued.

Prior to 1906 the Secretary of State for War had his office in Pall Mall in what is today the Royal Automobile Club, but the War Office over which he presided consisted of some eight hundred officials and clerks scattered about in three hundred rooms in nineteen different houses. Florence Nightingale described it as 'a very slow office, an enormously expensive office, a not very efficient office, and one in which the minister's intentions can be negatived by all his sub-departments and those of each of the sub-departments by every other'.

The primary hold of the War Office on the army was control of the purse strings – not until 1895 did the army have even a voice in financial decisions affecting it – and often enough economy replaced efficiency. Some of the cheeseparing was absurd. For example, prior to 1896 the night urinals in barracks were in total darkness after 'lights out'; to provide lights, said the accountant-general, would cost £3,000 for the initial outlay and £200 a year to maintain. One result, however, was that the army was extremely cost-conscious, as every recruit quickly learned. At the battle of Abu Klea in the Sudan, when Dervishes broke a British square, a gunner broke a rammer over the head of a Dervish who was about to spear him. When called before one of his officers the next day, he was sure he knew the reason and hastened to apologize: 'Please, sir, I'm sorry I broke the rammer, but I never thought the nigger's head could be so hard. I'll pay for the rammer'.

In 1887 a select committee of the House of Commons found: 'In one case an inquiry as to the expenditure of 4s. 7d. bore eight signatures upon it, and was not fully disposed of till six months after the payment was made'. It was said that the army was run on a system characterized by extravagance controlled by stinginess. There was little planning for what was going to be done, tight financial control over what was being done, and very little thought given to what ought to be done. As late as 1903 St John Broderick, Secretary for War, wrote to A.J. Balfour, the Prime Minister, to express his puzzlement: 'I do not find that any definite instruction exists as to what is the exact purpose for which the army exists, and what duties it is supposed to perform'.

Prior to the Anglo-Boer War (1899–1902) the army was not divided into field armies, corps, divisions, or even brigades on a regular basis. The 'division' at Aldershot was not a real division and consisted merely of the troops who happened to be stationed there for training at any one time; the Brigade of Guards was not intended to be a tactical unit and never fought as such. The British army was basically a mere collection of regiments which were assembled in any order a general saw fit when the need arose. In the summer of 1909 a combat division was put together as an experiment and the required men, horses and equipment had to be gathered up from scattered units around the country. This was the first time that anyone had ever seen in Britain a division at war strength – and it was the last until just before the First World War.

In the 1890s there was agitation for the formation of at least an army corps which would be available in case of need for a major war, but Henry Campbell-Bannerman said he did not feel that such a unit was suited to any purpose likely to be required by Britain: 'What is an army corps in this country? Sir, the expression is like the great word Mesopotamia – it is a blessed word. It deludes the earnest and it imposes on the simple'.

The British army was a small army, and though its numbers fluctuated wildly over the years, it remained small in comparison with those of other European powers. Most of it served most of the time outside Britain. In 1854 it had only 140,000 officers and men; a quarter of a century later, in spite of the steady growth of the Empire, it numbered only 186,000. By comparison, Prussia mustered 888,000 men for its war with France in 1870, Russia in the 1870s had 780,000 men under arms, and even Italy had 629,000 soldiers. In the 1860s Bismarck is reported to have said that if the British army ever landed on the Prussian coast, he would send a policeman to arrest it.

By the time Queen Victoria assumed the throne in 1837 many of her regiments were already mossy with ancient custom, and they continued to get mossier. It was with heavy loads of tradition that in 1914 the gallant little British Expeditionary Force, composed entirely of regular army battalions, sailed for France for a trial of arms with the massive, highly professional German army.

THE REGIMENTAL SYSTEM

Keep your hands off the regiment, ye iconoclastic civilian officials who meddle and muddle in Army matters.

Lord Wolseley

Regiments are not like houses. They cannot be pulled down and altered structurally to suit the convenience of the occupier or the caprice of the owner. They are more like plants: they grow slowly if they are to grow strong . . . and if they are blighted or transplanted they are apt to wither.

Winston Churchill (1904)

We must be very careful what we do with British infantry. Their fighting spirit is based largely on morale and regimental esprit de corps. On no account must anyone tamper with this.

Lord Montgomery of Alamein

Military historians have quibbled over the birthdate of the British army, but probably St Valentine's Day in 1661 would be as good as any. Only a few months earlier, King Charles II had returned to England to claim the throne of his beheaded father. Parliament had decided gradually to disband the 65,000-man army of the Commonwealth, and General George Monck, who had served Cromwell but who now, knighted and made Master of the Horse, was loyal to the King, was in the process of paying off and discharging the troops when he was forced to use some of them to put down a small rebellion. Although this event demonstrated the need to retain a permanent armed force, the Act of Parliament had to be obeyed. However, as often happened in the British army, legal niceties were overcome with a ceremony, and on 14 February 1661 Monck's own regiment of foot formed up on Tower Hill in London and on command laid down their arms forever as Commonwealth soldiers; they paused, then, on order, solemnly picked them up again as soldiers of the King. This regiment, soon to be named the Coldstream Guards, was to be the sole survivor of Cromwell's army. After more than three hundred years of existence, it can be seen today, dressed in its Victorian uniforms, guarding the Queen.

Although the motto of the Coldstream Guards is *Nulli Secundus*, the regiment is, in fact, second in order of precedence in the infantry, first place going to a regiment which the King had formed in 1656 for his protection. Known originally as His Majesty's Regiment of Guards, it has been called since 1815 the Grenadier Guards. The Scots Guards – or Scots Fusilier Guards, as they were called prior to 1877 – was even older than the other Foot Guards regiments, though ranking third in order of precedence. It was originally composed of mercenaries in the service of King Gustavus Adolphus of Sweden (from 1625 until 1633); then from 1633 it served Louis XIV in France. Louis loaned it to Charles for a time, and after that it was shipped back to France before eventually finding its permanent place on the British establishment.

The senior regiments of the British army, however, are the 1st and 2nd Life Guards, cavalry regiments descended from the three troops which Charles II brought with him from France. By far the oldest on the regular establishment (although it did not become a British regiment of the line until 1665) was the 3rd Regiment of Foot – the Buffs (Royal East Kent Regiment). Raised by London Guilds in 1572, it became one of three English and four Scots regiments to serve the Dutch Republic, and prior to 1708 it was known as the Holland Regiment.

As the regiments, one by one, took their place in the order of battle of the British army, they began immediately to take on those characteristics and peculiarities which were to make the Victorian–Edwardian army so distinctive and to create the extraordinary regimental spirit which dominated that army and stamped it with its unique character.

The core, the heart, the very essence of the British army was the regimental system as it existed in the cavalry and infantry. For officers, the regiment was a private, exclusive club, a fitting home for gentlemen. For officers and other ranks alike it was a clan, a hierarchical extended family, offering a meaningful place in life. Whatever the rest of the world might think, a man could here earn and learn self-respect, could take pride in himself, his regiment and its traditions. And he could look forward to adding his mite to its glory. Every one was different – unique, in fact – and a man did not so much join the army as join a particular regiment, which he generally stayed with throughout his entire career; after the abolition of the purchase system, this was often true of officers as well. Although an officer could request a transfer, he seldom did so. He might spend most of his military career on the staff or at other duties outside his regiment, yet remain on its roll, wear its uniform, and consider himself a part of it until he was promoted to general officer rank, retired or died.

A regiment was more a community than a bureaucratic sub-unit and, like a community, it had no fixed size. Although most infantry regiments consisted of only one or two battalions, they were capable of expanding. During the First World War the Hampshire Regiment raised thirty-six battalions, the Middlsex Regiment forty-five, of which forty were operational. The Northumberland Fusiliers had the most: fifty-two. A regiment could indeed include an entire arm, for all the artillery was encompassed in the Royal Regiment of Artillery. Names could be deceptive, for they were seldom descriptive. The King's Royal Rifle Corps was not a corps but a regiment; the Rifle Brigade was not a brigade, for it too was a regiment; and the ancient and peculiar Honourable Artillery Company (founded in 1537), although not on the regular establishment, was indeed honourable (that title was officially conferred upon it by Queen Victoria in 1860), but it was more than a company and not always artillery, for in the First World War it fielded two battalions of infantry as well as five batteries of artillery.

The size of a battalion also varied, but generally in the Victorian era infantry battalions consisted of between 700 and 1000 men divided into eight to twelve companies. Cavalry regiments were smaller, with about 300 to 500 of all ranks. A typical two-battalion regiment of infantry in 1900 would be commanded by two lieutenant-colonels and would include seven or eight majors, eighteen to twenty captains, and some thirty to thirty-five subalterns. A typical cavalry regiment of the same era would be commanded by a lieutenant-colonel and have four majors, eight captains and thirteen to sixteen subalterns.

Sons often followed fathers and grandfathers into the same regiment. Members of the Adye family served in uninterrupted succession from 1757 until World War II in the Royal Regiment of Artillery. Amos Norcott commanded a battalion of the Rifle Brigade at Waterloo; his son, William, commanded one in the Crimea; his grandson, C.H.B. Norcott, served in the regiment during the Anglo-Boer War; and his great-grandson, H.B. Norcott, fought with it in the First World War. In the Rifle Brigade (where the uniform was green) it was not only officers who were 'born in a green jacket'. William Peachy enlisted in the 1st Battalion in 1813 at the age of fiteen; his son, David, at the age of thirteen; David's son in 1864, aged twelve; and William, great-grandson of the original William, in 1892 at the age of fifteen. In all, the Peachys contributed more than a century of service to the same regiment.

In the 93rd (Sutherland) Highlanders there were at one time no more than a dozen family names in the entire regiment, and nearly all came from Sutherland or Caithness. It retained its family atmosphere together with the customs and beliefs of its place of origin. When it was forced to merge with the 91st (Argyll) Highlanders the marriage was not a happy one. Few of the Argylls were Highlanders and most were not even Scots: a count made in the 1860s revealed that the battalion consisted of 241 Scotsmen, 323 Irishmen, and 501 Englishmen. Each battalion continued to call itself by its old name or number even into the First World War.

Camaraderie extended beyond those a man lived with, beyond the present, beyond the grave, deep into the past. A soldier felt a kinship with all those who, like him, had served in the regiment. He was proud of himself, of his companions in uniform, and of those who had fought and won the battle honours that graced his regiment's colours or drums. Lord Wolseley, speaking of the 'uneducated private soldier', once rhapsodized:

> What can be finer than his love for his regiment, his devotion to its reputation, and his determination to protect its honour! To him 'The Regiment' is mother, sister and mistress. That its fame may live and flourish

he is prepared to risk all and die without a murmur. What earthly cause calls forth greater enthusiasm? It is a high, an admirable phase of patriotism, for, to the soldier, his regiment is his country.

Somewhat more prosaically, Ian Hamilton said: 'One way or another the roots of tradition strike him deep. The soldier feels the Regiment solid about him'. Officers developed a similar affection. When Captain Frederick Lawrence, of the Rifle Brigade, died aged thirty-four on a punitive expedition in East Africa, it was discovered that he had left the reversion of his entire estate (£77,267) in trust to his regiment for the welfare of all its members and for the encouragement of 'manly sports'.

Names and numbers were confusing, and not simply because they changed from time to time over the centuries. For example, the 2nd Life Guards was a regiment, but the 2nd Sherwood Foresters was the 2nd Battalion of the Sherwood Foresters Regiment, for there were two regiments of Life Guards (the only two in the army with the same name) and only one of Sherwood Foresters.

Night in the Guard Room at Aldershot, 1872 (*Photo: Illustrated London News Picture Library*)

In the late Victorian era – and indeed until 1922 – there were thirty-one regiments of cavalry. The two regiments of Life Guards and the Royal Horse Guards constituted the Household Cavalry; the Royal Horse Guards, usually called The Blues, was the only one without a number of any kind attached to it. Next in order of precedence were the Dragoon Guards, numbered from one to seven; then came twenty-one regiments of dragoons, lancers and hussars, numbered without regard to whether they carried sabres, carbines or lances. Thus, the 1st Dragoon Guards was different from the 1st Dragoons. Later, when regiments were merged, both numbers were kept, so that the 17th Lancers and the 21st Lancers became the 17/21st Lancers. Slashed numbers for infantry battalions in the First World War did not, however, indicate mergers but Territorial units attached to regular regiments.

It should perhaps be explained that dragoons were originally mounted infantry. Hussars began as light cavalry, but by the end of the century they were distinguished from other cavalry only by their romantic costumes. It should also be noted that not all Highland regiments contained Highlanders, nor all Welsh regiments Welshman. In 1903 it was found that 700 out of 1000 Royal Welch Fusiliers were cockneys and midlanders. The Cameron Highlanders was noted for the number of Englishmen in its ranks. In 1899 a Gordon Highlander was seen praying in a London synagogue.

The infantry consisted of the Foot Guards and the regiments of the line. Before the Anglo-Boer War there were three regiments of guards infantry: Grenadier Guards, Coldstream Guards and Scots Guards. The Irish Guards were formed in 1900, the Welsh Guards in 1915. None of the Foot Guards had numbers. The regiments of the line were numbered from 1 to (eventually) 109, plus the unnumbered Rifle Brigade and the West India Regiment. By General Order No. 70 of 1881 numbers were abolished, but some regiments were inordinately fond of them and continued to use them long afterwards; others did not use their numbers even when they were part of their official titles. The 3rd Foot, for example, was generally known as the Buffs; similarly, the 19th Foot was always called the Green Howards, although this did not become its official name until 1921. The King's Royal Rifle Corps, however, liked both its name and its number and was often called the 60th Rifles. When two regiments merged, the officers and men usually re-

ferred to their battalion by its old regimental number for years afterwards.

Perhaps mention should be made of the Royal Marines, which were
divided into Royal Marine Artillery and Royal Marine Light Infantry.
Although the Marines belonged to the Admiralty and never had a number, they had a place on the Army List, and when on parade with army
units took precedence after the 49th Regiment.

By the last half of Victoria's reign names such as rifles, fusiliers,
grenadiers and light infantry no longer had any real meaning. Originally, of course, rifle regiments were armed with rifles when the rest of
the army had muskets. Fusiliers were originally armed with a fusil, a
light flintlock musket, and were used to guard artillery. These names
were retained only because of the strong historical traditions that prevailed. Grenadiers, of course, were originally soldiers who threw grenades
and thus tended to be long in arm, big, tall men. Long after grenades
went out of fashion, there continued to be tall grenadiers. Battalions
usually had 'flank companies', one, consisting of the tallest men, called
the grenadier company, the other, consisting of short, nimble men,
useful as skirmishers, called the light company. By the First World War
the term 'grenadier' had so changed its meaning that when grenade
throwers returned to the battlefield there were objections to calling
them grenadiers and they became known as 'bombers'.

The Rifle Brigade was once the 95th Foot, but after 1815 its order of
procedence was last and it always stood on parade to the left of all other
infantry regiments. When there were a hundred regiments, its place was
the 101st; when a new regiment was added, it moved to remain at the
end. One might imagine that at one time it had disgraced itself and so
was doomed forever to be last, but such was not the case. The regiment
was taken 'out of the line' as a reward for its gallant conduct at the battle
of Waterloo.

In the Royal Regiments of Artillery some batteries were numbered
and some were lettered. Until the late Victorian era there were no for-
mations of artillery larger than a battery (usually six guns); then brigades
of three batteries each under lieutenant-colonels were formed. The batteries of Horse Artillery — those designed to keep pace with and fight beside the cavalry — bore letter designations, e.g., 'U' Battery; batteries of
Field Artillery, Garrison Artillery and Mountain Artillery were num-

bered. A curiosity in the matter of lettering is that although there was a 'J' Battery in the Royal Horse Artillery, there was never a 'J' Company in the infantry, the sequence jumping from 'I' to 'K'. Although several theories have been put forward, no one really knows why, nor does anyone know why the American army adopted the same custom.

Prior to about 1750, regiments were known by the names of their colonels, for the regiments were, in effect, owned by the colonels, who raised or bought them and were given a lump sum to house, feed and clothe their men. At one time in the eighteenth century, however, there were two infantry regiments commanded by men named Howard. The one commanded by the Hon. Charles Howard, second son of the Earl of Carlisle, had green facings and became known as the Green Howards, a name that stuck; the other, under George Howard, had buff facings, but was known not as the Buff Howards but simply as The Buffs.* The Cameronians were named after a religious reformer, Richard Cameron, a seventeenth-century Scottish Covenanter who founded the Reformed Presbyterians. Cameron was killed leading a revolt against Charles II, but his fighting followers were amnestied and formed the nucleus of the regiment, raised in Lanarkshire on 14 May 1689, 'all in a day, and without tuck of drum, nor expense of levy money'. In 1881 The Cameronian Regiment was merged with the 90th Perthshire Light Infantry, the two becoming respectively the 1st and 2nd battalions of what was officially The Cameronians (Scottish Rifles), but only the 1st battalion called itself The Cameronians; the 2nd was known as the 2nd Scottish Rifles. There was always tension between the two and a rivalry that was sometimes quite bitter. The 1st Battalion retained its religious tone, and at the turn of the century, when regiments began to publish their own magazines, that of The Cameronians was called *The Covenanter*.

In addition to their formal or unofficial names, every regiment had one or more nicknames. Some of these were borne with pride; others were fighting words. The 17th Lancers were called the Death or Glory Boys because their cap badge was a death's head with the words 'or glory' below it. The Worcestershire Regiment was called The Vein Openers, a name they earned when, as the 29th Foot, they shot four American colonists in an affair that has come down in American history

---

*Facings were the cuffs, lapels or collars, and the turnback of the coat. A regiment's colours were of the same colour as its facings.

as the Boston Massacre. Soldiers of the Northamptonshire Regiment were known as the Steelbacks because of their pride in being able to bear up under severe floggings. The name stuck even after floggings were abolished. The Royal Scots, who prided themselves on their ancient origins, were called Pontius Pilate's Bodyguard. The King's Royal Rifle Corps, an expensive and exclusive regiment, was sometimes referred to as the King's Rich Rude Rifles; during the First World War, because the cap badge was in the shape of a Maltese cross, it became derisively known as The Kaiser's Own. The 21st Lancers had seen no action prior to the battle of Omdurman in 1898, so it was said of them that their motto was 'Thou Shalt Not Kill'.

The 10th Hussars was considered one of the most expensive regiments in the army. In 1900, when the pound sterling was worth considerably more than it is today, it was believed that it was barely possible for one of its officers to live on £500 a year in addition to his pay; the average private income was considerably more. Officers in the 10th Hussars were not only rich; they were also thought to be dandified. Beau Brummell once served with them, but resigned because of a posting to Manchester, for, he said, he was 'not prepared to go on foreign service'. Officers in the regiment did not dance, perhaps because it was too difficult in their tight-fitting uniforms, and it became known as the Don't Dance Tenth.

The King's Royal Rifle Corps and the 10th Hussars were not the only expensive regiments: all cavalry regiments were, at least when stationed in Britain, where each officer was expected to provide himself with at least one charger and usually two hunters and three polo ponies as well. Infantry regiments too could be expensive, particularly the Household Brigade, where it was possible (barely) to live on an extra allowance of £300 per year. The Coldstream Guards considered £400 a year of private income to be the minimum for an ensign on joining. The entrance fee for the Guards Club was thirty guineas and the annual subscription £11. As young guardsmen could hardly be expected to content themselves with only one club, most joined the Bachelor's or White's plus one of the service clubs. Those who played tennis and cricket joined Prince's, and most belonged to one or more of the principal racing clubs – Sandown Park, Hurlingham, or Ranelagh. There were, however, some line regiments that lived more frugally; these were known as 'younger sons' regiments'.

REGIMENTAL CUSTOMS, CHARACTER AND POSSESSIONS

Each regiment had its own customs and traditions, usually based upon some event in its past. Battles long forgotten and neglected in history texts were remembered by every soldier of the regiments that took part in them. It was a tradition to preserve traditions. Some 'history' was more in the nature of folk tales, but it was colourful. It was said and believed, for example, that the Gordon Highlanders had been raised in 1794 when Jean, beautiful wife of the 4th Duke of Gordon, donned a regimental jacket and Highland bonnet and rode around the estate and to county fairs offering a gold guinea and a kiss to every man who enlisted.

Many of the distinctions and peculiarities grew up without official sanction. Though the War Office tried hard to weed them out, they persisted, often receiving official approval after many years. For example, in 1856 all infantry regiments changed the sash from the waist to the shoulder: over the left shoulder for officers; over the right for sergeants. But in the Somerset Light Infantry the sergeants wore their sashes over the left shoulder to commemorate the battle of Culloden in 1746 when all the officers were struck down and the regiment was commanded by its sergeants.

The band of the Leicestershire Regiment always played 'Wolfe's Lament' before the national anthem, and the officers in the regiment (as also in the Gordons, Norfolks, and Somerset Light Infantry, all of which had fought under Wolfe in Canada) continued to wear a black line in their gold lace in mourning for his death.

Throughout the British army, Last Post was always sounded at ten o'clock at night – except in the 11th Hussars. Lord Cardigan was not a popular officer during his lifetime, but he was remembered in his own regiment, the 11th Hussars, for Last Post was sounded at 9.50 p.m., the time of his death.

In the Gloucester Regiment the officers and men wore badges on both the front and back of their caps, and on 21 March each year they celebrate Back Badge Day, for it was on this day in 1801 that, during the battle of Alexandria in Egypt, the regiment was forced to beat off simultaneous attacks from the French on their front and rear.

The Cameronians, when they went to church, posted double sentries at the four corners of the church. This custom went back to the seventeenth century, when Scottish Covenanters were proscribed but held secret prayer meetings in fields and posted sentinels to guard against surprise attacks.

Regiments had their own individualities and personalities. Men of the Suffolk Regiment were known as 'kindly, reliable men who never gave up'. The Royal Norfolk Regiment was renowned for 'steadiness and reliability in difficult situations'. The Cameronians (not to be confused with the Cameron Highlanders) were regarded as puritanical, but perhaps the most religious were the Sutherland Highlanders, which constituted a movable parish, complete with its own minister and elders chosen from the ranks (two sergeants, two corporals and two privates), and was believed to be the only regiment with its own regular service of communion plate. It was, incidentally, the stand of the Sutherland Highlanders at Balaclava which William Howard Russell, the first war correspondent in the modern sense, described as 'that thin red streak tipped with steel', a phrase which came to be widely misquoted as 'the thin red line'. The band of the 12th Lancers bore witness to its piety by playing hymns every evening at tattoo. The band of the 10th Hussars also played hymns every evening. In contrast, the soldiers of the Norfolk Regiment had the nickname of the Holy Boys, not because of their devoutness, but because once, when about to leave for duty overseas, each soldier was given a Bible, every one of which was sold for beer.

Every regiment was proud of being different, but no one took such delight in what it called its 'separateness' as did the Rifle Brigade. It was jealous of its distinction of being 'out of the line' and having no number or fixed place (except last) in the order of precedence. Like its sister regiment, the King's Royal Rifle Corps, it dressed in green and wore black buttons, and spoke with disdain of red-coated regiments as 'the red army'. Certain commands, such as 'Attention' and 'Slope Arms', were never used. Indeed, the rifle was never carried on the shoulder but always at the trail. Bayonets were called swords; privates were called riflemen; Rifle Brigade officers prided themselves on never using slang, and junior officers never said 'sir' to their seniors. The regiment even had a marching pace that was faster than other line regiments, which made it unpopular at parades. A very close fraternal feeling developed: in an era when most officers paid little attention to the concerns of the soldiers under them and some even regarded other ranks as 'a damned nuisance', those of the Rifle Brigade prided themselves on their close relationship with their men.

The Royal Welch Fusiliers is perhaps one of the best known regiments because Robert Graves and Siegfried Sassoon both served in it during the First World War and both wrote of their experiences. Members of this regiment took pleasure in the peculiar spelling of Welsh as 'Welch', although no one seemed to know the reason. (The change did not become official until 1920; nevertheless, new officers were sent off parade if their buttons read 'Welsh'.) Robert Graves felt that the spelling 'disassociated us from the modern North Wales of chapels, liberalism, the dairy and drapery business, Lloyd George, and the tourist trade'. A distinctive part of the uniform of every Welch Fusilier, which he continued to wear even with khaki, was the 'flash'. This consisted of five black ribbons, each exactly two inches wide and seven and a half inches long, sewn to the back of the collar. When soldiers wore pigtails, the queue was tallowed and then powdered; to prevent it from staining the coat, a leather patch was worn on the back collar, and the flash was said to be a stylized reminder of that patch. But pigtails disappeared from the British army in 1808, and why anyone wanted to be reminded of them is a mystery.

In the nineteenth century the shamrock was considered a symbol of sedition and forbidden in the army, but Queen Victoria was so proud of the performance of her Irish soldiers in the Anglo-Boer War that she gave all Irish regiments the privilege of wearing the shamrock on St

Patrick's Day, just as Welsh regiments wore a leek on St David's Day.

Sometimes the desire of regiments to be different became absurd. Between 1854 and 1882 the blade length of swords in the 1st Life Guards was 38¼ inches – just ¼ inch longer than that in the 2nd Life Guards and the Royal Horse Guards. Although there were four regiments with facings and colours officially described as 'grass green', the Worcestershire Regiment used a unique shade and prided itself on having 'the brightest green worn by any regiment in the Army'. Equally, the green of the Northumberland Fusiliers, called 'Gosling Green', was specially made for the regiment by one particular firm for generations.

The gallant South Wales Borderers acquired a well-earned share of battle honours and Victoria Crosses, but one must conclude that it was an unlucky regiment. In 1741, when it was the 24th Foot, it lost 800 out of 1000 of its men in the descent on Cartagena. In 1849, during the Second Sikh War, it performed the infantry equivalent of the charge of the Light Brigade at Balaclava. Ordered not to fire its muskets, the regiment charged the Sikh guns at Chilianwala with bare bayonets and was nearly wiped out. General Charles Napier said that 'Their conduct has never been surpassed by British soldiers on the field of battle', but no one wrote a poem about the event. At Isandhlwana, during the Zulu War of 1879, a battalion was totally destroyed except for one company left behind at Rorke's Drift, and it was decimated. On 3 December 1917 the 2nd Battalion of the regiment, which had been nearly 1000 strong, stumbled out of the trenches with a strength of two officers, a doctor and seventy-three other ranks.

Every regiment had its own special day that it celebrated with ceremony once a year. If the unit was in England, it was a time of reunion for old soldiers and a time to remember old wars and past victories. On 1 March (St David's Day) any officer in the Welch Fusiliers who had never eaten a leek was required to do so – and with some ceremony in the mess. Standing with one foot on his chair and the other on the table, he was to munch a leek while behind him drums rolled and the regimental goat (of whom, more later) stood as a witness. On 7 April the Somerset Light Infantry celebrated Jellalabad Day. Historians make slight mention of Jellalabad and it is hard to find on a map, but for more than a hundred years its story was told and retold in the Somerset Light Infantry, which even added the name to its cap badge. In 1842, during the First Afghan War, in this walled town in eastern Afghanistan, just west of the Khyber Pass, the regiment (then the 13th Foot), together with the 35th Bengal Native Infantry, survived an earthquake and several attacks by the Afghans. In spite of its hardships, it fared better than the rest of the British army. Of 17,000 who started out from Kabul for Jellalabad, only one man, Dr William Brydon, reached there in safety.

Each year on 20 October the Gordon Highlanders celebrated Dargai Day, a day in 1897 during the Tirah campaign on the North-West Frontier when the Gordons made a notable charge. The Pathans were in a strong position on top of a cliff. Other British units had tried and failed to dislodge them; the dead and wounded of the Derbyshires and Dorsets dotted the glacis that led to the foot of the cliff. Then the Gordons were ordered to try. Lieutenant-Colonel Henry Mathias called together his officers and his pipe-major and told them: 'The general says this hill must be taken at all costs. The Gordon Highlanders will take it'. With a flourish the pipe-major threw his plaid and drones over his shoulder and began that peculiar music that stirs the blood of Scots. Kilted Highlanders dashed up the slope and stormed the heights of Dargai. It was a day ever remembered.

The regimental day of the Green Howards was 20 September, the anniversary of the battle of the Alma in the Crimean War. Annually on this day there was a ceremonial parade which included a trooping of the drums of the Vladimir and Minsk regiments which had been captured at the Alma.

Every regiment had its mementos of war, many of them captured flags and drums; the eagle standards which Napoleon presented to each of his regiments were eagerly sought prizes in Britain's battles with the French, and they made fine trophies. A Sergeant Masterton of the 87th Foot (1st Royal Irish Fusiliers) killed the ensign carrying an eagle standard at the battle of Barrosa (5 March 1811) and cried out: 'Bejasus, boys, I have the cuckoo'. During the Indian Mutiny the Black Watch found a huge gong in a bullock cart (or so it was said) and appropriated it; ever after it was used to sound the hours wherever the regiment was stationed. The Dorchester Regiment had a silver-headed drum-major's staff presented by the Nawab of Arcot for its part in the battle of Plassey in 1757, when it was the 39th Foot. At the battle of Arroyo dos Molinos during the Peninsular War the 34th Foot fought the 34th Regiment of the French army and captured its drums and drum-major's staff. The 34th became the Border Regiment, and the drums and staff were its most cherished trophies. The 17th Lancers proudly displayed the bugle that had sounded the charge of the Light Brigade at Balaclava.

The 14th Hussars had the most curious trophy. During the Peninsular War, as the 14th Light Dragoons, they captured part of the baggage train of Joseph Bonaparte, king of Spain, and found there a silver chamber pot which they carried off, thus earning the nickname of 'the emperor's chambermaids'. The pot, considered thereafter as part of the regimental silver, was on special occasions filled with champagne and passed around the mess. The 92nd (2nd Gordon) Highlanders possessed a bizarre snuff box given to them as an act of friendship by the 2nd Dragoons (Royal Scots Greys); it was made from the hoof of their last Balaclava charger. The 10th Hussars boasted a huge silver-gilt centrepiece given them by George IV in 1822. It consisted of a large pedestal surmounted by a candelabrum, each corner adorned by an allegorical figure. A plaque listed the regiment's battle honours. The whole supported a statuette of the King dressed as a Roman emperor. Less grand but more beautiful was the silver Magdala Cross of the Sherwood Foresters, looted from the palace of King Theodore during the Abyssinian campaign of 1867–8.

Regiments, like people, acquired friends and enemies over the years. The Worcestershire Regiment and the Lincolnshire Regiment were traditional friends, having fought side by side at Ramillies in the Spanish Netherlands (now Belgium) and again at Sobraon in India, and their adjutants in official correspondence always addressed each other as 'My dear cousin'. The Berkshire Regiment and the 15th Sikhs were friends from the day in 1885 when they fought off attacking Dervishes at McNeill's Zeriba in the Sudan. The 17th Lancers and the 8th Hussars were so close that, combining their numbers, they often referred to themselves as 'the 25s'. The Gordon Highlanders and the 2nd Gurkhas too were friends, and officers were honorary members of each others' messes. In 1905, when an earthquake destroyed the Gurkha station at Dharmsala in the northern Punjab, the Gordons subscribed 680 rupees to a Gurkha relief fund. During the Anglo-Boer War the Gurkhas from their meagre pay subscribed to a fund for the families of fallen Highlanders and soldiers of the King's Royal Rifle Corps, for the 2nd Gurkhas also had a special relationship with that regiment. The 2nd Gurkhas possessed part of the mess table on which had been laid the corpses of the King's Royal Rifle Corps officers slain at Delhi during the

Mutiny. The Seaforth Highlanders were friends of the 5th Gurkhas, for they had often fought side by side on the North-West Frontier. Kipling probably had these comradeships in mind when in 'With the Main Guard' he had Private Mulvaney say: 'Scotchies and Gurkys are twins bekaze they're so onlike, an' they get dhrunk together when God plazes'. When General Roberts was made a baron he took as supporters for his coat of arms representations of soldiers from the Seaforths and 5th Gurkhas, both of which had served him so well in Afghanistan.

Regiments which had served together in Moore's Light Division in the Peninsula remained close. In the 1870s, in the midst of an altercation at the theatre at Aldershot, two Rifle Brigade soldiers found themselves being worsted. One called for help from the Light Division, and this appeal to history and traditional friendship brought soldiers of the 43rd and 52nd Regiments to join the fight. Soldiers often fastened on a belt the badges of regiments with whom their own regiment had lain, and these became prized possessions.

There were also traditional enemies, regiments that could not be bivouacked side by side without provoking trouble. The Royal Irish Rifles and the Green Howards had no love for each other, nor did Coldstreamers and Royal Scots. Highlanders and cockneys always got on well together, but not the Scots and Welsh. (The adjutant of the Welch Fusiliers once told Robert Graves: 'The Jocks are all the same, the trousered variety and the bare-assed variety. They're dirty in the trenches, they shit too much, and they charge like hell – in both directions'.) There were only four regiments in the army with more battle honours than the Highland Light Infantry, yet it was looked down upon by other Scots regiments, who resented the description 'Highland', maintaining, quite rightly, that it was recruited from the sweepings of Glasgow's slums. 'Glesca Keelies' they were called, and with perverse pride called themselves ('keely' being a Glaswegian term for one who regards a brawl in a public house as a sociable evening).

It seldom took much to provoke a fight between unfriendly regiments. There was once a mighty brawl when a soldier in the Lancashire Fusiliers told a Gordon Highlander that Scots had to wear kilts because their feet were too big to fit in trousers.

Sometimes regiments were enemies without really knowing why. Private Frank Richards of the Royal Welch Fusiliers wrote: 'We and the Highland Light Infantry were bitter enemies, I don't know why—it was

something handed down from bygone days'. Fights could be bloody affairs, for the usual weapon was the broad belt with its heavy buckle that
every soldier wore. A scrap could easily be started by a reference to some
unfortunate incident, real or imagined, in another regiment's past.
Welch Fusiliers wishing to pick a quarrel with the Black Watch had
only to enter a pub and call out for a pint of 'broken square', and at this
reference to the battle of Tamai, where in 1884 Dervishes temporarily
broke a British square of which the Black Watch formed a part, belts
would be whipped off and a row begin. Kipling described such a fight in
Dublin:

> There was a row in Silver Street – the regiments was out,
> Between an Irish regiment an' English Cavalree;
> They called us 'Delhi Rebels' and we answered 'Threes about'!*
> That drew them like a hornet's nest – we met them good and large,
> The English at the double an' the Irish at the charge.
>
> The English were too drunk to know, the Irish didn't care;
> But when they grew impertinent we simultaneously rose
> Till half o' them was Liffey mud, and half was tatthered clo'es.

In Kipling's poem a soldier is killed in the drunken brawl, and doubtless
this occasionally happened, but, as Wolseley said, 'It is this intense feeling of regimental rivalry that is the life-blood of our old, historic army,
and makes it what it is in action'.

Many regiments had official mascots. The Irish Guards had an Irish
wolfhound, the Grenadier Guards a goose named Jacob. Both the 5th
Lancers and the Buffs once had tigers. The 17th Lancers at one time
had a bear cub whose mother had been shot by Prince Adolphus Teck
in India. The cub, called Lizzie, was taught a number of tricks and became a favourite of all ranks until one day she disappeared. A year and a
half later a band of Indian jugglers appeared with a trained bear which
some soldiers thought resembled Lizzie. When she proved able to perform an unusual trick with a bottle which one lancer had taught her,

---

* Kipling never used the names of real regiments in his stories and poems, but the
'Delhi Rebels' were the Royal Irish Fusiliers, who won their proudest battle honour fighting the Delhi rebels during the Indian Mutiny. 'Threes about' refers to the 9th Lancers,
who misunderstood an order at the battle of Chilianwala (1849) and retreated when they
should have advanced.

she was confiscated. Lizzie was taken back to Britain when the regiment returned home, but eventually turned mean and had to be given to the Dublin zoo. Even so, she was cheered in parting and was played out of barracks by the regimental band.

The Warwickshire Regiment, which had a stag as its cap badge, acquired an antelope. The Coldstream Guards at one time had a cat named Pinkie, who earned a reputation for toughness and durability. In 1904 four companies of the Royal Fusiliers accompanied Colonel Francis Younghusband on his expedition to Lhasa and brought back a Tibeten wild ass, which marched with the troops through the City of London on their return. During the Anglo-Boer War a battery of artillery had a chicken as a mascot; it rode in a special box of its own attached to a limber and earned such fame that it was suggested that the Royal Zoological Society put it in its zoo after the war.

Cavalry regiments tended to adopt horses as pets. One named Bob, who had charged with the Light Brigade at Balaclava, was at one time the oldest in the British cavalry. When he died at the age of thirty-three he was buried with full military honours. The 10th Hussars owned a horse named Old Times who had been a fine, prize-winning show jumper until he was wounded on the North-West Frontier. Retired, he became a pet and roamed at will around the barracks.

The famous goat of the Welch Fusiliers was not an ordinary goat; it was, in fact, quite royal. When Queen Victoria ascended the throne in 1837 the Shah of Persia presented her with a herd of goats, which flourished at Windsor. In 1844 the Queen presented one to the regiment; when he died, he was replaced from the royal herd, as were all subsequent goats. He stood on parade and even marched to church with the troops. (The goat was, of course, Church of England.) When the regiment was sent to India, the goat went along, and because of the lavish care it received, many Indians assumed that the regiment worshipped it. On the march it rode in a cart and in bivouac it had a tent of its own. When a goat died he was given a military funeral and a cross was erected over the grave. It was always well tended, even after the regiment moved on, for it was the custom in India to care for the graves of other regiments' mascots. The goat (one of whom was named Gwillym Llewellyn Jones) was always looked after by a soldier, usually a lance-corporal, who was called the goat-major. Sad to relate, one goat-major was court-martialled for 'disrespect to an officer: in that he, at Wrexham

The goat and drum-major of the Welch Fusiliers on St David's Day when leeks were also worn (*Photo: Mary Evans Picture Library*)

. . . did prostitute the Royal Goat, being the gift of His Majesty the Colonel-in-Chief from His royal herd at Windsor, by offering his stud services to . . . [a] farmer and goat breeder of Wrexham'. The goat-major pleaded guilty but claimed that he had been motivated by compassion for the goat. Unimpressed, the court ordered him reduced to the ranks.

The Welch Fusiliers were not the only ones to own royal animals. Queen Victoria once presented the Rifle Brigade with two red deer. The Derbyshire Regiment (2nd Sherwood Foresters) always had a ram and it was always called Derby, the rams being distinguished by Roman numerals; in 1913 the battalion was given Derby XII by the Duke of Devonshire.

Mascots and pets tended to accumulate. In 1899, when a battalion of the Rifle Brigade left Crete to fight the Boers in South Africa, it carried with it a badger, two ibexes, and, of course, a full complement of dogs. Soldiers and dogs always seem to go together and can be seen in most armies. Many dogs faithfully followed their masters into battle, for although soldiers were never able to smuggle their wives or sweethearts on board troopships, they were remarkably successful in bringing their pets on board.

The Bedfordshire Regiment once got three animals – an ugly-looking tom cat, a fox-terrier and a poodle – onto a troopship by putting all three in the band's bass drum, in spite of a cat and dog fight inside as the drum was being carried up the gangplank. The Connaught Rangers spirited a pet bear on board when the regiment left Canada by chloroforming the beast and stuffing him in a cask. Only a limited number of dogs were permitted to accompany the Welch Fusiliers when they sailed from India to Burma in 1904, but Private Frank Richards noticed that 'in some mysterious way every owner smuggled his pet on board'.

A Maltese terrier belonging to a drummer in the Coldstream Guards made the soldiers laugh as he chased Russian cannon balls at the Alma. The same story is told of a dog named Bob in the 1st Scots Fusilier Guards. The 1st Gordons had a dog, Juno, who charged with them at Tel-el-Kebir in 1882. The 2nd Gordons acquired a Russian mastiff in Afghanistan; he was later severely wounded and captured by the Boers at the battle of Majuba in South Africa, but he managed to escape and limp back to the British lines. The Royal Engineers had a dog named Sandy who joined the fight at Inkerman and was wounded by a bayonet when he attacked a Russian soldier. After the war he was awarded for his valour a silver medal (which was stolen), and when he died he was given a military funeral and his picture appeared in the *Illustrated London News*. Jock, who belonged to the Scots Guards, always accompanied them in battle and was credited with saving a guardsman's life by bowling over a couple of Russians. His regiment fashioned an imitation Victoria Cross for him. A springer spaniel trotted along with the British infantry as it advanced in the battle of Bergandal in the Anglo-Boer War and ran to sniff the ground where the bullets kicked up dust. Even after a bullet struck him in the shoulder, he continued valiantly to follow the attack.

A dog described as a 'well-bred pointer' belonging to Lieutenant-Colonel Henry Degacher of the 24th Foot (South Wales Borderers) took part in the battle of Isandhlwana during the Zulu War. He was lost during the debacle but rejoined a fortnight later. A mongrel named Bobby, attached to the 66th Foot (2nd Berkshire Regiment), was wounded in the neck and back at the battle of Maiwand during the Second Afghan War. He was left on the field in the course of a retreat, but managed to survive and eventually rejoined his regiment at Kandahar, fifty miles away. Later in England, when the Berkshires paraded before Queen Victoria to receive their campaign medals, the Queen herself presented Bobby with his own medal; he expressed his appreciation by barking and wagging his tail. English cities proved more dangerous than Afghans: Bobby was run over and killed by a hansom cab eighteen months later. The regiment had him stuffed, hung his medal around his neck and put him in a glass case, which stood first in the sergeants' mess and later in the regimental museum.

Prior to 1880 the first twenty-five infantry regiments of the line were all two-battalion regiments; the Rifle Brigade and the King's Royal Rifle Corps had four battalions each, while the others had but one. A part of Edward Cardwell's reforms was to marry single-battalion regiments to each other. Only one, The Queen's Own Cameron Highlanders, escaped amalgamation, and between 1881 and 1897 (when a second battalion was raised) it was the only single-battalion regiment in the British army.

These regimental marriages were not popular with soldiers. Although an attempt was made to merge units that had been traditional friends or had some affinity for each other, there were many shotgun weddings and there was, initially, much bitterness. Even among regiments that had been friends, there was a feeling that friendship and marriage were quite different matters. The amalgamation of the 52nd and 43rd Regiments, blood brothers since serving together in Moore's Light Division in the Peninsula, to form the Oxfordshire Regiment (soon changed to the Oxfordshire and Buckinghamshire Regiment and known universally as the 'Oxs and Bucks') was often held up as an example of a happy marriage, but one officer who had been in the 52nd was fond of saying years later: 'I strop my razor fifty-two times and when I come to forty-three I spit'. Even as late as the First World War, officers of the 2nd 'Oxs and Bucks' insisted on calling themselves the 52nd Light Infantry.

Some of the amalgamations did appear odd. When in 1881 the 100th Royal Canadians and the 109th Bombay Infantry (formerly the 3rd Bombay European Regiment in the Honourable East India Company's army) were merged to form the Prince of Wales Leinster Regiment, it seemed a curious mating, but as both were filled with Irishmen it was perhaps not so bizarre.

Throughout the years there had been separations and marriages, occasionally within the same family, as it were, and so for some the amalgamation was a kind of homecoming. In 1758 the second battalion of the 24th Foot was divorced to form the 69th Regiment. In 1881 this regiment was merged with the 41st Foot to form the Welsh Regiment (a title later varied to the Welch Regiment), and then in 1969 the Welch Regiment completed a full circle and married with the old 24th, which had become the South Wales Borderers. It currently exists as the 'Royal Regiment of Wales (24th/41st Foot)'.

There was much talk about the *tone* of a regiment. It was a typically Victorian word, 'tone', no less important for being vague, and its use implied a considerable amount of class-consciousness. Although most soldiers regarded their own regiment as the best, there was, in fact, a social ranking, a pecking order among them that did not depend entirely upon their official order of precedence. In general, cavalry looked down on infantry, Guards looked down on regiments of the line, and regulars looked down on the Indian army, which they called 'black infantry'.

The West India Regiment was on the home establishment though it was never in Britain. It was in a category by itself, and definitely on the lower end of the social scale. Formed in 1779, it was not disbanded until 1928. Its officers were Britons (usually men who were unable to obtain commissions in any other regiment) and its other ranks blacks from the West Indies. It was used to garrison British possessions in the West Indies and in West Africa because it was believed that black soldiers were better able to resist tropical diseases. Probably lowest of the low on the military social scale however was the Royal Indian Army Service Corps. Few of its officers were educated at public schools or Sandhurst and many regulars felt that they were not quite gentlemen. It

Paying the West India Regiment in service during the Ashanti War (*Photo: Graham Brandon*)

was said that the initials of the corps, R.I.A.S.C., stood for 'Really, I am so common'.

Among the regulars prior to the abolition of the purchase system, snobbery could be seen in the value of commissions in different regiments, a commission in the Guards, for example, often selling for twice that of one in a line regiment. It could also be seen in the social ranks of the officers. As a rule of thumb for English infantry: the further the regiment's depot from London, the lower it stood on the social scale.

A look at the Army List for 1899 shows that H.R.H. The Prince of Wales was colonel-in-chief of the 2nd Life Guards; the regiment's colonel was Lord Howe, an earl; among its twenty captains and lieutenants were three peers of the realm, two baronets and two 'Honourables'. Officers without titles had aristocratic names such as Charles Frederick St Clair Anstruther-Thompson and Claud Champion-de-Crespigny.

The Royal Horse Guards had an even more aristocratic roster. The Prince of Wales was colonel-in-chief of this regiment too; Lord Wolseley was its colonel; and of the twenty-five serving officers, seven were peers and six were the sons of peers. Neither of these regiments possessed a single officer who had passed through the Staff College, nor had any been given an award for gallantry.

Such regiments – splendidly dressed and over-drilled – seldom fought in the nasty little wars of the nineteenth century. The 2nd Life Guards went for sixty-seven years (from Waterloo to Tel-el-Kebir) without seeing action, and the 3rd Hussars did not fight as a regiment between the Second Sikh War (1846) and the end of the Anglo-Boer War in 1902. In contrast to these glittering regiments, the Northamptonshire Regiment, formed by a merger of the 48th and 58th Regiments – a fine unit which had fought (or its forebears had fought) in Canada, Egypt, Spain, the Crimea, New Zealand and South Africa – had no colonel-in-chief, its colonel was not even a knight (which was most unusual), and none of its sixty-three officers was titled. However, four had passed Staff College and one had won the Victoria Cross. It was the kind of regiment a serious officer seeking an active career would join.

For young men of aristocratic families, with ample wealth, and a taste for sport and society, the Guards regiments had much to offer. They were usually stationed in London or Windsor, there was plenty of leisure time, and even some of the duties were pleasures. Guards infantry regiments found the guard for St James's Palace and the Bank of England, the former commanded by a captain and two subalterns, the latter by a single subaltern. At both places an elegant dinner was provided. At the Bank of England the directors furnished not only food but two bottles of wine for two guests. At St James's the infantry officers were joined for dinner by the officers of the Household Cavalry from the guard at the Horse Guards. All guests had to leave by eleven o'clock however.

Many relatively poor but ambitious officers strove to obtain commissions in the Indian army or to join regiments with battalions in India, for there an officer could exist on his pay if he lived frugally. Such was the case with Bernard Montgomery (later Lord Montgomery of Alamein). He passed out of Sandhurst in 1908 with marks too low for the Indian army and so chose the Royal Warwickshire Regiment because it was a 'good, sound County Regiment and not one of the more expensive ones', because it had a battalion in India, and because he admired its cap badge.

Regiments changed their character over the years, some quite dramatically. In the days of Queen Victoria and King Edward, the King's Royal Rifle Corps was one of the most expensive and snobbish regiments in the army. General Sir Brian Horrocks described it as

> one of the most exclusive family regiments in the military world. No one could hope to become an officer in the 60th without close family connections, and even then only after most searching inquiries had been made by the Colonel Commandant of the Regiment. It is more difficult to obtain a commission in this Regiment than in any other corps in the army, including the Household Cavalry, Cavalry, or Guards.

In 1900 the Duke of Cambridge was its colonel-in-chief and it numbered quite a few aristocrats, including His Highness Prince Christian Victor Albert Ludwig Ernest Anton of Scheswig-Holstein, G.C.B., G.C.V.O., a captain in the regiment and a brevet major. It had not always been so stylish, however. It was formed in North America as the Royal American Regiment in 1755. After the American Revolution it evolved from a colonial corps into a kind of foreign legion. Even its officers were foreigners: Swiss, French, German, *et al.* Then the foreigners were swept out and it became an English regiment, the 60th Rifles, which grew ever more popular among the rich and titled.

Officers of socially prominent regiments tended to obtain the most desirable appointments outside their units. A comparison of non-regimental appointments held by officers in the Scots Guards with those of officers in the Manchester Regiment in 1899 illustrates this. One officer of the Scots Guards was aide-de-camp to the governor-general of India, another to the governor-general of Canada, another to the governor of Bombay, two more to major-generals, and one was adjutant of the Guards Depot. The Manchester Regiment was reputed to be on the bottom rung of the social scale among regiments of the line. It was even said that its officers could live on their pay. In contrast to the splendid appointments held by Scots Guards offficers, offficers of the Manchester Regiment at this time were serving as head of the Aldershot military prison, in the army pay department, as adjutants of militia battalions;

one was a recruiting officer in Liverpool, another deputy assistant adjutant general in Mauritius. One was seconded to the Gold Coast Constabulary, one to the Egyptian army, and one was serving in Uganda. None was an aide-de-camp to a governor or a general.

A man's family and the size of his income mattered if he wished to become an officer. Family and money determined his regiment and the work he would do. One thing alone was essential to the officer corps: its members had to be gentlemen.

OFFICERS
AND GENTLEMEN.
Part I: Officers

Their officers are good as good can be, because their training begins
early, and God has arranged that a clean-run youth of the British middle
classes should in the matter of backbone, brains, and bowels, surpass all
other youths. For this reason a child of eighteen will stand up, doing
nothing, with a tin sword in his hand and joy in his heart until he is dropped. If he dies, he dies like a gentleman.

Rudyard Kipling, 'Drums of the Fore and Aft'

To be an officer in the British army it was essential to be a gentleman,
as the British define that term, for it was believed that only gentlemen
possessed the qualities needed to lead British troops in battle. According
to Wellington, 'the description of gentlemen of whom the army were
composed, made, from their education, manners and habits, the best
officers in the world, and to compose the officers of a lower class would
cause the Army to deteriorate'. Long after the Great Duke's death his
arguments were still used to defend the purchase system, for most gentlemen (or their families) had sufficient cash to purchase commissions
in the days when that was required, and sufficient means to enable
them to live in their regiments.

If a man was a gentleman it did not much matter what other deficiencies he might have. Physical defects counted hardly at all. Charles Napier was nearly blind; Garnet Wolseley and Frederick Roberts, the two best generals of the late Victorian era, had but two eyes between them. Roberts, in addition to having only one seeing eye as a result of a childhood illness, was only five feet three inches tall and would not have been accepted had he tried to enlist as a private. However, he came from a good family and his father was a general.

The loss of an arm was no impediment, either, and the army had many one-armed officers, including such generals as Lord Raglan and Ian Hamilton. The famous Sam Browne belt, invented by Samuel Browne so that he could draw his sword more easily with his one arm, was adopted (sometimes with adaptations) for all officers in most western armies. Ian Hamilton, whose wrist was shattered in the disastrous battle of Majuba Hill (1881) when the British army suffered one of its most humiliating defeats, always maintained that 'Majuba was worth an arm any day'. Adrian Carton de Wiart lost a hand in one war and an eye in another, but he became a lieutenant-general. Benjamin Bromhead had one arm sliced off and the other rendered useless by Dervishes in the Sudan, but he did not consider retiring and eventually commanded his battalion. His brother, Gonville, a captain and a company commander in the 24th Foot (South Wales Borderers) during the Zulu War of 1879, was left behind at Rorke's Drift when his battalion invaded Zululand because he was almost totally deaf, but he won the Victoria Cross by his gallantry when his little post was attacked by swarms of Zulus. Major-General Walter Kitchener, Lord Kitchener's brother, was also deaf. Once during the Anglo-Boer War a huge 120 mm. shell exploded only fifty yards from him; turning to a fellow officer, he remarked serenely, 'I thought I heard a shell'.

Age was no handicap, either. In 1877 – sixty-two years after the battle of Waterloo – there were still a number of officers on full or half pay who had fought under Wellington. Both Hugh Gough and Lord Roberts were seventy when they fought their last battles, and so was Hugh Wheeler when he was attacked at Cawnpore. Charles Napier was sixty-seven when he conquered Sind, Sir Colin Campbell sixty-five when he fought in the Indian Mutiny. All but one of the British generals in the Crimean War were more than sixty years of age, and Sir John Burgoyne, the chief engineer, was seventy-two. Still, none was as old as General William Blakeney, who was eighty-four when he defended Fort St Philip in Minorca in 1756.

Lord Roberts (*Photo: Graham Brandon*)

Since there was no such thing as being over-age in grade, by mid-century there were many middle-aged men in the lower ranks of the artillery, where promotion was only by seniority. At Woolwich in 1845 all three troops of horse artillery were commanded by captains who had been present at Waterloo thirty years before and were more than fifty years old. Once when Lord Raglan asked Richard Dacre how he was getting on, Dacre replied: 'My Lord, when a man has been twenty-one years a subaltern, he can never get on'. But Dacre did get on; in 1850 he was still a captain after fourteen years in that rank, but ten years later he was a lieutenant-general and he died a field-marshal.

Until the middle of the Victorian era not much education was required of officers, although most had attended a public school, and sometimes it seemed that not much intelligence was required either. General Sir John Moore once described Lieutenant William Warre as a blockhead, and said 'there can be no hope of improving such a slathering goose, who erred, as he always will do, from no bad design, but from want of brain'. But Warre subsequently received a knighthood and rose to become a lieutenant-general. General Hope Grant was a brave cavalry officer, but he never learned to read a map and had difficulty in making his subordinates understand what he wanted done. He was 'puzzle-headed', said his officers. Henry Havelock-Allan, son of the Henry Havelock of Mutiny fame, was said to suffer from 'fits of mental excitement and eccentricity'. He appears to have been quite mad, but he became a lieutenant-general.

The commissioned ranks in the nineteenth century were not formed into an orderly pyramidal organizational structure. An officer might hold two or three ranks simultaneously (ranks could be honorary, brevet, local or temporary), and frequently held one in his regiment and another in the army. In different regiments at different times the names of ranks also differed. In the days of the Honourable East India Company there were 'Company officers' and 'Queen's (or King's) officers', and the latter took precedence over the former if of equal rank, regardless of length of service. Thus a newly promoted captain might arrive in India, never having heard a shot fired in anger, and find himself senior to a captain in the Indian army with perhaps fourteen years' service, much of it fighting on the North-West Frontier. It was a rule much resented by officers in the Company's army.

Awkward situations could develop where officers held a rank in the army superior to their rank in their regiments. As long as an officer was with his regiment he served in his regimental rank, but when on a staff appointment or on any assignment outside his regiment, he served in his rank in the army. He also reverted to his army rank whenever his unit was brigaded with another unit of equal or smaller size, and his army rank was senior to any other.

For his services in the Ashanti War, George Pomeroy Colley was promoted to the rank of full colonel in the army, but when in 1874 he rejoined his regiment in Dublin, he reverted to his regimental rank of captain and had to serve as orderly officer and perform other duties of a company officer. Not infrequently an officer would become his own commanding officer's commanding officer. Lord Dundonald, 2nd Life Guards, was a major in his regiment but a colonel in the army, and often found himself in command of a force that included his own regiment. 'I never liked commanding my own colonel, and told him so', he said, 'but he was always very good about it and did not seem to mind'. This was not always the case. Neville Lyttelton told of a battalion stationed at Jullunder where a junior major was senior in army rank to his own colonel and was for a while a brigadier, in which capacity he criticized the light drill of the battalion's left wing. When a more senior officer arrived and the temporary brigadier reverted to his substantive rank, his colonel published an order: 'The late Brigadier having found fault with the light drill of the left wing of the battalion, it will parade under him every day at 6 a.m. for light drill until further orders'. This was not a pleasant activity during a Punjab winter.

At one point in his career Adrian Carton de Wiart was a substantive captain in the 4th (Royal Irish) Dragoon Guards, a brevet major, an acting brigadier general, and in temporary command of a division, a major-general's command. Neville Chamberlain (no relation to the late Prime Minister), a famous frontier fighter and inventor of the game of snooker, was once a captain in his regiment, a lieutenant-colonel in the army, and a local brigadier-general on the North-West Frontier. The rank of brigadier or brigadier-general was always local or temporary, never substantive. If was not used between 1880 and 1899 but was reintroduced during the Anglo-Boer War.

Prior to 1871 officers in Guards regiments held army ranks one or two grades higher than their regimental ranks and were named in army lists as 'ensign and lieutenant', 'lieutenant and captain', or 'captain and lieutenant-colonel'. This was not a practice appreciated by officers in line regiments, and when purchase was abolished, so were double ranks for officers in the Guards.

Prior to 1880 there was considerable variation in the titles of those holding the lowest commissioned rank – they could be ensigns, cornets, sub-lieutenants or second-lieutenants – but by 1894 all were officially second-lieutenants, although in the Foot Guards they continued to be called ensigns even during the First World War. The rank of cornet existed only in the cavalry, and ensign only in the infantry, though never in the Rifle Brigade, and never in the Royal Engineers or Royal

Artillery. In the engineers and artillery prior to 1870 there were no majors except brevet majors, but in the artillery there were first captains and second captains. Brevets were awarded for distinguished service. The most common was to the rank of major, the lowest for which they were given; there were no brevet lieutenants or captains, nor were there brevet generals. Subalterns (second-lieutenants and lieutenants) could not be breveted, though they were sometimes promised a brevet of major when they reached the rank of captain for services performed as lieutenants.

In cavalry regiments the riding master, and in both cavalry and infantry regiments the quartermasters, held honorary rank as lieutenant or captain. They were not infrequently rankers. In the 1870s, honorary rank one grade higher was given to Yeomanry and Militia field officers after twenty-five years' service and to captains after twenty years service.

Frequently – one might almost say usually – when a regiment of infantry was referred to, a battalion was meant, and when a regiment's colonel was mentioned the lieutenant-colonel commanding a battalion was meant, for colonels of regiments were always generals and their title and position in a regiment were largely honorary. Many of the socially prestigious regiments, such as the Guards, certain cavalry regiments, and the King's Royal Rifle Corps, had not only colonels but also colonels-in-chief appointed from the ranks of European royalty. In 1899 the Prince of Wales was colonel-in-chief of the 1st and 2nd Life Guards as well as the Blues; Francis Joseph, the Emperor of Austria, was colonel-in-chief of the 1st Dragoon Guards; Czar Nicholas II had the Royal Scots Greys, and the Duke of Connaught the Inniskilling Dragoons. When the Royals went to the continent to lick the Kaiser in 1914, they were attacking not only a British field-marshal but their own colonel-in-chief, the German Emperor William II. Five days after Britain declared war on Germany the War Office asked King George V publicly to deprive the Kaiser of his honorary titles and commands. The king refused, saying that his name should remain on the Army List until he voluntarily resigned. Lord Roberts was prevailed upon to talk sense into the King, and finally it was agreed that the names of belligerent royalty would be dropped from the next edition of the Army List, but the King firmly refused to make a public announcement.

Although colonels of regiments were all real officers, usually with distinguished records (as were also the colonels-commandant in the artillery and engineers), for the socially prominent regiments they were most often drawn from the peerage. In 1899 Earl Howe was colonel of the 2nd Life Guards, Viscount Wolseley had the Blues, and the Duke of Cambridge had the Scots Guards. By contrast, the less expensive regiments were commanded by lesser figures, though most had been knighted and had reached the rank of lieutenant-general. Still, the colonel of the South Lancashire Regiment in 1899 was only a major-general with no post-nominal letters, not even a C.B.

In 1899 the Royal Regiment of Artillery had the Duke of Cambridge as its colonel-in-chief and thirty-one colonels-commandant, all but three full generals. The most senior colonel-commandant was General Sir Collingwood Dickson, G.C.B.,V.C., who had been sixty-four years on the Army List.

Before 1871, when the government decided to pay £6,150,000 to buy back the army from its officers, commissions and promotions were purchased in the cavalry and infantry. Given the assumptions about leadership which the British entertained, the purchase system had its advantages. The Duke of Wellington stoutly defended it. Said he: 'It is promotion by purchase which brings into the service . . . men who have some connection with the interests and fortunes of the country'. The system effectively excluded those who, though they might be brilliant, dropped their aitches or preferred beer to wine. Since the army provided no pensions for officers, the purchase of commissions was an investment and the purchase of higher ranks added to it, so that a lieutenant-colonel could sell his commission and retire with a comfortable sum. For the government the system had other charms, for it spared the Treasury the expense of adequate wages.

The system was not inflexible, however, and provided both risks and opportunities. There were two risks: death and promotion to general officer rank. The highest rank available for purchase was that of lieutenant-colonel; the rank of colonel came automatically after a certain number of years in grade. When an officer was promoted to major-general he lost his investment. Some colonels, threatened with promotion, hastened their retirement, but others were given advancement before they had an opportunity to do so. Sir James Scarlett, made a major-general for distinguished services during the Crimean War, was bitter over his lost investment, even though he was a man of considerable wealth. Sir James Hope Grant too was bitter; the £12,000 lost by

Officers' living quarters at Balaclava (*Photo: Graham Brandon*)

his surprise promotion represented an important sum. Both Scarlett and
Hope Grant appealed for justice without success. An officer who died
on active service also lost his investment – or rather, his heirs did; his
rank was not sold but was given to a deserving officer, usually the senior
of the next lowest rank in the regiment. Thus, young officers light-heart-
edly drank toasts to 'a bloody war and a pestilential season'. Officers
were also promoted without purchase by augmentation; that is, when an
extra battalion was added to a regiment or a new regiment was formed.

Since a certain amount of time in grade was required before the next
step on the promotion ladder could be bought, it became the custom in
the late eighteenth and early nineteenth centuries to purchase commissions for very young boys, and in at least one instance a commission was
bought for a boy on the day of his birth. Although the purchase system
enabled Wolfe to be commissioned at the age of fifteen and Wellington
to become a battalion commander before he was thirty and a general
while still young, it also enabled rich incompetents rapidly to climb the
military career ladder. Thomas Brudenell (subsequently Earl of Cardigan), who led the charge of the Light Brigade at Balaclava, is said to

have paid £40,000 to become the lieutenant-colonel of the 11th Hussars (then Light Dragoons). The purchase system also held back poorer officers of ability. Henry Havelock, once said that before he became a captain he had been 'purchased over by two fools and three sots'. He eventually became a major-general, but others were less fortunate. James Algeo of the 77th Foot (2nd Middlesex Regiment) was nineteen years a subaltern, and after thirty-nine years of service only a captain. Archibald Stewart of the 92nd (2nd Gordon) Highlanders was still a lieutenant after thirteen years' service on full pay and more than seventeen on half pay.

In 1856 a royal commission concluded that purchase was 'vicious in principle, repugnant to the public sentiment of the present day, equally inconsistent with the honour of the military profession and the policy of the British Empire, and irreconcilable with justice'. But nothing was done about the practice for another fifteen years.

Luck came to the aid of some poor officers though. George Cornwall of the 93rd (Sutherland) Highlanders, unable to purchase his majority, was only a captain after thirty-six years of service; his messmates called him 'Daddy' Cornwall. Corporal William Forbes-Mitchell noted that 'he sometimes swore', but added that 'considering how promotion had passed over him, that was perhaps excusable'. Cornwall was severely wounded at Cawnpore, but the wound proved to be his ticket to fame, fortune, promotion and happiness. He was invalided home, and on the long voyage from India to England around the Cape of Good Hope made the acquaintance of a rich widow. He was greeted as a hero when he reached his native Dublin, presented with a valuable sword, and given the Freedom of the City. Soon after, he recovered from his wounds, married the widow, purchased his majority, returned to India with his bride, and lived to command the regiment.

The prices paid for the different ranks varied. There was an official price list established by regulation, but varying amounts were paid 'over regulation', depending upon supply and demand, the real price often being double the regulation price. This was the rule rather than the exception, and an auction room in Charles Street, London, handled these transactions. The cost also depended upon the regiment: ranks in the Foot Guards were the most expensive, followed by Life Guards, Horse Guards, dragoons, and infantry of the line. Prices for ranks in the Foot Guards and the line infantry in 1840 averaged something like this:

	Foot Guards	Infantry of the line
Ensign	£1,200	£ 450
Lieutenant	£2,050	£ 700
Captain	£4,800	£1,800
Major	£8,300	£3,200
Lieutenant-Colonel	£9,000	£4,500

In 1869 Hugh McCalmont paid £5,125, including 'over regulation', for his captaincy in the 9th Lancers. In the same year Lord Dundonald, at the age of 17, paid £1,260 for his commission in the 2nd Life Guards. Not only was this expensive, but he had joined a regiment in which it was impossible for an officer to live without a considerable amount of extra income. He earned only 8s. per day, and he was required to keep a batman and a civilian groom, and to pay for mess subscriptions, coach subscriptions, band subscriptions, and several others. In some regiments these could include subscriptions for theatricals, a wine cellar, and a pack of hounds. Only sons of the wealthy could afford to live in the Foot Guards, Household Cavalry, Scots Greys, 4th or 10th Hussars. In 1899 Lieutenant-Colonel William Bellairs estimated the amount of allowance or private income a subaltern would require annually to remain in the service:

Royal Marines (when afloat)	£ 50–60
Artillery, engineers, infantry	£ 60–100
Cavalry	£300–400

The abolition of the purchase system did not change the character of the officer corps, for the need for a private income to live in a regiment stationed in England acted as an effective social filter. Not only was an officer required to pay both his mess bill (which frequently exceeded his pay) and the many subscriptions, but he also had to buy an array of expensive uniforms and much of his equipment. Even as late as the First World War officers had to buy their own revolvers. The 1903 committee that looked into officers' expenses found that clothing and equipment in the infantry cost £200 and in the cavalry £600 to £1,000; even in a county regiment stationed in England a private income of at least £200 was needed. The committee concluded:

The whole evidence before the Committee proves incontestably in their opinion, that the expenses of the Army form a very serious deterrent to parents in selecting a profession for their sons, and that many otherwise suitable candidates are precluded from entering the Service by no other consideration than the insufficiency of their private incomes.

Still, nothing was done to pay officers a living wage. It was simply too convenient to underpay them and run the army on the cheap.

Pay varied according to the service, the type of regiment, and where it was stationed. In England a second-lieutenant of a line regiment received 5s. 3d. per day (only 4s. 6d. before the Crimean War); Foot Guards of the same rank received an extra £70 per year. Engineers and field artillerymen received 4d. per day more as second-lieutenants, and engineers doing engineering work an extra 2s. Cavalry second-lieutenants were paid 6s. 8d. Second-lieutenants in the Royal Horse Artillery received the highest basic rate: 7s 8d. Pay rose as an officer rose in rank, but not all that much. A lieutenant-colonel of an infantry line regiment was given only 18s. per day. There was, however, a dramatic increase when an officer reached general officer rank. Major-Generals received £1,095 and a full general £3,923.

In India officers were paid in rupees, the value of which declined over the years. In 1850 a rupee was worth 2s.; by 1900 its value had slid to 1s. 4d. An infantry second-lieutenant in India in 1900 with less than three years' service received 202 rupees per month, or about £160 per year. This was considerably more than the £96 per year he received in England. Even so, Ian Hamilton, as a subaltern in the Gordon Highlanders in India in the 1870s, calculated that he needed a private income of £200. On the other hand, the commander-in-chief of the Bengal army was quite handsomely paid 8333½ rupees per month. (One can only speculate on how such a curious sum with its half rupee was arrived at as the pay of the commander-in-chief.) In pounds sterling this amounted to approximately £6,000 per year and made the appointment the most lucrative available; the commander-in-chief at the Horse Guards received only £4,500. Sometimes, as a result of the cheaper living and increased pay in India, officers developed a taste for a standard of living they could not support when they returned to England; William Butler of the 69th Foot (2nd Welsh Regiment) reported: 'Before we were a year at home half of our officers were in debt, and many of them had to exchange or leave the service'.

Extra pay was given for passing examinations in oriental languages in India, and everywhere officers holding certain staff appointments received special pay and allowances. In 1900 an aide-de-camp to a general officer received £273 15s. exclusive of allowances; a staff captain at headquarters was paid £500; a deputy assistant adjutant general at headquarters earned £700 and an assistant military secretary £800. It was thanks to these opportunities and to strict economy that William Robertson, a penniless ranker, managed to survive as a subaltern. He served in India, learned six languages in three years, became adjutant of his regiment, drank water in the mess and did not marry. He was also helped by a small lump sum (£150) given to a few rankers for their uniforms, and by his father, a tailor, who made his civilian clothes. Even so, officers without independent means had a very difficult time of it, particularly if they failed to marry women with fortunes. Colonel Robert Hume, an exceptionally brilliant officer with a large family, frequently sat up late at night at a sewing machine in order to keep his children in clothes.

To match the bewildering array of allowances there was an equally perplexing set of regulations governing deductions, which caused frequent, and often justified, complaints. In 1914 one officer emerged from a miserable week in a Belgian trench to discover that he had been charged 2s. 3d. a night for 'lodging'.

When there was no place available in the army temporarily, or if an officer wished to retire for a while, he was placed on half-pay, and in this status he might remain for many years. William Hambley of the 3rd Rifle Brigade served for eight years, fighting in eighteen battles and suffering five wounds, but was placed on half-pay when his battalion was disbanded. He remained unemployed for more than thirty-five years and then, at the age of sixty-two, was recalled to duty for the Crimean War.

Lieutenant Ian Hamilton with the Gordon Highlanders in India in the 1870s earned £350 per year (including the 40 rupees he received as a Hindustani interpreter), and his mess bill was £270. In a letter to his brother, Vereker, written on 19 August 1876, Hamilton said: 'The thought of all that spent on one's stomach is simply disgraceful but in a regiment like ours one *cannot* help it. Champagne always flowing. No *one* allowed to pass through the station without being made a regimental guest – all that sort of thing'. The Gordons did live in style. When the regiment learned it was to go to Delhi to take part in the celebration to proclaim Queen Victoria the Empress of India, a mess meeting decided to buy a huge tent to 'entertain the swells', as Lieutenant Hamilton put it in another letter to his brother. "It was also passed', he wrote, 'that open house be kept and champagne flow like water so that ruin stares me in the face'.

In the 1900s the King's Regulations said that the cost of food in the mess must not exceed 4s. per day, but it was a regulation frequently contravened. In addition to special subscriptions there was the expense of maintaining the mess itself, providing servants' liveries, newspapers, and stationery, and replacing broken glass and dishes. Most regiments required that an officer have a certain level of income and these were generally well known. The management of the mess was in the hands of a committee, usually composed of a major, a captain, and two subalterns. Each might be responsible for a department, such as wine or catering. Sometimes in England the entire operation was handed over to a private outside caterer, but in most battalions all the arrangements were made within the unit. A mess sergeant corresponded to a butler, and several soldiers acted as mess servants: a 'kitchen man' corresponded to a kitchen maid, a 'delft-man' took the place of a scullery maid, and the soldier who was 'silverman' performed no military duties but devoted himself to keeping the plate polished; often he slept in the midst of boxes designed specially for each piece. Two or three soldiers under a corporal acted as waiters and were often dressed in livery. The mess sergeant also kept a roster of officers' soldier-servants, who were required to do duty, usually for a week at a time, in the mess. The cook was often a civilian, sometimes French, whose salary was paid from mess funds.

For an officer, army life revolved around the regimental mess. It was much like a private club and was often the centre of his social activities. Some officers tended to divorce the life of the mess from soldiering. Lieutenant G.E. Hawes of the Royal Fusiliers, writing in 1901 from Cairo to his friend Lieutenant Edmund Malone in another battalion of the same regiment, said:

> I'm beginning to realize . . . that I do not like soldiering, though I very much like the life – the fun of always being with a lot of nice people of one's own age. . . . I feel I never want to leave this jolly battalion, and the thought of one day perhaps doing so, to work for the Staff College, and then afterwards living alone outside a mess fills me with horror.

Captain R.W. Campbell thought that it offered even more: 'The mess is the school for courage, honour, and truth', he said. 'In the British officer's anteroom you will find the foundations of that splendid chivalry which has given us fame'. Major-General George Younghusband felt much the same:

> Life in a big Mess has a very salutary effect on those who live in it. The prig ceases to be priggish: it isn't good enough. The cad, if by chance he has slipped in, ceases to be caddish: it isn't good enough. The real 'bad hat', or untamable 'bounder' quietly disappears from His Majesty's Service.

Although officers sat down to gleaming crystal, fine plate and expensive silver, conversation was limited – sex, women, religion, politics and 'shop talk' were all forbidden topics, leaving principally trivia, sport, and horses. Even when a regiment took the field, life in the mess remained much the same; every effort was made to duplicate the conditions and customs of the permanent mess. There was always at least one mess tent with tables and chairs, linen, silver, glassware, fine wines and sometimes even carpets and lounge chairs. The tent served another purpose when a regiment was on active service: slain officers were laid out on the tables.

A newly commissioned officer was taken in hand by the senior subaltern, from whom he learned the traditions and tabus of the regiment. Usually a new subaltern was not expected to speak unless spoken to, and in some regiments he was strongly advised not to express an opinion on anything during his first two or three years. In the 2nd Scottish Rifles an officer with less than three years' service was not allowed to stand on the hearthrug in front of the anteroom fire. In this battalion, as in others, there was no smoking from 7.30 until after dinner, when smoking was allowed only after the port had circulated twice. In all regiments wine passed from right to left. If the man on one's right asked for wine, the bottle had to go completely around the table unless permission was asked of the mess president for a 'backhander'. (A naval superstition held that the ship would sink within a year if the wine was passed the wrong way.) Fines were imposed on those who broke the rules. In the Norfolk Regiment officers forfeited a bottle of wine for tearing a newspaper or for speaking Latin.

In the mess the uniform rather than the officer's rank often fixed his position. If, say, the lieutenant-colonel commanding a battalion returned in civilian clothes after dining out and found only the junior subaltern in the anteroom, and the subaltern was in uniform, the colonel would ask his permission to enter. As one officer put it: 'As a matter of course this permission is never withheld, but equally as a matter of course it is always demanded'. Also, combatant officers socially outranked non-combatant officers. Thus, if a lieutenant was the senior combatant officer present, he, rather than, say, the battalion surgeon, though a captain, would escort a guest into dinner and occupy the senior place.

In most regiments, though not in all, the first toast of the evening after dinner was to the sovereign's health. The custom began with an order from the king as a pledge of an officer's loyalty. Those loyal to the Stuarts circumvented it to their satisfaction by passing their glasses over their finger bowls, the toast becoming for them: 'To the king across the water'. Some regiments refused to toast the sovereign at all on the ground that the regiment's loyalty was and had always been beyond question.

Officers serving in Sierra Leone drink a toast on the Queen's birthday, 1889
(*Photo: Mary Evans Picture Library*)

Some regiments drank the sovereign's health every night, some only once a week. Some drank the toast sitting (as always in the Royal Navy) but most drank it standing. The usual ritual after the wine had passed round was for the president of the mess to say to the vice-president (both of these offices usually rotated weekly by roster): 'Mr Vice, the Queen'. All officers then stood, said more or less in chorus, 'The Queen, God bless her', and then took a sip of their wine. In Welsh regiments this was generally followed by a toast to the Prince of Wales.

Toasts to royalty were followed by other toasts. Horace Smith-Dorrien had a ritual, which he claimed had been used by Wellington, of an unvarying toast for each day of the week. On Mondays it was 'Our men'; on Tuesdays, 'Our women'; Wednesdays, 'Our swords'; Thursdays, 'Ourselves'; Fridays, 'Our religion'; Saturdays, 'To sweethearts and wives', after which he always added, 'May they never meet'; and Sundays to 'Absent friends'.

In every regiment there was what was called the Regent's Allowance, consisting of two bottles of wine, usually one of port and one of madeira, which were served each night through the generosity of the sovereign. The custom began when George IV was Regent. Dining in a mess one night he noticed that a few officers did not drink the loyal toast. When told that they could not afford wine, he thought this such a shame that he pledged himself to provide each regiment's mess with two bottles to be used in drinking the King's health. Every sovereign continued the custom, even after Edward VII decreed that the toast could be drunk in water. By 1900, however, the wine had been converted to cash and the sum was simply added to the general mess fund.

The mess was every officer's home; thus, officers did not buy drinks for each other there. This attitude eroded in some regiments, and General George Younghusband (writing in 1917) spoke of an 'insidious and deadly' custom:

> That is the habit of Officers standing each other drinks, at any time of day, in the ante-room; for all the world as if one of His Majesty's Officers' Messes was a public-house, or American bar. And the vulgarity was emphasised by adding such catchwords as 'so long' and 'here's to you', which came from the same not very aristocratic haunts.

Younghusband doubtless disapproved of the Royal Warwickshire Regiment, where it was long the custom for an officer never to decline a drink offered by another officer and never to order a soft drink. Every newly joined subaltern was expected to have a drink with every other officer in the battalion. It was to this heavy-drinking regiment that the abstemious twenty-one-year-old Second-Lieutenant Bernard Montgomery reported for duty in 1908 and tasted liquor for the first time. The senior subaltern informed him that a drink could not be ordered before the fish course. Montgomery was suitably impressed: he had never eaten a meal that included a fish course. The Warwickshires were not the only hard-drinking regiment. In the 9th Lancers in the 1860s it was 'common practice', according to Hugh McCalmont, 'to drink claret at breakfast in the mess almost as a matter of course'.

Among the uniforms every officer was required to buy was his mess dress, different for each regiment but all generally conforming to the same design, with a short jacket that could not be buttoned. Officers of the Household Cavalry had mess uniforms, but when in London they wore civilian clothes ('mufti') to mess. For more than a century prior to 1850 officers in the Worcestershire Regiment wore their swords to mess, and even after the custom was generally abandoned, the orderly officer and the captain of the week always went sworded to table. The custom originated in 1746, when a detachment of the regiment (then the 29th Foot) was stationed in the Leeward Islands. While the officers were messing one night, a party of Indians attacked and massacred the garrison. After this the regiment decided it would be prudent to be prepared.

Etiquette varied from regiment to regiment. In the King's Royal Rifle Corps badges of rank were not worn on mess jackets, and all but the colonel were called by their first names. In the Leicestershire Regiment subalterns gave other subalterns and captains their last names only, never their rank; majors were called by their rank without using surnames. Except on parade, only the colonel was addressed as 'Sir'.

Highland Regiments always celebrated New Year's Day and St Andrew's Day. It was then the custom for the mess sergeant to pass around a quaich, a two-handled cup, filled with scotch. Each officer in turn drained it, then twisted the cup over and outward and kissed the bottom to show that it was completely empty. In most Scots regiments during Queen Victoria's reign the pipe-major was also given a drink, and he gave the toast: 'Deoch slainte na ban Righ' (Here's to the woman king). An English officer gazetted to the Black Watch was required to swallow a Scots thistle and wash it down with a glass of whisky. This, it was said, made a Scotsman of him.

In every Highland regiment pipers marched around the table after dinner playing their instruments, an experience many English visitors found painful. Others too. The regimental history of the Gordons records a visit to the mess in 1890 of a Russian naval officer who, although 'at first stunned and dazed by the crash and volume of the pipes, gradually became alert, fingers drumming in time more and more certainly, till he turned on his host excitedly: "They're playing a tune" '!

In some regiments it was the custom that no one could leave the table until the colonel left. In others the president and vice-president could not leave until all other officers had risen. Usually no officer was allowed to leave without special permission on guest nights until the last guest had gone. All officers, even if married, were required to be at mess on guest night, usually held once a week.

Cigars or cigarettes – Turkish cigarettes, never Virginian – were smoked; pipes were not allowed. In the Warwickshire Regiment, where hangovers were common, there was a civilized rule that no one spoke at breakfast. After dinner, when the bottle had passed round – 'when the cloth was removed' was the expression used – there was often singing, reciting, betting and occasionally rougher activities. Experienced servants transported to safety the more fragile furnishings, for while the senior officers usually retired to play billiards or whist (later bridge), the young officers engaged in wrestling matches and other sports more suited to the outdoors; it was not unknown for subalterns to ride their ponies into the mess to leap the sofas. Not all the rough play was for the young; Sir Hope Grant, when a fifty-two-year-old general, still enjoyed playing high cockalorum. But there were also quiet times. An 1889 watercolour of the Green Howards' anteroom after dinner presents a sedate scene: officers quietly drinking, talking, reading newspapers, while one plays a banjo.

Betting, sometimes of an unusual kind, was common in the mess, and in expensive regiments large sums were frequently exchanged. Often the wagers were on an officer's ability to perform some physical feat. In 1880 Lieutenant Josceline Bagot of the Grenadier Guards bet that he could walk or run from Hatchett's Hotel in Piccadilly to Marwell's Hotel in Brighton, a distance of fifty-four miles, in twelve hours. He won handily. Starting at 5.15 a.m. he walked the distance in nine hours and forty-six minutes and was back in London for dinner. Lieutenant Adrian Carton de Wiart of the 4th Dragoon Guards was dining at a mess in Johannesburg one evening in 1905 when he was bet that he could not walk to Pretoria (thirty miles as the crow flies) that night within ten hours. He accepted, and won with fifty minutes to spare.

Usually the betting was done only among the officers, but in 1877 Lieutenant Lord Grimston, 1st Life Guards, wagered £25 that he could out-walk any man in the regiment, and was accepted by Corporal Maxwell. The two men started out from Hyde Park Corner for the cavalry barracks at Windsor, a distance of 22½ miles. Although the betting among the officers was three to one on Grimston, the corporal won easily, walking the distance in four hours and fifteen minutes. Lord Grimston arrived forty minutes later.

In the 1870s Lieutenant Neville Lyttelton won five Canadian dollars by jumping a ditch twenty feet deep and sixteen feet across on his horse. In 1910 an officer in the 2nd Scottish Rifles bet that he could ride a mile, run a mile, swim a mile and row a mile within an hour; he won with seven minutes to spare. Some wagers were simply silly. In the 15th Foot (Prince of Wales Own West Yorkshire) there was betting as to who could stand on one leg the longest. Lieutenant Johnson Wilkinson won after standing one-legged for two hours.

The wearing of moustaches was an on-again off-again affair, depending not only on current fashion but on regulations as well. At the beginning of the nineteenth century it was a matter of individual taste, though sometimes the preference of a regiment's commanding officer prevailed. A regimental order of 11 May 1801 for the 13th Foot (Somerset Light Infantry) stated:

> Such few officers as have adopted moustaches are desired to discontinue them as they carry an appearance not only of affected singularity but of want of cleanliness.

Not long after, however, it became *de rigueur* for cavalry officers to wear moustaches, and in 1854 permission was given for infantry officers to grow them. In 1896, paragraph 60 of the Queen's Regulations made moustaches obligatory for all officers, though there were some who refused to comply. In the 1900s, when William Robertson was commandant of the Staff College, he dismissed 'a clever and gallant officer who foolishly persisted in refusing to grow a moustache'.

Although officers were underpaid, most did not work very hard and they had few responsibilities. Hubert Gough, speaking of the days when he was a subaltern in the 16th Lancers during the 1880s, said:

> We led a cheerful, care-free life; what duties we had to do . . . did not call for much mental effort. Afternoons were usually free for most officers. We played polo and some cricket at the Aldershot Club in summer. We took the coach, with four horses and two men, all taken from the ranks, to almost every race meeting round London.

Almost all the work involving discipline, drill, and the feeding and well-being of the troops was handled by the commanding officer, the adjutant and the quartermaster working through their non-commissioned officers. It was the adjutant's job to arrange the daily routine of the battalion, to issue written orders, and to ensure that the drill and dress of the battalion were of the desired standard. The quartermaster, of course, was responsible for stores and supplies; he was often a man promoted from the ranks and his rank as lieutenant or captain was usually honorary.

Hugh McCalmont, describing his days as a subaltern in the 1860s, wrote:

> There was plenty doing in Dublin in those days, any amount of dances and dinners going on during the season, and real good hunting to be had fairly close at hand, while soldiering was taken pretty easy even during the drill period.

Ian Hamilton wrote to his brother of a march made by his battalion in 1876 from Multan to Delhi. The officers got up at 3.30 in the morning and fell in fifteen minutes later:

> . . . one is always in before 9 a.m. and has tubbed and breakfasted by 10, and then the remainder of the day is entirely your own to do what you like with. No drills or anything of that sort, and duty will only come once every 10 days as we have so many subs [sub-lieutenants].

Leave was generous, generally at least two months a year. In the Guards a subaltern could obtain four months' leave out of every twelve and a captain could count on six. In addition, some regiments hunted two days a week during the season. When Captain John Adye, newly posted to Aldershot, asked his commanding officer, Major Thomas Studely, for leave to go hunting, he was told: 'As long as there is one subaltern left in barracks to do the work on a hunting day I do not want you to ask for leave. Always go'. Such was the life of an officer in times of peace.

OFFICERS AND GENTLEMEN.
Part II: Gentlemen

> Speaking roughly, you must employ either blackguards or gentlemen, or,
> best of all, blackguards commanded by gentlemen, to do butcher's work
> with efficiency and despatch.
>
> Kipling

Cromwell once said: 'I had rather have a plain russet-coated captain
that knows what he fights for and loves what he knows than what you
call a gentleman and is nothing else'. This was a point of view that died
with him. From 1660 until the First World War the British army was
led by gentlemen. Officers of all ranks agreed that this was essential, although then, as now, a gentleman proved difficult to define. Men came
from 'good families', they were 'of the right sort', they were 'sound'. It
was not necessarily a part of a gentleman's character to pay bills
promptly; officers had to be reminded from time to time that it was dis-
honest not to pay their tailors,* although gambling debts were promptly
paid.

Among the activities regarded as merely the pranks of high-spirited
young gentlemen (as related by officers who participated in them) were:

---

* Six years after joining the 4th Hussars Winston Churchill still had not paid all the
tailors' bills for his initial uniforms.

shouting 'fire' in a crowded hotel, removing a baby from its carriage and making off with the pram, stealing a large and expensive boat, tearing up lamp posts and tossing them in a pond, throwing potatoes at pedestrians who stood in the way of a dashing dog cart, wrenching off door knockers from private houses, and setting off explosives under card tables. Gentlemen frequently exhibited a lack of sympathy for the plight of their social inferiors and often were actually cruel to those who tried to better their station in life. Their snobbery was blatant.

Occasionally one of the 'wrong sort' got into a regiment, but he was usually driven out. Unwanted officers were first politely asked to 'turn in their papers', to resign; if they refused, they were subjected to a 'subalterns' court-martial' and rough handling by their peers. Lord Wolseley spoke with approval of attacks at Aldershot on subalterns who 'had practically no pretensions to the rank of gentleman'. In 1894 Second-Lieutenant George Hodge of the 4th Hussars did not meet with the approbation of his peers and was so severely handled that he resigned his commission. The following year, and in the same regiment, Second-Lieutenant Winston Churchill joined with other subalterns in driving out Second-Lieutenant Alken George Bruce, who had been a classmate of Churchill's at Sandhurst. Among other things, Churchill and his pals assured young Bruce that he would need at least £500 a year to live in such a grand regiment as the 4th Hussars. (Churchill himself at this time had less than £300 per year.) Bruce and his father both made complaint and took their case to the press. Not for the last time in his life, Churchill found his name in the news.

Certainly subalterns could make life most unpleasant for anyone they disliked. A former officer in the 18th Hussars described the treatment meted out to any young officer who failed to meet what were regarded as gentlemanly standards:

> He was never allowed to go to sleep, except in a wet bed; everything he possessed was broken up; and he sometimes found himself in a horse trough to cool his brain. I remember one chap who wouldn't go, and was shut up in a room full of hay, which got alight, and he was then put in a horse trough to put the fire out. He was a very bad case, a shocking cad, who joined with a wife off the streets, and with whom it would have been impossible to live. He had every hint, and the last, before the hay episode, was that he found all his luggage packed, and at the station; but no! We had to apply the 'ordeal by fire', and then he *did* go!

Social position carried weight. Even in the case of staff appointments, it was long considered more important to come from an aristocratic family than to have passed through the Staff College, to possess social graces rather than military abilities. Lord Wolseley, speaking of the period in the 1870s when Lord Airey was adjutant-general, said that Airey had 'what is of great advantage to the highly-placed staff officer at Army headquarters, he was well connected, and was intimate with what is commonly called "Society" '.

There was no doubt that being well connected helped an officer get to wherever he wanted to go in the army. Lord Roberts always inquired into the pedigrees of officers who applied to him for appointments and, as Ian Hamilton said, 'if he was a man who owned a good grandmother he would give him a trial'. When Arthur Eyre, 90th Light Infantry (only son of General Sir William Eyre), applied to go with Garnet Wolseley on his expedition to fight the Ashantis in West Africa, Colonel Evelyn Wood approved the application, merely noting, 'The son of a good soldier, his mother is a lady'. So young Eyre adjusted his monocle, went off to Africa and was killed by an Ashanti musket ball.

Engaging in sports – gentlemen's sports, naturally – was considered de rigueur, and it was still common up to the First World War for a superior to include in his confidential report on an officer: 'A good man to hounds'. Wolseley, in defining the desired qualities of leadership in an officer, listed 'good pleasant manners . . . a genial disposition'. Manners included an observance of tabus, and General George Younghusband warned young officers that 'to smoke a pipe in uniform in Pall Mall or Hyde Park is a more grievous offence than to elope with the colonel's mother'. Guards officers never carried their own suitcases or parcels, never smoked Virginia cigarettes, and never reversed in waltzing.

In spite of the emphasis on manners, it often seemed that those whose social position had always been high and assured possessed manners less elegant than those of run-of-the-mill middle-class gentlemen. The Duke of Cambridge once had the bad grace to rebuke a general at Aldershot in the presence of the Duke's staff, provoking the general to blurt out: 'I don't mind being called a damned fool, if it pleases your Royal Highness to call me so. But I do mind being called a damned fool before your Royal Highness' other damn fools'.

A few officers were such dandies that they astonished their contemporaries. John Palmer Brabazon (called 'Bwab' by his friends because, like many cavalry officers, he pronounced the letter 'r' as 'w') was a brave soldier who had served with distinction in the Ashanti War, the Second Afghan War, two campaigns in the Sudan and in the Anglo-Boer War; he was also a friend of Lord Randolph Churchill and, when in command of the 4th Hussars, was instrumental in getting young Winston into his regiment, which Winston wanted, instead of the King's Royal Rifle Corps, which Lord Randolph favoured. John Adye was once surprised during the Nile campaign, when he encountered him in the middle of the desert at a time when transport was so scarce that all ranks were reduced to a quart of water a day for all purposes, to see Bwab pull from his sleeve a silk handkerchief soaked in Cologne. He had, it seemed, found room for his scent in his baggage.

Of course, to say that all British officers were gentlemen born and bred ignores the exceptions. Neville Macready was the son of W.C. Macready, a famous actor, and Cornelius Clery was the son of a wine merchant; these were unusual antecedents for army officers, but both became generals and Macready was adjutant-general for the British Expeditionary Forces in 1914.

Social standards for officers in the militia and volunteers were somewhat lower than for the regular establishment. Still, Major-General Sir Henry Hallam Parr was surprised to discover during the Anglo-Boer War a company of volunteers led by a captain who was the son of a coach-maker in Dover with a senior subaltern who was the son of a greengrocer at Folkestone; but what really astonished him was that both were 'smart and efficient officers'.

There were also a few men who rose from the ranks to become general officers. It has always been one of the great strengths of the British social system, and perhaps the reason for its remarkable endurance, that it has never been a completely closed corporation. In the nineteenth century there was little upward social mobility. The obstacles in the paths of men who attempted to move out of their class were formidable, but the route was not barred. A young man of modest means could become a peer, a crofter's son could become a major-general, a footman could become a field-marshal. It happened.

The word *ranker* had a curious double meaning: it referred both to a gentleman who had enlisted in the ranks and to an 'other rank' who became an officer. Lieutenant-General Sir William Bellairs, writing in 1889, said, 'For a young man of good family and fair education to join the army . . . as a private, with only a moderate prospect of rising to become an officer, would be about as inadvisable as yoking a racehorse to the plough'. Yet some young men who could not obtain a commission in any other way, did try this last resort. Gentlemen also enlisted for other reasons, most of which were the same as those which led men to join the French Foreign Legion: to forget or escape a woman, to avoid the shame of having disgraced their families, or because they had developed an uncontrollable anti-social habit. Private William Brown told of a former attorney serving in the ranks of the Rifle Brigade. He was an able, intelligent man who was frequently promoted to non-commissioned officer and as frequently lost his stripes, for he was an incurable alcoholic. Corporal William Forbes-Mitchell told a strange tale of two gentlemen privates in the 93rd (Sutherland) Highlanders who knew and hated each other. When one was killed in the attack on the Secundrabagh, the other was seen to bend over him and heard to say, 'I came to the 93rd to see this man die'! As Forbes-Mitchell said, 'If the history of these two men could be known it would without doubt form material for a most sensational novel'. It was of such 'poor little lambs who have lost their way' that Kipling wrote in 'Gentlemen Rankers', a poem best known in the United States for its parody, 'The Whiffenpoof Song', in which Yale undergraduates replace gentlemen rankers.

A few gentlemen who could have been officers chose to serve in the ranks, though usually only in wartime. Stephan Graham, who served as a private in the Scots Guards during the First World War, was one such; while in London he was acutely aware of living in two different social worlds at the same time:

> One night I made one of a joyous party where my neighbour on one hand was an English princess, and the next night I was a sentry at Buckingham Palace.

The most famous gentleman ranker of all time was, of course, the man who called himself (sometimes) T.E. Lawrence.

The other type of ranker, the soldier promoted from the ranks, was rare, but he existed throughout the Victorian–Edwardian era. From time to time there were public complaints that not enough deserving non-commissioned officers were given commissions, but there were strong objections from within the army. General Sir Hugh Rose, in a report written in 1862, said of this class of ranker:

Neither the officer so raised, nor the officers of *a superior class in life* with whom he associates, nor the soldiers he has to govern, are benefited by what is a disadvantageous anomaly, the transfer of a man of a very different, inferior and less educated class in life to one superior in all these respects.

There was one almost sure way for an N.C.O. to win a commission, but it depended upon the right circumstances, considerable courage and much luck: it involved leading a forlorn hope. A forlorn hope is not, as some imagine, an impossible mission, but a body of men who engage in a dangerous, often desperate enterprise, such as plunging through a newly made breach in the wall of a fort and planting the colours on the ramparts. Sergeants sometimes led forlorn hopes when their officers had fallen. Their chances of survival were not good, but success was often rewarded with a commission.

Luke O'Connor won the Victoria Cross in the Crimea as well as a commission; he rose to become a major-general. William McBean was an Inverness ploughboy before he enlisted in the 93rd Highlanders. His rise was delayed by his religion and he was seven years a lance-corporal, for his commanding officer refused to promote him because he was, he said, 'a damned Free Kirker'. However, he eventually won the Victoria Cross as well as a commission and died a major-general.

Scotsmen, if not better educated than English, Welsh and Irish other ranks, appear frequently to have been of better character and, perhaps in consequence, to have more often succeeded when commissioned. Sergeant John Knox of the 2nd Scots Guards won a Victoria Cross and a commission in the Rifle Brigade for rallying men around the colours at the Alma; J. H. Levey, a lance-corporal in the Scots Guards during the Anglo-Boer War, won a commission and commanded a battalion of the Gordons in the First World War, earning the Distinguished Service Order.

John Shipp was the only man ever to earn a commission from the ranks *twice*. He had been placed in the parish poorhouse at the age of five. As soon as possible he was apprenticed to a farmer, who mistreated him. At the age of thirteen, he ran away and enlisted in the 22nd Foot (Cheshire Regiment), where he rose to the rank of sergeant. In India he distinguished himself by his daring: at the battle of Bhurtpore in 1805 he led three forlorn hopes in unsuccessful assaults, in the last of which

Military steeplechase in the Crimea (*Photo: National Army Museum*)

he was severely wounded. His courage was rewarded with an ensigncy in the 65th Foot (1st York and Lancaster Regiment), but he found his new role difficult to sustain, for, as he said, 'The gentleman did not seem to sit easy on me'. Returning to England after a further two and a half years of service, Shipp, now a lieutenant, found it impossible to live on his pay. He incurred debts and was forced to sell his commission. Soon finding himself penniless, he re-enlisted, this time in the 24th Light Dragoons, and rapidly rose through the ranks. He distinguished himself in the Gurkha War, won a second commission, and in 1821 was promoted to lieutenant. Two years later, having become involved in a horse-racing scandal and having made disparaging remarks about his commanding officer, he was court-martialed and cashiered.

The most brilliant career of a ranker was that of William Robertson, the only one ever to become a field-marshal, and the story of his struggles as a junior officer is poignant. He was born in 1860, the son of a village tailor and postmaster at Welbourne in Lincolnshire. He was educated at the village school until, at about the age of fifteen, he was employed as a footman in the service of the Cardigan family in Northamptonshire. He was unhappy with his lot, however, and decided to enlist. His mother was horrified. 'I would rather bury you than see you in a red coat', she told him. Nevertheless, he took the Queen's shilling on 13 November 1877 and was posted to the 16th Lancers at Aldershot, which since 1855 has been the principal training centre of the British army. Being a clever young man, he was made a lance-corporal only two months later. In 1885, at the age of twenty-five, and after only eight years service, he was promoted to troop sergeant-major: this was a rapid rise through the non-commissioned ranks in this era. Three years later – encouraged by his officers, it should be noted – he took the bold step of accepting a commission when it was offered and became a second-lieutenant in the 3rd Dragoon Guards, then stationed in India.

At this time only about three per cent of all officers were commissioned from the ranks, and most of these served as riding masters, paymasters or quartermasters; rarely were they combatant officers. The requirements were that the soldier be a non-commissioned officer not over thirty-two years of age who had passed a first class army school certificate of education and an examination in regimental duties and drill.

At first glance it might seem odd that a penniless young man such as Robertson would take a commission as a combatant officer in an expensive cavalry regiment, but it was sometimes easier for a poor officer to rise in a cavalry regiment than in a county infantry battalion. Many wealthy and aristocratic officers, with which most cavalry regiments were well stocked, chose to transfer or go on half pay when their regiments were ordered to India. This left vacancies for the poor but ambitious officers who, in any case, preferred India because of the increased pay and allowances there.

Before Robertson left for India, he took a musketry course at Hythe. He was, of course, well aware of the social barrier he had crossed. On the night of his arrival he found himself unable to pluck up the courage to go to the officers' mess. He found a place to stay in town. In a letter to his mother he tried to explain what it was like for him:

> You see it's all among strangers – strangers in more ways than one. . . .
> The officers who now know me are very nice, but it's a difficult business because you see I feel that I am acting under a false flag if they do not know my previous life. However I soon out with it if the occasion demands, so it will soon be known throughout the school, and then I shall be all right because of knowing to whom they are talking. . . . I have just been asked by a very nice officer to go over to Folkestone with him this afternoon, on the impulse I assented. Well that was wrong. If I go there money will be spent and a Sunday spent wrong, so I have made escape and do not intend going. . . . I find that the clothes Father made for me

compare very favourably with any others here and feel very thankful for the trouble he has taken and hope to repay him one day. . . . Have not got into eating about a dozen courses after 8 at night. . . . Of course I should like a bit more companionship during my walks but that will come in time, anyway, it does not matter as I do not care much about it at any time, only one is liable to despondency with too much of one's own company.

Later, from India, he wrote to his father:

It is so miserable out here – *you don't know*. . . . I'm afraid I do not remember how often I *must* feel cut off from *all* friendship. So far as I know, not *once* has anyone in my present sphere taken offence at being in my company, but there is much difference between this and sincere mutual interest; this cannot naturally be between a born gentleman and one who is only now beginning to *try* to become one. . . . here amid all the gaiety and apparent friendship I feel that were I not an officer tomorrow, there would be perhaps none to recognise me. Poor human nature is so very weak, it must have somewhere to look for support and sympathy and it *does* require some sign to reassure it.

For seven years Robertson struggled, through hard work and self-denial, to maintain himself financially and to overcome his loneliness. Like many who feel themselves outsiders by virtue of their race or social origins, he tended to blame each piece of bad luck on discrimination, but in fact he appears to have encountered very little, and in only nine years rose from being one of the oldest subalterns in the army to being one of its youngest colonels. The turning point in his life occurred in 1895–6. In those two years he was promoted to captain, won the Distinguished Service Order, entered the Staff College – the first ranker ever to do so – married the daughter of a general officer in the Indian army (over the strong objections of the bride's family), and his wife presented him with a son. In the First World War Robertson the ranker became Chief of the Imperial General Staff and subsequently a baronet. He died full of honours as Field-Marshal Sir William Robertson, G.C.B., G.C.M.G., K.C.V.O., D.S.O.

OTHER RANKS:
Beef, Beer and Lust

Sons of the sheltered city – unmade, unmeet
Ye pushed them raw to the battle, and ye picked them raw from the
street.

Kipling, 'The Islanders'

There were officers and then there were the 'other ranks' – the warrant officers, non-commissioned officers and privates. They were so different, officers and other ranks, that they seemed to be of two different races. They were alike in that most were born of British parents, usually in the British Isles or in India, but their accents (even language in some cases), their habits, manners, tastes and, of course, financial circumstances were far apart. The British army operated on what was basically a caste system. (The British were more at home in India than one might imagine.) In Britain, as in India, differences in wealth and social position were assumed as facts of life. There was little resentment. Subordination to those above seemed to come naturally. Armies have always been viewed with suspicion in democratic societies because they are the least democratic of all social institutions. They are, in fact, not democratic at all. Governments which have tried to eliminate the officer class or to blur the distinction between officer and man have not been successful. Armies stand as disturbing reminders that democratic processes are not always the best, living and perpetual proof that, in at least this one area, the caste system works.

To Welsh and Irish regiments came recruits who could not speak English, and in English ones were youths from places such as Yorkshire whose English was unintelliglble to most other Britons. Irish, Scots and Welsh regiments were called 'tribal regiments', but the various races were not evenly divided, for all contained a disproportionate number of Irishmen. In the first decade of the nineteenth century the 13th Regiment of Foot (Somerset Light Infantry) contained eighty Englishmen, six Scotsmen, two foreigners and 485 Irishmen. In 1878, which may be taken as a typical Victorian year, 39,121 out of 178,064 other ranks were Irish – almost one in four. They came, for the most part, from depressed rural areas and city slums.

In the century between the battles of Waterloo and First Ypres, the British officer had not changed much. In 1914, in spite of technological advances, he still wore spurs, was usually mounted, wore uncomfortable and impractical uniforms, came from the same social classes with the same values as in the past, and, most important of all, retained much of the same set of attitudes, beliefs and prejudices. If an officer of Wellington's army could have walked into the mess of his former regiment a century later, he would have noticed little change; he would have quickly adjusted, and by the time dinner was finished and the cloth removed he would have felt quite at home. But if a private of 1815 could have found himself in a barracks in 1914 he would have been perplexed indeed, for the changes that had taken place in the life of a British private were dramatic. Nearly all would be able to read and write, and no backs would carry scars from the lash. Food was much improved, but Wellington's soldier would notice the absence of women. The average age of the twentieth-century soldier would be much lower, and there would be few 'old sweats' of the sort Kipling described in *Soldiers Three*. Some of the old attitudes remained, but the private of 1914, although he swore, gambled and whored as did Wellington's men, bore little resemblance to the private who fought at Waterloo. There were a number of reasons for this, one being the change in the terms of service.

It was and had always been an army of volunteers; not until the middle of the First World War (January 1916) did Britain resort to conscription. From 1783 until 1806 men enlisted for life; then for a twenty-three-year period enlistments were seven years for the infantry, ten years for the cavalry and twelve years for sappers and gunners. In 1829 Parliament restored the life engagement; in 1847 this was changed to twenty-one years – which was much the same thing. In 1870 'short service' was introduced. Men enlisted for twelve years but spent only three to seven years with the colours and the remainder in the reserve.

Recruitment improved considerably, and short service attracted volunteers of a higher quality; they were no longer almost exclusively life's losers, but included a number of young men who wanted a few years of adventure in far-off places before settling down. Nevertheless, recruiting remained a problem in peacetime. Although the terms of service were improved, bounties, which had been as high as twenty guineas, were abolished, These had been strong inducements to enlistment, although, whatever the original intention of the recruit, he was almost invariably persuaded by his new comrades in arms to spend the money on gin and beer. An exception was the case off the four Ross brothers, who in 1805 enlisted together in the 74th Regiment (2nd Highland Light Infantry) and used their bounty to buy a cottage for their parents. Three of the brothers died fighting in the Peninsula, but James, the survivor, was living in the cottage in 1882 at the age of 95.

Recruiting difficulties sometimes caused the War Office to lower the physical standards, for potential recruits were most often rejected because they were 'under-developed', unable to meet the requirements of height, weight or chest measurement. In 1900, even with lax standards, half the volunteers were rejected. At one point the artillery was permitted to accept men of shorter stature if they were exceptionally broad in the shoulders and chest, leading one old recruiting sergeant to complain to his officer: 'Beg yer pardon, sir, but the Almighty don't make men in the shape you order 'em'. Officers continued to deplore the inferior physical qualities of the recruits. In 1910 General William Butler said that 'men are now taken who would have been rejected with scorn a few years ago; we get recruits no longer from rural districts, but from the slums of the big cities, and even from these sources we find it difficult to obtain them in sufficient numbers'.

It was true that more and more recruits came from the cities. Following the agricultural depression in the 1870s and the industrialization of Britain in the last quarter of the nineteenth century, increasing

Recruits, 1882 (*Photo: Graham Brandon*)

numbers of young men left the countryside to seek work in factories. Those who failed to find it often joined the army. Physical standards did decline and soldiers became shorter and shorter. In 1850, for example, more than half the men in the 92nd (2nd Gordon) Highlanders were five feet eight inches or taller; in 1890 less than a quarter of the men were that tall, and only thirty-seven out of 810 were six feet or more in height. In the 1st Gordons only nine out of 841 were six feet or taller. In 1891 the average height of a soldier in the second battalion of the Queens was only five feet six and three-quarter inches. In 1907 the average height of recruits in the Oxfordshire Light Infantry was only five feet five and three-eighths inches.

Although height alone was a doubtful military asset, particularly in the days of the repeating rifle, high military headgear was favoured as making men seem taller, and tall soldiers were always much admired. The pride of the 93rd (Sutherland) Highlanders at one time was Sergeant Samuel Macdonald, who stood six feet ten inches tall and possessed a forty-eight-inch chest. The Countess of Sutherland, who took a personal interest in the regiment, thought his large frame required more support than the normal army ration could supply, so she gave him an extra two shillings and sixpence a day for food. The regiment grieved when at the age of thirty-five he died of 'water on the chest'.

Butler's comment on the reduced quality of recruits was, at least in part, the complaint of all old soldiers in all armies in all eras: that the army had rapidly gone down hill since the days of their youth. In one important respect recruits were much improved, for in the last decades of the nineteenth century an increasing number were literate. Although the army profited by the higher standards, it also found that the better educated young men were not so easy to recruit. It was more difficult to deceive the clever slum dweller than it had been to trick the simple country boy. The recruiting sergeant required the talents of a confidence man and the morals of a horse trader as 'by beat of drum and otherwise' he went about seeking volunteers. In the days before short service, many a young man, after a friendly drinking bout with an affable sergeant, awoke to find the Queen's shilling in his pocket (token of his acceptance as a recruit) and himself a soldier for life.

Recruiting sergeants were fond of boasting of their successes. One described his methods in Scotland. He caught Scots weavers by sending a former Glasgow weaver to their haunts:

It was never much trouble enticing them to enlist. The best way was to make up to the man you had in your eye . . . and ask what sort of web he was in. You might be sure it was a bad one. . . . Ask him how a clever, handsome-looking fellow like him could waste his time . . . in a damp, unwholesome shop . . . weaving was going to ruin and he might soon be starving . . .

Ploughboys had to be hooked in a different way. Tell your man how many recruits had been made sergeants, how many were now officers. If you see an officer pass tell him how he was only a recruit a year ago, but now he's so proud he won't speak to you . . . tell him that where your gallant, honourable regiment is lying everything may be had for almost nothing, that the pigs and the fowls are lying in the streets ready roasted, with knives and forks in them, for the soldiers to eat whenever they please . . . keep him drinking – don't let him go to the door without one of your party with him, until he is past the doctor and attested.

Recruiting posters were misleading too. One, designed for the 7th Light Dragoons in the early nineteenth century, after listing the usual blandishments, added that temporarily 'men will not be allowed to hunt during the next season more than once a week'. An 1825 poster for the 66th Foot (2nd Berkshire Regiment) announced that the regiment was looking for 'gallant and spirited young men' and that 'young men of good character and conduct are certain to be promoted as there are at present upward of forty sergeants and corporals wanting to compelete the corps'.

Not all recruits were made drunk or were taken in by the language of the posters or the wiles of the sergeant. There can be no doubt, as Sir Henry Wilson once said, that Jack Frost was the best recruiting sergeant and that many joined to get out of the cold and rain and to put food in their stomachs. According to a staff sergeant in the 13th Foot (Somerset Light Infantry) in 1846, more than half the recruits were unemployed labourers and mechanics seeking support; others, he said, enlisted because they were idle and considered a soldier's life an easy one; then there were the bad characters and criminals, the discontented and restless, and those perverse sons 'who seek to grieve their parents'. He estimated that only one out of a hundred and twenty were ambitious and hoped to improve themselves.

Kipling called these recruits from the over-populated industrial areas 'the sons of those who for generations had done over-much work for over-scanty pay, had sweated in drying-rooms, stooped over looms, coughed among white-lead, and shivered on lime barges'. Often enough it was the dregs of the social and economic system that were taken on, the army serving as an alternative to prison. In came the pathological outcasts, the poorest, the stupidest, the criminally inclined. The welfare state and the emergence of the claiming classes were in the undreamed-of future and, barring the workhouse, the army provided the state's only welfare service. Daniel Defoe said that 'the poor starve, thieve or turn soldier'.

In a study of late Victorian poverty by B. Seebohm Rowntree, it was calculated that in 1900 about 90 per cent of all recruits came from the working classes, that 7 per cent were shopmen or clerks, 3 per cent boys and 1 per cent from the 'servant-keeping class'. A closer look at 'working class' is necessary to obtain a true picture. John Bayne, a modern writer, made the following estimate of the social origins of men in the 2nd Scottish Rifles in 1914:

Upper working class	5%
Working class	24%
Real lower class	70%

Non-commissioned officers, he noted, tended to come from the two higher classes. With allowances for the fact that Scottish regiments tended to have a higher percentage of true working-class men, Bayne's estimate is probably close to the average prevailing in the Victorian–Edwardian army. This means that most recruits were a foul-mouthed, noisy, rough lot, usually smelly and frequently verminous.

The young men brought in by the recruiting sergeants had grown up ignorant amid squalor and wretchedness. They had been fortunate to escape or to have survived the usual childhood diseases (rickets was called the 'Glasgow disease'), and they had taken to drink when they were small boys. Their knowledge of sanitation, even personal cleanliness, was almost non-existent. The average recruit was born in a slum housing two persons to a room, where perhaps fifty or more shared one cold water tap and a single toilet. He might have washed his face from time to time, but baths were rare indeed, and even babies were almost never bathed more often than once a week. Toothbrushes were unknown and teeth simply rotted. The smell of a crowd of slum dwellers was overpowering. In the army the frequent body inspections and the emphasis on excessive cleanliness were probably necessary to reverse the habits of the young soldiers and to change what was for them their natural way of life.

For many young male slum dwellers the army was appealing. The pay was small but regular; the food was unappetizing, but by the turn of the century it was ample; the army offered security in an insecure world. The Edwardian soldier was not unhappy with his lot. There was, in fact, some eagerness to enlist on the part of some sections of society. When one young man who wanted to join the Gordon Highlanders was rejected as being too small and the colonel told him to go home, drink more milk and return when he was fully grown, the lad said, 'Oh sir, an' ye'd just tak' me! I'm wee, but I'm wicked'! He was taken. In 1912 another would-be soldier tried to enlist at the Gordons' depot at Aberdeen but was rejected for 'hammer toes'. He was sent away, but before leaving the barracks he asked the quartermaster to hold £7 for him. Two days later he reappeared. 'Ah, my lad, come back for your money, eh'? asked the quartermaster. 'Na, na. I'm back tae 'list. The taes is off'. He had had his deformed toes amputated, for, as he said, he would rather 'be a sodger wantin' twa taes than to remain a "civvy" with the full complement.' Sandy Herd, a famous golfer (Open Champion, 1902), once wanted to enlist in the Gordons but was unable to because, as he later explained, 'Me mither hid me claes.'

Those who joined the army under the impression that a soldier's life was an easy one were soon deprived of their illusions. A soldier in the 71st (2nd Highland Light Infantry) during the Victorian era wrote:

> Frequently have I been awakened through the night by the sobs of those around me in the tent; more especially by the young soldiers, who had not been long from their mother's fire-sides. They often spent the darkness of the night in tears.

Still, there were those who craved adventure and the uniform; they joined the army willingly, never regretted it, and loved the life it offered. Frank Richards joined the Royal Welch Fusiliers in 1901 because 'they had one battalion in China . . . and the other battalion in South Africa, and a long list of battle honours on their Colours; and also that they were the only regiment in the army to wear the flash'. He never rose above the rank of private, but he was happy and continued to re-enlist.

Throughout the nineteenth century the private soldier's lot slowly but steadily improved: his pay was raised a bit, the food got rather better, the discipline became less ferocious and living conditions less unhealthy. But even as late as 1877, when William Robertson joined the army, soldiers were issued their uniforms, a mattress, a pillow, four blankets and two sheets. The blankets were seldom washed, clean sheets were issued only once a month, and clean straw for the mattresses only once every three months. Robertson's work day began at 6.30 a.m. and ended at 6.15 p.m. – unless he had guard duty. Sunday was supposed to be a holiday, but it included a full-dress turn-out for a compulsory church parade, which was followed by an inspection of the stables and quarters by the commanding officer; it was, in fact, the worst day of the week.

'Pipe clay, antiquated and useless forms of drill, blind obedience to orders, ramrod-like rigidity on parade, and similar time-honoured practices were the chief qualifications by which a regiment was judged,' said Robertson. The posting of unneeded sentries was all too common. In 1886 General Evelyn Wood found a sentry stationed at the door to a ward at the Colchester Hospital that had been set aside for military prisoners. The ward was empty – and had been for the previous three months.

Soldiers did not starve to death – at least in peacetime – but they did not grow fat on the rations issued. As one man said: 'When a man entered a soldier's life he should have parted with half his stomach'. Until 1840 there were only two meals a day: at 7.30 a.m. and 12.30 p.m. Until 1870 the only food issued was three-quarters of a pound of meat (usually inferior beef), a pound of bread, and a pound of potatoes, for which sixpence per day was deducted from the soldier's pay. If he wanted vegetables, he had to buy them himself. Even in 1900 the last meal of the day was tea at four o'clock in the afternoon, and nothing further was issued until six o'clock the following morning, when the soldier was given tea, bread and sometimes some butter. However, by this date regimental institutes were beginning to be formed, and here a hungry young soldier could get a bowl of soup and a chunk of bread for a penny.

The meat served in the army was infamous. In the late 1870s the boiled meat was called Harriet Lane, this being the name of a woman hacked to pieces by the notorious murderer, Henry Wainwright. In India in 1903 the ration was increased to one pound per day and it was of better quality; it was also cheap, for a pound of the best beef could be purchased for one anna (about one penny).

The only cooking utensils issued were two copper pots to each company. At Aldershot until 1889, a soldier sent to hospital had his dinner cooked in his battalion and it was carried to him in a tin; it was, of course, seldom warm by the time it reached the patient. Cooks were selected without regard to their culinary skills and were often notorious as the dirtiest men in the regiment. However, as one man said: 'It takes a deal o' dirt to poison sogers'.

The officers, most of whom took considerable interest in their own food, were remarkably unfeeling about the miserable fare of their men. During the Crimean War the renowned French chef, Alexis Soyer, went to Turkey to help Florence Nightingale and, after establishing the kitchen in her hospital at Scutari, applied himself to the cooking arrangements of the soldiers. He invented a stove that was practical in the field and he showed the soldiers how to improve their preparation of food. But Soyer encountered opposition. General Vincent Eyre said, 'Soldiers don't require such good messes as these while campaigning . . . you will improve the cook, but spoil the soldier'. Lord Dundonald, writing in 1926 of the meat, bread and potato ration issued in the 1880s, said that with this ration, a beer and a pipe the men 'were as content as, perhaps more content than, guests at some great banquet'.

When *The Times* correspondent, William Howard Russell, began to send home from the Crimea horrifying accounts of the hardships suffered by the soldiers, most officers were surprised. After all, conditions were not much worse than they had been on many a previous campaign. The difference was that they were being reported in the press to an increasingly literate public who found the customary treatment of soldiers unacceptable.* From this time onward, the quality of daily life of a British soldier steadily improved, but major improvements were made on the initiative of civilians, and always there was resistance, in varying degrees, from the officer corps.

*Throughout the nineteenth century literacy steadily increased, first slowly and then, in the last quarter of the century, with a rush. The number of newspapers also increased, as did circulation. During the Peninsular War *The Times* had only about 5,000 readers; forty years later, during the Crimean War, circulation had risen to 40,000.

Alexis Soyer demonstrating his bivouac kitchen in the Crimea (*Photo: Illustrated London News Picture Library*)

There was also resistance to change from the non-commissioned officers. The narrow gradations of social standing found in civilian life were repeated, formalized and made rigid in the army. The system among the other ranks was complicated, and there was considerable variety in the titles and badges among the warrant and non-commissioned officers. Each man, however, knew his place and that of everyone else in the hierarchy. A single chevron on the sleeve, point down, indicated the lowest noncommissioned officer, called a lance-bombardier in the artillery but elsewhere a lance-corporal. There were no corporals in the artillery, so two chevrons indicated a bombardier. In the Household Cavalry (Life Guards and Blues) there were no sergeants, and the equivalents were called corporals-of-horse; the sergeant-major was corporal-major; and there were titles such as farrier quartermaster-corporal, a rather grand personage who ranked as a warrant officer, of which there were three classes. All these ranks still exist, but a rank peculiar to the nineteenth century was that of colour-sergeant. It was first introduced in 1813 as a reward for distinguished service, but in 1914 it was abolished and colour-sergeants became company sergeant-majors or company quartermaster-sergeants, although in many regiments the quarter-master-sergeant is still addressed as 'colour-sergeant'.

Rank had its privileges and its responsibilities, social as well as military. Sergeants had their own messes and were never seen drinking beer with privates. The sergeants' mess was a modest duplicate of the officers' mess, a place for feeding and recreation presided over by the regimental sergeant-major, its absolute master. Usually there were more married sergeants than married officers, so only a few lived in the mess building. Some of the bachelors had small private rooms in the same buildings as their men.

Food in the sergeants' mess was less varied and less expensive than in the officers' mess, and beer was drunk instead of wine, but the same rules of conversation applied – no talk of women and no shop talk. There were social evenings, dances, and games nights (to which officers were often invited). The government supplied the furniture and billiard tables, and there were tables for dominoes, whist and euchre, but the plate, china, glass, cutlery and pictures on the walls were the property of the mess. The life of a sergeant could be a pleasant one; many even had their own batmen, or shared one with other sergeants.

It was below the dignity of sergeants to drink in the canteen, and they were never seen there except on duty. Corporals messed with the privates and drank at the canteen, but many canteens had separate rooms where the corporals could drink by themselves. Even a lance-corporal was expected to observe the dignity of his rank and to remember that he was a cut above the common soldier. Robert Graves told of the fury of his colonel in the Royal Welch Fusiliers when he heard a private address a lance-corporal by his first name. Private Frank Richards said that he always refused promotion because he did not want to leave the society of his chums, although he admitted that many of his chums did not feel the same way and he lost many friends who accepted promotion. It was indeed a class-conscious army.

Although privates were the lowest on the army's social scale and, criminals and mental defectives aside, on the civilian social scale as well in Britain, still Tommy felt himself superior to all foreigners and quite superior indeed to those whose colouring was darker than his own, whom he usually called 'wogs' or 'niggers' or some other derogatory name. Once at Secunderabad, when a private was giving evidence

Recreation room at Aldershot (*Photo: Mary Evans Picture Library*)

before a military court, he referred to three coolies. An officer reminded
him that one of the three was the Nizam of Hyderabad, one of the
richest men in the world and ruler of the largest independent state in
India. The private amended his statement to 'the Nizam of Hyderabad
and two other coolies'.

In British cantonments in India, Indians were not allowed to enter
tents or barracks with their shoes on. For, said Private Richards, "They
had to realize that they were our inferiors; and while they did so all was
well with them, and with us, and with the whole of India, where they
outnumbered us by a couple of thousand to one'. The only 'natives'
whom Tommy accepted as equals or near equals were the Gurkhas.

Prior to the First World War the British army, unlike the Royal
Navy, never experienced a serious mutiny among its regulars. The
nearest thing was the so-called 'White Mutiny' which occurred shortly
after the Indian Mutiny when the government automatically transferred

all the European troops of the Honourable East India Company's army
to the forces of the Crown. The soldiers protested that they had enlisted
to serve the Company, not the Crown. A few of the ringleaders were
shot and most of the others were eventually shipped back to Britain.

Because of the large percentage of Irishmen in the ranks, a number of
Fenians deliberately enlisted in the 1860s with the intention of foment-
ing mutiny. In 1863 John Boyle O'Reilly, aged nineteen, enlisted in the
10th Hussars. He was, by all accounts, intelligent and popular with all
ranks. His attempts at subversion were inept and certainly do not appear
to have been heinous: he embroidered shamrocks on the underside of
his saddle cloth and on the lining of his greatcoat. Nevertheless, he was
charged with 'knowledge of an intended mutiny' and, in spite of the tes-
timony of his colonel, Valentine Baker, that he had always been a good
soldier, a court-martial sentenced him to be shot. His sentence was
commuted, first to life imprisonment, then to twenty-three years transportation to Western Australia. In Australia he contrived to escape,
aided by an Irish priest and some officers on an American whaling ship,
and fled to the United States. He arrived in Philadelphia to find that the
story of his escape had preceded him and he was welcomed as a hero.
He took out his first naturalization papers that same day. Later he
married an American girl of Irish extraction, became editor of *Pilot* in
Boston, published several volumes of poetry, planned the successful rescue of other Irish patriots in Australia, and became one of the leaders of
the Fenian movement in the United States.

Soldiers in Irish regiments were called 'Paddy' or 'Mick' and in Scottish regiments 'Jock', but the common name for the British soldier, regardless of his origin, was 'Tommy' or, more formally, 'Thomas Atkins'. There are different accounts as to the origin of this name, but
Tommy seems to have been born sometime in the early nineteenth century in the 23rd Foot (Royal Welch Fusiliers), though some say it was
the 33rd Foot (1st West Riding Regiment), the Duke of Wellington's
old regiment, and that the Duke himself provided the name of an old
soldier he had known in the regiment. All agree, however, that the
name appeared on a model for a form of some sort and that the British
soldier readily accepted the name as his own.

Kipling said of Tommy Atkinses that 'Their duty is to keep themselves and their accoutrements specklessly clean, to refrain from getting
drunk more often than is necessary, to obey their superiors, and to pray

for war' ('The Incarnation of Krishna Mulvaney'). Did the other ranks pray for war? Certainly their officers thought so, and undoubtedly many, perhaps most, actually did, but we have fewer personal accounts of life in the ranks. Wolseley said of the men in the 90th Foot (2nd Scottish Rifles): 'Our whole battalion was composed of young men full of life and spirit, and impressed with the one idea that the world was especially created for their own pleasures, of which, to most of us, war with all its sudden changes, and at times its maddening excitement, was the greatest'. Ian Hamilton, writing of the day when the Gordons' battalion in India learned that it was to take part in the First Boer War (1881), said: 'War put me very nearly out of my mind with delight. Bar one private from Glasgow who was said to be in love with a nautch girl, every single living soul was excited and happy'.

The memoirs that exist of Victorian soldiers tend to confirm the officers' belief that their men also enjoyed war. Sergeant Forbes-Mitchell said that 'there is nothing to rouse tired soldiers like a good cannonade in front; it is the best tonic out! Even the youngest soldier who has once been under fire . . . pricks up his ears at the sound and steps out with a firm tread and a more erect bearing'. In July 1897, when the 1st Battalion of the Highland Light Infantry was to entrain for the North-West Frontier to fight in the Malakand campaign, invalids left their beds and boarded the train. When the adjutant discovered them, he placed them all under arrest, but soon relented and let them come. 'Have to admire the damn fellers' spirit', he said.

Most of the army spent most of its time outside Britain, and what remained, being small, was not always a visible presence, but the attitude of civilians towards soldiers remained consistently ambivalent. A rhyme popular in the days of Marlborough ran:

> God and the soldier we both adore
> When at the brink of ruin, not before.
> The danger over, both are alike requited,
> God is forgiven, and the soldier slighted.

It was this attitude towards soldiers that Kipling wrote of in 'Tommy':

> For its Tommy this, an' Tommy that, an' 'Chuck him out, the brute'!
> But it's 'Saviour of 'is country' when the guns begin to shoot.

It was true enough that those who wore the 'Widow's uniform' were often denied service in public houses and places at the theatre. Many saloon bars had signs saying 'Men in uniform not admitted'. Since, except when on furlough, only non-commissioned officers of the rank of colour-sergeant or higher were allowed to wear civilian clothes, the soldier was a marked man, and the number of respectable places where he could go for recreation or amusement was strictly limited. Dr Johnson considered Life Guardsmen, felons and horrible stinks to be equally undesirable in a home. His attitude was not uncommon, and the public's attitude was unchanged a century later. In the late Victorian era mistresses sometimes dismissed maids for walking out with soldiers, men 'filled with beef, beer and lust'. When William Robertson's mother lamented that she would rather bury him than see him in a red coat, she was reflecting the low regard in which soldiers were held by respectable working-class families.

In English literature the private soldier was often a comic character. Shakespeare's Feeble, Mouldy, Bardolf, Pistol and others are figures of fun. It was an attitude that endured, and in the pages of *Punch* soldiers were caricatured and belittled. Thackeray, who satirized and pilloried officers, scarcely mentions private soldiers except to say that 'they get the word of command to advance or fall back, and they do it; they are told to strip and be flogged, and they do it; or to flog and they do it; to murder or be murdered, and they obey; for their food and clothing and twopence a day for tobacco'. So it was a novel departure from literary tradition when Kipling, while admitting that 'single men in barracks don't grow into plaster saints', presented in his stories and poems a sympathetic picture of Private Thomas Atkins.

Robert Graves, who served in the Royal Welch Fusiliers, had this to say of Tommy:

> He was known on the one hand for his foul mouth, his love of drink and prostitutes, his irreligion, his rowdiness and his ignorance; on the other for his courage, his endurance, his loyalty and his skill with fusil and pike, or with rifle and bayonet. Wellington referred to the troops who served under him in the Peninsular war as 'the scum of the land' but they won him a dukedom. . . .

They were, after all, heroic scum, and they could at times be as chivalrous as their officers.

Other ranks did not talk of the 'Chivalry of Arms', but they were sometimes on friendly terms with their enemies. In New Zealand during one of the Maori wars, pickets of the 65th Foot (1st York and Lancaster) would occasionally come in refreshed and rested after a night's outpost duty, for they would simply call out to the Maoris to ask if they planned to attack; if they said no, the pickets could sleep in safety. The Maoris had no love for the settlers who were stealing their land, but towards the 65th – pronounced 'hickety pip' by the Maoris – they bore no malice, and they even tended the graves of their fallen. Soldiers of the 65th were equally accommodating when the Maoris inquired about surprise attacks and, taking a liking to their Maori name, began to call themselves 'the hickety pips'.

There were soldiers who found a home in the army and there were those who did not or could not adjust. One night after a battle in India Sergeant Forbes-Mitchell heard a soldier mutter in his sleep: 'Oh, mother, forgive me, and I'll never leave home again'. There were, of course, desertions, and the reasons men gave for them provide glimpses of the soldier's life, The *Journal of the Household Brigade* for the year 1874 said:

> Out of 743 soldiers sentenced last year for desertion, 229 alleged they disliked the army, 57 were annoyed by comrades or hardly treated by non-commissioned officers, 44 married without leave or had 'love affairs', 87 through drink, 39 on the 'spree' and 18 through 'whim and folly'.

Somehow one's heart is touched by those who succumbed to 'whim and folly', but there is no evidence that the hearts of officers of courts-martial were affected.

DISCIPLINE

Perhaps the greatest improvement in the lot of the soldier in the Victorian era was the reduction in the number and severity of punishments. Although there remained eight offences for which the penalty, even in time of peace, was death – including 'personal violence to a superior or disobedience of his lawful commands' – and a dozen additional capital offences in time of war – such as 'shamefully casting away his arms in the presence of the enemy' and 'sleeping on his post' – the threat of flogging and branding was almost entirely removed. Branding was completely abolished in 1871, but it had never been, as was flogging, a common punishment.

Even before flogging was abolished, it came to be imposed less and less as a punishment, but before the Crimean War it was used even for trivial offences. Private James Honeygold of the 9th Foot (Norfolk Regiment) was sentenced to 150 lashes for failing to answer ten o'clock roll call one evening; because of his previous good conduct, he was given only 50. Private John Bird of the same regiment received 400 lashes for stealing 19s. 6d. from a comrade, During the Peninsular War two privates were given 170 lashes each for stealing a pig; another received 75 'on suspicion of killing a pig'. At Gibraltar, sentinels who did not call 'All's well'! every thirty seconds could be given 200 lashes. At one time there was at Gibraltar a drummer who in the course of his fourteen years' service had received 25,000 lashes and was reported to be 'hearty and well, and in no way concerned'. Sentences of up to 2000 lashes were sometimes ordered until George III decreed that no punishment should exceed a thousand. A colonel of the Gordon Highlanders once remitted a sentence of one hundred lashes awarded by a court-martial on the grounds that the punishment was too trivial.

Being flogged was spoken of by soldiers as 'going to the triangles' or 'going to the halberds' because originally the whipping post was made by tying a man to sergeants' halberds made to form a triangle. In this tradition-bound army the shape was retained for half a century after halberds had disappeared.

A flogging was administered by the strongest drummer or bugler in the battalion; behind him stood the bandmaster armed with a stick with which to beat the beater if he did not lay on hard enough; and behind the bandmaster stood the adjutant, also armed with a stick to beat the bandmaster. A doctor was in attendance and was authorized to order the flogging stopped at any time, but this was only a respite, for the victim, once recovered, whether in hours or in days, was hauled back to receive the remainder of his punishment.

The regiment was always paraded to witness a flogging. It must have been a dread sight to see, for a man's back could be reduced to a pudding of bloody flesh. Neville Lyttelton, speaking of the 1860s when he was a young officer, wrote: 'I only saw two men flogged; it was early in the morning and made me feel quite squeamish'. Bindon Blood as a young officer in the same era also saw two men flogged at Aldershot. It was witnessed by some six hundred troops, many of them young soldiers, and more than a hundred fainted; officers too fell out and tried to recover their composure while sitting on the shafts of empty carts. Blood reported that one of the men he saw flogged that day reformed and became a sergeant-major. Another sergeant-major once confided that he 'never was a man' until he received fifty lashes for insubordination in the Crimea.

Blood found it curious that in the engineers 'the officers disliked corporal punishment, whereas the non-commissioned officers and the old sappers were generally in favour of it'. It was indeed curious, but true. In Ireland, sixteen-year-old John Green once saw a man receive fifty lashes for striking an officer; the flogging was also witnessed by a crowd of civilians, who, horrified by the spectacle, shouted abuse at the officers present. Green, writing after he had retired as a sergeant, when he had no cause to falsify his opinion, said that 'the people might mean well, but it is absolutely necessary to punish such conduct or no man could live in the army or navy'. Later Green saw a man given eight hundred lashes by 'the strongest drummers and buglers in the brigade' and he was 'astonished how soon the man recovered after such a severe flogging'.

Sergeant William Forbes-Mitchell of the 93rd (Sutherland) Highlanders also spoke in favour of the lash:

> Whatever opponents of the lash may say, my own firm opinion is that the provost-marshal's cat is the only general to restore order in times like those I am describing [looting in Lucknow]. I would have no courts-martial, drumhead or otherwise; but simply give the provost-marshal a strong guard of picked men and several sets of triangles, with full power to tie up every man, no matter what his rank, caught plundering, and give him one to four dozen, not across the shoulders, but across the breech, as judicial floggings are administered in our gaols; and if these are combined with roll-calls at short intervals, plundering . . . would soon be put down.

And James Anton, a quartermaster sergeant of the Black Watch, wrote:

> Philanthropists, who decry the lash, ought to consider in what manner the good men – the deserving, exemplary soldiers – are to be protected; if no coercive measures are to be resorted to in purpose to prevent the ruthless ruffians from insulting with immunity the temperate, the well-inclined, and the orderly-disposed, the good must be left to the mercy of the worthless. . . .

John Stevenson, who was twenty-one years in the Foot Guards, sixteen as a non-commissioned officer, said: 'I never was any more afraid of the lash than I was of the gibbet; no man comes to that but through his own conduct'.

In the Indian army flogging was abolished in the 1830s. Though it was later re-instated for a ten-year perod, it was rarely used, and when it was, the Indian soldier was immediately discharged. It was thought unwise to retain as a soldier a man who had been so humiliated. British soldiers, however, did not always feel humiliated, and some actually took pride in their ability to bear up under the lash.

Private Richard Hovenden of the 58th Foot, 'The Steelbacks', distinguished himself at the crossing of the Bidassoa during the Peninsular War by clubbing one Frenchman to death and strangling another. Later, he and some friends celebrated victory so uproariously that they were charged with 'creating a disturbance in a wine shop' and were sentenced to one hundred lashes each. All but Hovenden bore the flogging without flinching, but Hovenden sobbed as the lash struck and after the twentieth stroke fainted. The remainder of his punishment was remitted and he returned to the ranks, where his comrades ostracized him; he had failed as a 'steelback'. This was too much. Hovenden marched up to his commanding officer and said, 'Meaning no offence, sir, I wish to tell you that you are a fool'. He earned a sentence of 150 lashes. Before it could be administered, the French attacked: Hovenden broke out of his cell, took part in the fighting, saved his colonel's life by killing a Frenchman who was about to sabre him, and staggered back to his cell severely wounded. The following morning the colonel pardoned him and ordered him to be released, but it was too late. He had died of his wounds during the night.

In 1859 flogging was restricted to certain offences; nine years later it was decreed that it could only be used on active service. Three times Bills were introduced in the House of Commons to abolish it – in 1876, in 1877 and in 1879 – but all were defeated. In 1879, during the Zulu War, men were flogged for the last time while on active service. Finally, in 1881, flogging was replaced – almost – by Field Punishment No. 1, under which men were tied spread eagle to the wheel of a gun or wagon and exposed without food or water for several hours for up to twenty-one days.

Many historians have assumed that flogging disappeared completely from the army in 1881, but, as the following quotation from the *Field Service Pocket Book* for 1914 makes clear, the 'regulation cat' was not quite gone:

> In India, on active service, the provost-marshal can punish corporally, then and there, any person below the rank of N.C.O. who, in his view, or that of any of his assistants, commits any breach of good order and military discipline. Punishment not to exceed 30 lashes . . . and to be inflicted with the regulation cat.

A deserter being flogged during the Zulu War in 1879 (*Photo: Illustrated London News Picture Library*)

For major crimes men were shot or hanged, but it was often difficult to find a hangman. No man in the 93rd (2nd Argyll and Sutherland) Highlanders could be induced to play that role. When Private Jack Brian was asked, he replied indignantly: 'Wha' do ye tak us for? We of the 93rd enlisted to fight men with arms in their hands. I widna become your hangman for all the loot in India'. In 1856 a man in the 80th (2nd South Staffordshires) who killed a gunner was sentenced to be hanged. Even though a free discharge and £20 was offered, it was difficult to tempt a volunteer. When at last one was found, he was locked in a stable for safe keeping. The regiment was paraded and the condemned man had been brought out when the assistant adjutant-general galloped up to General Lord William Paulett and told him that the hangman had changed his mind. He positively refused to do his job, On hearing this, General Paulett calmly turned to the provost-marshal and said, 'Captain Maude, will you have the goodness to hang the prisoner'? Captain Maude blanched, but turned quickly to one of his sergeants and ordered him to do the job. When the hanging was over the hang-man *manqué* was flogged, the lashes laid on with a will by the sergeant.

No description by a private soldier of his reaction to a hanging exists, but probably the emotions described by Kipling in 'Danny Deever' were accurate. Doubtless some men did faint, and certainly afterwards the young recruits as well as the old sweats would want their beer. Capital punishment was more common in wartime. During the First World War, more than three hundred men were shot or hanged for cowardice, desertion or mutiny.

In the Victorian era bad characters were sometimes ignominiously dismissed the service. Neville Lyttelton described the manner in which men were drummed out of the army in the 1860s:

> The battalion was drawn up in two lines, five paces apart and facing inward. The culprit was marched down between the lines, sometimes led by a drummer boy holding a rope round the man's neck, with the band playing the 'Rogues March' behind him. On arrival at the barrack gate the boy kicked him out into the road where he was taken charge of by the police, his facings and buttons having been previously cut off. Occasionally he showed signs of shame and remorse, but by no means always. I heard of a culprit who, when leaving, bowed to his special friends in the ranks as he passed them, and once a man was reported as saying to the Colonel, 'A fine battalion, sir; you may dismiss them, I do not require them any more'.

Sometimes an entire regiment was punished. The 64th Foot (1st North Staffordshire Regiment) 'in consequence of bad behavior and disaffection' once had their colours taken from them. They were won back in Sind when their commander, pointing to the enemy perched on a rocky height, called out, 'Soldiers of the 64th, your colours are on top of yonder hill!' In 1902, at Sialkot in the Punjab, an Indian civilian was beaten so badly by some soldiers that he subsequently died in hospital, but he had time to describe the uniforms worn by his assailants, who were identified as 9th Lancers. The individuals, however, could not be detected, and so the entire regiment was subjected to extra drills, stoppage of leave and other hardships.

The defenders of flogging had insisted that it was the only way in which discipline could be maintained. Yet over the years the number of serious offences steadily decreased, and markedly so after short service was introduced and flogging was, in effect, abolished. In 1874 there were twenty desertions per thousand men; by 1893 there were only twelve per thousand. In 1869 there were 144 courts-martial per thousand men; by 1892 there were only fifty-four per thousand. During the late Victorian era the amount and kinds of punishment which regimental officers could administer were much reduced, and by the 1900s a company commander could do no more than sentence a soldier to seven days' confinement to barracks; a battalion commander could award field punishment for up to twenty-eight days; any offence requiring severer punishment had to be dealt with by a court-martial.

Every offence, from appearing on parade with a dirty button to the murder of a comrade, was regarded as a 'crime', and discipline remained strict. At guard mount it was common for an inspecting officer to turn over a button to be sure that the back had been polished as well as the front. In the Guards, even the coal in the coal buckets was washed. Indeed, the spit-and-polish discipline in these regiments was ferocious. Private Gerald Kersh of the Coldstream Guards told what he learned about discipline at the Guards' training barracks:

> Above all, discipline; eternally and inevitably, discipline. Discipline is the screw, the nail, the cement, the glue, the nut, the bolt, the rivet that holds everything tight. Discipline is the wire, the connecting rod, the chain, that coordinates. Discipline is the oil that makes the machine run fast, and the oil that makes the parts slide smooth, as well as the oil that makes the metal bright. They know about discipline here. . . . The principle of discipline here is divinely simple: you lay it on thick and fast, all the time.

Private Kersh also had something to say about the atmosphere discipline creates, for although dirt and mud and vermin usually prevailed on active service (when a soldier was doing what an army is paid to do), an obsession with cleanliness was characteristic of the army in peacetime: 'Discipline has an odour of its own', Kersh said, 'a smell of scrubbing soap and floor-polish mixed with just a little too much fresh air . . . the smell to end smells.'

Private Stephan Graham of the Scots Guards told how all the spit and polish was achieved;

> We spend hours every day polishing. The five ration tins have to be shined with bath-brick. We clean our buttons and hat badges with sol-

diers' friend four times a day, and bring our boot leather to a high polish the same number. We polish the many brasses of our equipment with 'bluebell' or bath-brick; we polish the table ends and the metal of our entrenching tools. We burnish the handles of our bayonets with the burnisher. We polish our dummy cartridges, our oil bottles, and the weights of our pull-throughs. For kit inspection we polish the backs of our blacking-brushes, clothes, and hair-brushes with 'nutto' or 'soap'. We polish the instep of the soles of our duplicate pair of boots. The eight metal wash-basins which we never use we bring to a high lustre with 'globe polish', and the backs of our Bibles which we do not read we diligently bring to a polish with 'nugget' or 'soap'. Our knife, fork, and spoon are of the sort that rapidly tarnish, so the smart men never use them, but keep a duplicate set for use at table, which they generally keep dirty. Many of us also use brushes of our own and we wear also our own socks and shirts, so that the army kit may be always ready for inspection.

Every night we carefully soap the insides of our trouser-creases, wet the outsides, and we obtain smartness by laying the damp garments on our mattresses and sleeping on them. We carefully fold our tunics in a certain way and no other, and we strap our overcoats on the pegs behind our beds, so that they may show not one slightest crease. We keep rags and dusters and silk dusters, shining the wood of our rifles with them until it glimmers, and gently polishing our hat bands to a colour matching that of the wood. We scrub our equipment, and then paste khaki blanco on it. We wash our kit boxes and bath-brick our shelves. Thus it may be understood that if we turn out smart on parade it is not without pain on our part.

No one could parade like the Foot Guards. They were the most over-drilled regiments in the army. Not much of the drill they learned so well was of use in war, but there was a general feeling that, as one officer put it, 'When a regiment can march and drill like the Guards Brigade, there is no fear of its conduct in the sternest battle'. Even privates in the Guards were impressed with the necessity for strict discipline, as Stephan Graham made clear:

The sterner the discipline the better the soldier. . . . A strong discipline is the foundation of heroic exploits in the field. . . .

In fact, for the private soldier in action the one thing needful is obedience. Imagination, thought, fear, love, and even hate are out of place, and through stern discipline can be excluded. . . . Discipline is the necessary hardening and making dependable. . . .

> Personal conscience is one of the hardest things to modify or eliminate
> . . . it may whisper in a soldier's ear the dreadful admonition, 'Thou
> shalt not kill'. It may give him sleepless nights and unfit him for duty.

Throughout the army, discipline and steadiness were the qualities considered vital; initiative and intelligence were looked upon as civilian qualities, and therefore suspect.

Those who upheld and enforced discipline were the non-commissioned officers (N.C.O.s), the corporals and sergeants. The regimental sergeant-major was a god-like figure more feared than any officer and endowed with special powers and privileges. Private Stephan Graham described him:

> The regimental sergeant-major is like a big yard dog. He rushes forward
> and barks menacingly at any who appear on his line of vision. . . . He
> does not act the part of a father to the soldiers. His position forbids it. He
> is paid to be terrible. . . . And he learns to love authority.

Although there was nothing new in the process by which non-commissioned officers transformed civilians into soldiers, the British sergeant was, as Kipling said, exceptionally good at his job. A recruit was first impressed with his own insignificance and worthlessness; he was deliberately humiliated, as Private Graham of the Scots Guards relates:

> To be struck, to be threatened, to be called indecent names, to be drilled
> by yourself in front of a squad in order to make a fool of you . . . to have
> your ear spat into, to be marched across the parade ground under escort,
> to be falsely accused before an officer and silenced when you try to speak
> in defence – all these things take down your pride, make you feel small,
> and in some ways fit you to accept the role of cannon-fodder on the
> battle-ground. A good deal of it could be defended on grounds of usefulness. But of course it doesn't make a Christian army, and it's hell for the
> poor British soldier.

An American volunteer in the same regiment heard his first news of a tragedy at home when a sergeant on parade bluntly told him: 'I suppose you know your wife's dead'.

ATTITUDES, BELIEFS
AND PREJUDICES

It was the firm belief of British officers that they were not only braver than their men, but braver than officers in other armies. Lord Wolseley wrote:

> I do not know, I cannot tell from experience, whether courage or coward-ice is the more quickly contagious. But this I do know, that of all horrible sights, that of a man in action who exhibits a want of nerve and daring is the worst. Thank heaven, it is a disease from the effects of which the Brit-ish gentleman does not require any sort of inoculation.

Whether or not a British officer was brave because he was a gentleman is open to question, but that he was indeed brave is not. He may well have been the bravest in the world. He exhibited courage not only when it was needed, but often when it was not. Many seemed to take a posi-tive pleasure in courting danger. Casualty figures invariably showed a disproportionate number of officers killed and wounded. Queen Victo-ria once urged that officers be instructed to be more careful in exposing themselves in action, but not even the Queen herself could suppress their self-destructive tendencies.

The desire to be where spears and bullets were flying thickest was not confined to junior officers. Generals, instead of staying back and directing battles, often abandoned their posts and rushed forward to take part in the bloody work of their subordinates. During the battle of Magersfontein in the Anglo-Boer War, Lieutenant-General Lord Methuen at one point led a subaltern's command of Highlanders in a mini-charge at the Boers. His staff searched for him most of the day. It was not until he was shot in the thigh that he returned to headquarters, where he belonged. In the battle of Colenso during the same war, a decision affecting the entire battle could not be made because General Sir Redvers Buller, who was in command – or was supposed to be – could not be found: he was playing the rôle of a battery commander.

The Victorial Cross became the most difficult of gallantry medals to earn largely because the general standard of bravery was so high. Officers were expected to remain cool under fire and not to 'bob' – that is, not to duck when bullets whistled close or shells exploded near them. Major-General Arthur Fitzroy Hart was known as 'No Bobs' Hart because he never flinched under fire and cursed his men when they did. Shortly before leaving England to fight the Boers in 1899, General Buller instructed all his officers that they must not permit their men to be what he called 'jacks-in-boxes', men who jump up to shoot and duck down again. It was hardly worthy of remark that at the battle of Isandhlwana every officer possessed a horse and could have fled. None did. All stayed and all died with their men. Perhaps the standard can best be illustrated by the story of a man who failed to live up to it.

In 1879, Louis Napoleon, the young French Prince Imperial, wanted to observe the British campaign against the Zulus. In spite of some resistance on the part of the government, permission was granted, but senior officers in South Africa were told to keep an eye on him to make sure that no harm came to the one great hope of the French monarchists. The officers did their best, but the Prince was an active, high-spirited young man and he became a nuisance and a worry. It seemed safe enough when one day he was permitted to accompany a mounted patrol led by Captain Jaheel Carey, 98th Foot (2nd North Staffordshires), to make some sketches. The area they intended to cover had been declared free of Zulus.

Early in the afternoon, when the patrol was dismounted and resting, they were attacked by a swarm of Zulus on foot. All tried to mount their horses; the Prince Imperial had one foot in a stirrup and an insecure grip on the saddle holster when his frightened horse dashed off. The

Lord Chelmsford following the body of the Prince Imperial at Iteleze camp
(*Photo: Graham Brandon*)

Prince fell, first under the horses hooves when the holster gave way, and then under the stabbing assegais of the Zulus. Carey galloped on. There was, in fact, little he could have done except to return and be killed as well. But that was what was expected of him.

Carey was found guilty by a court-martial of misbehaviour in the presence of the enemy and was sent home to be cashiered. However, the Empress Eugenie, the Prince's mother, pleaded for mercy with Queen Victoria, and the sentence of the court-martial was set aside. Carey was greeted almost as a hero by the press and public when he arrived in England, for most people blamed his superiors and they did not understand the military code of conduct. Unfortunately for the position taken by the press, Carey was a poor hero in every respect, for in the development of the scandal a letter he had written immediately after the event came to light and he was revealed to be a liar, a hypocrite and a cad as well as a coward – a most untypical British officer. He was eventually returned to his regiment, which regarded him as a disgrace, and he remained with it for six years until he died in Bombay. He stuck it out even though his brother officers turned their backs at his approach and refused to speak to him except in the line of duty.

The death of the Prince Imperial created a sensation in Britain, and the newspapers talked of it for days, but General Wolseley in a letter to his wife expressed sentiments which were undoubtedly shared by many soldiers: 'He was a plucky young man, and he died a soldier's death. What on earth could he have better? . . . Perhaps I have insufficient sympathy for foreign nations; I reserve all my deep feelings for Her Majesty's subjects'.

William Butler, speaking of the 'British subaltern in a marching regiment', said: 'He drops easily into the belief that he represents the highest form of civilization, and that he has only to snipe-shoot or pig-stick his way through the world, while at the same time in some mysterious manner he is bearing aloft the banner of British freedom and Western culture'. This attitude was carried a step further in the minds of most, and it was thought that Britons had a natural talent for ruling what Kipling called 'lesser breeds' and that they had a responsibility to do so.

George Younghusband said: 'There is perhaps no nation on earth which has come under British rule and guidance which has not benefited by it'. He also stated flatly that 'the Indian cannot govern himself', and added that Indians should be governed on the 'paternal system', which he defined as 'one clean-bred, perfectly honest and unbribable Englishman, standing under a tree and, according to his lights, without law or legal procedure, deciding cases on commonsense lines, and to the best of his ability'. It is, of course, questionable how well the ends of justice were served by such a system. A British magistrate in Ceylon – doubtless a 'clean-bred, perfectly honest and unbribable Englishman' – once described his methods to Johnson Wilkinson of the 15th Foot (East Yorkshire Regiment):

> He said niggers were such liars it was useless questioning them, and as he was a good judge of character and countenance, he used to put litigants alongside one another, and not allow them to say anything. After looking at them earnestly for a moment or two, and having made up his mind, he would say to one of them, 'You are the guilty man', and dispose of him accordingly.

British officers in general tended to look down upon all who were not like themselves. Africans and Asians were called 'wogs' or 'niggers', campaigns against them were called 'nigger smashing', and it pleased some subalterns in India to train their dogs to 'go for niggers'. Englishmen sometimes expressed surprise when they encountered people of a different race who behaved like themselves. Captain Frederick Stephenson of the Scots Fusilier Guards wrote home from Singapore:

> The other day I met a Chinaman at dinner . . . he eat (*sic*) and drank and chatted like other people . . . he is very rich and a justice of the peace . . . still, he is thoroughly Chinese in appearance.

General Osborne Wilkinson, writing in 1896, thought 'the day is still very remote when the *warlike races* [of India] will be qualified to supply the place of the European officers'. Lord Wolseley considered the Indians as 'a race whom we regard as inferior in every sense', and he thought that the African would be better off as a slave: 'His vanity, pretensions, his vulgar swagger, make one feel how much more useful he would be if we had never emancipated him'. Wolseley even referred to the Sultan of Turkey as 'this little cowardly black man'. Indeed there was a disdain for all foreigners, even those of British descent: Canadians, Australians and others in the Empire came to resent being sneered at as 'colonials'. Americans ranked even lower, and Wolseley confided to his wife: 'I thank God I am not one of them'.

Field-Marshal Sir John French, speaking of some of the French generals, told Kitchener: '*Au fond* they are a low lot, and one always has to remember the class these generals mostly come from'. After all, Marshal Joffre was the son of a tradesman. An often told story – illustrative, whether or not true – is that of the sergeant-major who, on the eve of the B.E.F.'s embarkation for France, prepared his men to meet their allies by telling them: 'Remember, wogs begin at Calais'. And General William Robertson as Chief of the Imperial General Staff during the First World War gave some advice to General Douglas Haig: 'As a whole the French commanders and staff are a peculiar lot. . . . The great thing to remember in dealing with them is that they are Frenchmen and not Englishmen, and do not and never will look at things in the way we look at them'.

Although most British subjects were brown, yellow or black, all British officers were white, and most were Church of England. There were few Jews. In the army lists of the era the names are almost entirely English, Scots, Welsh or Irish; there are few traditional Jewish names. Even those which appear so could be deceptive. Ian Hamilton spoke of an officer in the Gordon Highlanders in the late 1870s whose nickname was 'Jew' because of his name and features: 'Billy Isaacs was hampered by his name, but, as he said himself, one of his female ancestors got mixed up in a money-lending affair with a Hebrew . . . and thus hampered a decent fellow with a hooked proboscis and an ikey name'. The attitude here reflected by Hamilton goes far to explain why there were no Jewish generals, no military equivalents to Disraeli or Rothschild.

In the officers' disdain for foreigners there were degrees of dislike, a hierarchy of contempt. In general, coloured races were more looked down upon than white races, but even among the Asians and Africans, the more peaceful were less well thought of than the savage. The Indian army recruited only from the 'warlike races', and the anonymously written official records of campaigns on the North-West Frontier speak with utter contempt of the peaceful tribes that caused little trouble, but with grudging admiration of the Pathans, who, ever turbulent, plagued the British for more than a century. Wolseley in West Africa was totally scornful of the peaceful Fantis, who were under British protection, and thought they should be the slaves of the fierce Ashantis he had come to fight, for they, he said, 'however barbarous have at least the virtue of courage'.

Some have thought it curious that Kipling's poems often praised the bravery and fine fighting qualities of the Dervishes ('Fuzzy-Wuzzy') and the Boers ('Piet'), but British soldiers understood, for they too admired such qualities in their opponents. Stirring up hatred of the enemy might be necessary to raise volunteers, but professional soldiers did not need to indulge in it. Ian Hamilton bore no ill will against those he fought, adding that 'mercenary troops fight better than irregular volunteers or conscripts'.

Hamilton believed in what he called 'the Chivalry of Arms'. He was not alone. Sir John French described this old-fashioned sentiment: 'Soldiers should have no politics, but should cultivate a freemasonry of their own and, emulating the knights of old, should honour a brave enemy only second to a comrade, and like them, rejoice to split a friendly lance to-day and ride boot to boot in the charge to-morrow'. This near-incredible sentence was written, not in the eighteenth or nineteenth centuries, but in 1919 by the man who led the B.E.F. to

France in 1914. If this is to be taken seriously – and why not? – the field-marshal preferred a brave German soldier to a British civilian.

Military courtesy between foes existed as late as the Anglo-Boer War when Sir John French and a Boer general, Christiaan Beyers, exchanged Christmas presents, but it was in decline. Certainly in the Victorian–Edwardian era it never again created the scene said to have been played out by the opposing British and French commanders at the battle of Fontenoy (1745), when each politely invited the other to fire first.

There was one conspicuous exception to the distaste for non-white foreigners. One can search in vain through the military literature of the era for a disparaging remark about the Gurkhas. The British had a sincere affection for these doughty little mercenaries from Nepal. They were always spoken of with respect and admiration. Apparently the feeling was mutual, for although no foreigners were allowed to set foot in Nepal and all recruiting was done informally by the Gurkhas themselves when they went home on furlough, the Gurkha battalions were always filled.

Gurkhas marching through Jellalabad (*Photo: Graham Brandon*)

Civilians ranked only slightly higher than foreigners in the officers' social scale. 'It is wonderful with what rapidity the contagion of panic spreads through a civilian population', said Sir John French contemptuously. But there was a notable exception to the low opinion of civilians in general and of those in government in particular: the soldiers loved their Queen. Secretaries of State and Prime Ministers were frequently damned, but no soldier cursed his sovereign. When Wolseley sent off his dispatches following the successful Ashanti campaign, he recorded that 'one thought banished all other reflections . . . "Will the Queen be satisfied with what her soldiers and sailors have accomplished in the trying campaign just finished" '? Ian Hamilton once said: 'The Queen believed in herself and we believed in her. There lay the secret of the Victorian Age'.

The hearts of some civilians harboured an unreasoning fear that the army might seize political power, but there was never a threat, even a thought, in the regular army of a *coup d'état*. Officers were concerned about Acts of Parliament which affected them, but they had no desire for power outside their own tight little world. They were, as a group, conservative in their political outlook – to put it mildly. Sir John French held views which twenty years later would have branded him a fascist. He was convinced that intrigues 'ran riot in all branches of the public service when "votes" rule everything . . . [exercising] their usual baneful influence'. Although the army continued to obey its political masters and to do its duty, it resented all change. The Duke of Cambridge, who was for nearly forty years the commander-in-chief at the Horse Guards, once protested that he was not against change, but that change must come at the right time; the right time, thought the Duke, was when it could no longer be avoided. He was not alone in this attitude.

The army was reluctant to vary its methods or even its weapons. The Duke of Cambridge in 1889 objected to night marches because they interfered with the horses' rest. The artillery in 1890 was still practising a drill that had been in use since the Peninsular War at the beginning of the century. In 1854, when the new Minie rifle was issued and regiments were ordered to send an officer to one of the newly-opened schools of musketry, the officers in the 90th Foot thought it hilarious when their colonel sent a one-armed officer. The cavalry was the most conservative arm. When carbines were issued to one cavalry regiment, the first consignment was dumped on the stable manure pile. In 1874 Joseph Farwell Glidden, a New Hampshire farmer, patented an improved form of barbed wire, but its military potential never occurred to the British until they saw the Boers using it to defend their trenches in 1900. The British army was the last in Europe to abandon the muzzle-loading cannon, and as it clung to the notion that it was a disgrace to lose guns, it often used artillery ineffectively through excessive fear of losing it.

Paradoxically, the British army was both the first and the last to use breech-loading guns. The story is a curious one. As early as December 1854 a three-pounder, breech-loading gun was ordered for the field artillery. An Armstrong breech-loader was used in action for the first time in the China War of 1860 and was reported to be effective. It was then decided – on the initiative of the Secretary of State for War, not the soldiers – to convert to breech-loaders, and by 1862 the government had purchased £2½ million worth of these new weapons for the army and navy. However, in 1867 a commission was appointed to compare the smooth-bore, muzzle-loading guns firing round shot with the rifled breech-loaders using cylindrical shells. Incredible as it seems, the commission unanimously sided in favour of the old muzzle-loaders, and in 1866 they were restored to service. They were, the commissioners said, easier to work and cheaper to produce. By 1875 the regular field and horse artillery (but not the artillery in the Indian army) had been re-equipped with muzzle-loaders. Not until 1885 were they declared obsolete, and even as late as the Anglo-Boer War (1899–1902) the British in South Africa tried to fight the primitive Boers (who had wisely equipped themselves with fine, breech-loading guns manufactured by Krupp in Germany and Creusot in France) with some old muzzle-loaders.

In the same war the Boers employed a handy, quick-firing gun which came to be called a pom-pom because of the sound it made. This gun spewed out one-pound shells from a belt, and the British officers, who had never seen such a gun, were impressed with its effectiveness. It was made by Vickers in England, and originally designed for naval use, but as the army and navy rarely spoke to each other, the pom-pom appeared on the velt as a secret weapon as far as the army was concerned.

In campaigns prior to the Anglo-Boer War, batteries of artillery revealed their position with their first round because of the smoke. Smokeless powder, invented in 1886, was not adopted until five years later, and even then it was embraced with an astonishing lack of enthusiasm. Not until 1899, when the Boers used it, did it occur to the British that such ammunition made it quite difficult to locate the position of an artillery battery.

There was considerable resistance to the machine gun. Hiram S. Maxim, an American, conducted successful field tests of his invention in 1884, but the gun was not adopted. It was thought to be too expensive to use (£5 per minute), and there was some confusion as to whether it should be considered an infantry or an artillery weapon. General John Adye, an artillery officer writing in 1894, said that machine guns 'had not, in my opinion, much future in a campaign against a modern army' and that they 'would add considerably to the impedimenta of troops in the field'.

The halberd was carried by sergeants until 1830, but the weapon most favoured was really the pike, or rather its less efficient modern equivalent, the bayonet, which replaced it about 1700. When, during the First Sikh War, at the battle of Sobraon (10 February 1846), it was reported to General Sir Hugh Gough that the artillery was running short of ammunition, he exclaimed, 'Thank God! Then I'll be at them with the bayonet'! This faith in the most primitive and least efficacious of available weapons persisted into the First World War and beyond. The bayonet is more intimidating than lethal; comparatively few have ever been killed by it.

It took a long time for the army to accept the transition from the old 'Brown Bess' musket to the rifle, and then it was slow to accept the many improvements made on the rifle. The inventors, improvers, developers and manufacturers were seldom soldiers; most were civilians and included an American dentist, a Scottish preacher, a Swedish banker and even a Quaker – Christopher M. Spencer, who invented the outstanding repeating rifle of the American Civil War. Even when new weapons were officially adopted, they were often not issued, for it was felt that it would be wasteful not to wear out the old ones first.

There was, however, one novel piece of ordnance developed by a British soldier: the rocket. It was not new to warfare, but Sir William Congreve made it practical to use and easy to transport. As early as 1800 the Royal Horse Artillery had a rocket troop. Rockets proved to be useful when employed against primitive peoples and Americans (who embodied their 'red glare' in the words to their national anthem). Their psychological effect was greater than their destructive power, however, and soldiers distrusted them, for they were never entirely reliable and sometimes burst among one's own instead of the enemy's troops. By 1914 they were no longer in use.

A most exceptional and technologically progressive officer who did not conform to the usual pattern was Douglas Mackinnon Bailie Hamilton, Lord Dundonald, of the 2nd Life Guards. He was an advocate of machine guns, favoured carbines for cavalry, and was a musketry enthusiast. His inventions included waterproof bags for carrying men and equipment across rivers, a compass with a luminous dial; a light, one-horse galloping gun carriage; a sanitary water cart; a light ambulance with rubber tyres; and a light headquarters van. None was accepted by the army. Dundonald's grandfather, an admiral, had also been an inventor. During the First World War Dundonald revealed to Kitchener a secret weapon his grandfather had passed down to him: a device for sending over the enemy lines 'asphyxiating vapour under cover of dense smoke clouds'. Kitchener, then Secretary of State for War, was not interested. It was of no use for land warfare, he said.

There was a general distrust of 'gadgets'. When Robertson became Chief of the Imperial General Staff he installed himself in a room at the War Office 'from which all the telephone apparatus was expelled . . . so that I might be left in peace', and when it was proposed to try tanks in France, he thought this 'rather a desperate innovation'. Sir John French's naïve retrospective, written in 1919, would be hilarious were it not so tragic: 'I cannot help wondering why none of us realised what the most modern rifle, the machine gun, motor traction, the aeroplane and wireless telegraphy would bring about. It seems so simple when judged by the results'.

It would be difficult today to find many soldiers who would honestly confess to a love of war. There seems something brutal, inhumane, unnatural in anyone who would delight in killing other human beings or who would knowingly and willingly expose himself to physical hardships for the thrill and excitement of being shot at or threatened with spears. Yet the Victorian–Edwardian professional soldier often went to remarkable lengths and made extraordinary personal sacrifices to take part in fighting. Ian Hamilton even thought there must be something wrong with those who disapproved of war: 'The average pacifist is not a very good man – not really'.

During the Crimean War Lieutenant Gerald Graham wrote to his sister: 'There is no doubt about it, excitement apart, war is the most dis- agreeable employment in the world'. But to his father he spoke of his envy of those of his colleagues who were off on an expedition to Kertch. Graham may have thought war disagreeable employment, but he stayed in the army, won a Victoria Cross and became a lieutenant-general. Later, when the First Boer War began in 1881, the subalterns of the Gordon Highlanders in India sent a personal cable to General Evelyn Wood begging him to send for their battalion. He did. Captain the Honourable Julian Grenfell, 1st Royal Dragoons, wrote in a letter to his mother: 'I *adore* war. It is like a big picnic. I have never been so well or so happy'.

This love of war had little to do with patriotism and even less with politics. Few soldiers concerned themselves with the justness of the cause, which was generally assumed to be righteous. William Butler was a somewhat different professional soldier. He thought that battle was 'by far the most exciting of life's possibilities to its mortals' and he participated in many, but he also thought that the Gordon Relief Ex- pedition (1884–5) was the 'very first war during the Victorian Era in which the object was entirely noble and worthy'.

No man delighted in war more than Garnet Wolseley. Of his youth he said, 'Like all young soldiers, I longed to hear the whistle of a bullet fired in earnest'. He soon did. In Burma as a subaltern in his first battle, he was severely wounded in the leg and had to be invalided home. He had scarcely recovered when he had an eye shot out in the Crimea. Yet these grievous wounds did not diminish his love of fighting. Of his charge on a stockade in Burma, where he was first struck, he wrote: 'What a supremely delightful moment it was'! And his duty in the trenches before Sevastopol gave him 'intense pleasure'. Writing later in life of this period of his youth, he stated: 'I can honestly say that the one dread I had – and it ate into my soul – was that if killed I should die without having made that name for myself which I always hoped a kind and merciful God might permit me to win'. He did indeed live to make a name for himself, and there can have been few men who took part in so many wars and campaigns. Near the end of his life he wrote: 'That "war is a horrible thing", is a very nice heading for the page of a schoolgirl's copybook, but I confess that in my heart I always thoroughly enjoyed it'. He once spoke of his 'intense love of fighting and all out-of-door amusements'. He found it impossible adequately to explain his feeling about battle:

> It is only through experience of the sensation that we learn how intense, even in anticipation, is the rapture-giving delight which the attack upon an enemy affords. I cannot analyse nor weigh, nor can I justify the feeling. But once experienced, all other subsequent sensations are but as a tinkling of a doorbell in comparison with the throbbing of Big Ben.

Many officers went to extraordinary lengths to take part in a war or a battle. Lieutenant-Colonel Philip Doyne, commanding the 4th Dragoon Guards (1892–6), had never seen a battle, so he went on leave and contrived to serve as a private in the King's Own Scottish Borderers during the storming of the Malakand Pass. In 1899, when the Anglo-Boer War broke out, Colonel Dundonald took leave and went to South Africa at his own expense, as did many others; once there, he was given command of a cavalry brigade. In the same war, Lieutenant-Colonel the Honourable Lewis P. Dawnay, a retired officer, went out to visit his son, a second-lieutenant in the Coldstream Guards; when he arrived with a large stock of champagne on the Modder river, General Sir Henry Colvile, commanding the Guards Brigade, attached him to his staff as an extra aide-de-camp and he took part in the battle of Magersfontein. Another Coldstreamer who managed to get in the war was Captain Raymond Marker. Although he held a coveted position as aide-de-camp to the Viceroy of India, he obtained leave and joined his regiment at Bloemfontein. Captain David Plenderleath Sellar, 4th Dragoon Guards, took leave, went to South Africa, contrived to be taken on by the 2nd Gordon Highlanders, and was besieged in Ladysmith with this battalion. The siege outlasted his leave, so that, returning to his regiment, he was charged with being absent without leave.

When the Gordon Relief Expedition was being formed in Egypt, Ian Hamilton took six months' leave from his battalion in India and went to Cairo looking for employment. He found the city teeming with officers who had done the same. Most were disappointed, but Hamilton found the second battalion of his regiment there and was given a job in it. When George Pomeroy Colley arrived just too late for the Zulu War of 1879, he told Evelyn Wood: 'I'm sorry to have arrived too late for the fun'. Wolseley said of the end of the Crimean War: 'I remember how

sad I felt when peace was announced'. When Lieutenant J.F.C. Fuller
of the 1st Oxfordshires in South Africa heard from another officer that
the Anglo-Boer War had ended, he said sadly, 'Well, I am sorry'.

Not only did officers strive to participate in Britain's wars, they
frequently went off to take part in, or at least to observe, the wars of
others. Winston Churchill went to Cuba to see the Spanish-American
War in that part of the world, and George Younghusband went to the
Philippines to look at the same conflict in that setting. Kitchener observed the Franco-Prussian War; Wolseley and a number of other British officers visited both the Union and the Confederate armies during
the American Civil War. It was here that Wolseley first saw infantry
fighting from trenches – a bad practice, he thought, for it encouraged
'a very dangerous tendency to unfit soldiers for all rapid offensive action'.

A number of officers and former officers actually fought in the Rus-
sian-Turkish War in the late 1870s, most serving in the Turkish army.
One of these was Valentine Baker, brother of the famous explorer, Sir
Samuel Baker. Valentine Baker had had a fine career in the British
army and was a keen soldier who had distinguished himself in the Kaffir
War of 1855–7 and at the battle of Chernaya during the Crimean War.
For thirteen years he commanded the 10th Hussars and then was assistant quartermaster-general at Aldershot. He was also happily married
and the father of a daughter. In August of 1875 he was convicted of 'in-
decently assaulting a young lady in a railway carriage'. There is reason
to believe that the charge was false, but he was fined £500 and sentenced to a year in prison. Naturally, he was told that Her Majesty had
no further occasion for his services. In the Turkish army he rose to the
rank of lieutenant-general. Later he commanded the Egyptian gendar-
merie and led them against the Dervishes in the Sudan, suffering a cata-
strophic defeat at El Teb in 1884. In that same year he was rehabili-
tated. Three years later he died.

There were two opposing views of an officer's function in battle.
There was a feeling among many that the actual killing was not gentlemanly. Some believed it was the officer's duty to lead his men to slaugh-
ter and perhaps be slaughtered, but that it was demeaning personally to
engage in the butchery. This is perhaps best exemplified by Lord Cardigan, who led the charge of the Light Brigade at Balaclava armed with

a cigar, and who, having brought his troops face to face with the Russian gunners, considered his duty done and rode back alone, leaving his men to muddle through as best they could. A.A.H. Hanbury, a lieutenant in the Berkshire Regiment during the Edwardian era, held similar views: 'Officers, you feel, shouldn't engage in the rough-and-tumble – that's for the men'. Not infrequently, officers would lead an attack armed only with their sticks; sometimes they simply forgot their revolvers, but Sir Adrian Carton de Wiart, who fought in four wars, had his own reasons for going into battle unarmed: 'I never carried a revolver, being afraid that if I lost my temper I might use it against my own people, so my only weapon was a walking stick'.

Many actually enjoyed the butcher's work in war. Wolseley was one such. As a twenty-three-year-old captain during the Crimean War he wrote to his dowager aunt: 'Man shooting is the finest sport of all; there is a certain amount of infatuation about it that the more you kill the more you wish to kill'. Yet Wolseley was nauseated by the sight of raw meat. In Canada he could not watch a deer being skinned, and to pass a butcher's shop was always a trial for him.

George Younghusband was only eighteen years old when he joined his regiment on the North-West Frontier. The very next day he fought in the battle of Ali Musjid, and found the experience 'more exciting than any of our schoolboy games'. Evelyn Wood said of his first battle experience: 'I was conscious of a decided feeling of exultation in the presence of danger, such as men feel when they do well in manly sports, or women feel when they realise they are pre-eminent among their compeers'. Lieutenant George Gleig of the 85th Foot became a clergyman, but he fought in the Peninsula and described his feelings when he learned that he was about to go into battle for the first time: 'I am no fire-eater . . . but I confess that the news produced in me very pleasurable sensations'. Later, when he had fought in several battles, he still retained that 'inexpressible eagerness to close with your adversary'.

Lieutenant Charles Gordon, later to win fame as 'Chinese' Gordon, fought his first war in the Crimea and found it 'indescribably exciting'. Abu Klea, a bloody battle in the Sudan where the Dervishes broke a British square, was Lord Dundonald's first fight. He later recorded his feelings as he looked around after the battle at the hacked and riddled bodies on the sand, many of whom had been his friends:

I remember asking myself . . . 'Now you have seen what fighting is, how do you like it? and I remember answering myself, 'It is pretty hot work, very hot work', and then my mind turned to the work I had to do and I never thought of the matter again.

Lieutenant T. W. E. Holdsworth of The Queen's described the attack of his regiment on Gazni, a fortified town in Afghanistan, in 1839:

Whilst we were marching down to the attack, the fire on both sides was at its height; the noise was fearful and the whole scene the grandest, and at the same time the most awful, I have ever witnessed. . . . As I got nearer the gate it grew worse, and the enemy from their loopholes began to pepper us with matchlocks and arrows. The scene now was splendid. The enemy at the commencement of the firing, threw out blue lights in several places, which looked beautiful, and the flames of these, together with the smaller flashes from the matchlock men, added to the roar of their big guns, the sharp cracking of their matchlocks, the whizzing of their cannon balls and ours . . . the singing of their bullets, and the whizzing of their arrows, all combined to make up as pretty a row as one could wish to have.

Seventy-five years later Lieutenant Duff Cooper described a First World War battle in a letter to Diana Manners, his future wife:

At the last minute as we were forming up for the attack I discovered that my sergeant was blind-drunk—a dreadful moment. And it was followed by the most glorious of my life. A full moon, a star to guide us, a long line of cheering men, an artillery barrage as beautiful as any fireworks creeping on before us, a feeling of wild and savage joy. It is a picture that will hang in my gallery for ever. . . . The whole battalion won their objective under the scheduled time . . . it was what the old poets said war was, and what the new poets say it isn't.

In spite of the difference in time and place, the face of battle appears to have changed remarkably little.

If officers could not take part in a war somewhere, they looked for danger and excitement in other ways; they were seconded to constabularies in small, turbulent colonies, served on boundary commissions in remote parts of the world, and embarked on exploring expeditions. Several accompanied Henry M. Stanley to Central Africa for the rescue of Emin Pasha in 1887; Lieutenant Palgrave of the Royal Fusiliers was on Douglas Mawson's Antarctic expedition in 1911–13; Lieutenant the Honourable F.R.D. Prittie of the Rifle Brigade served on the Uganda–Congo Boundary Commission of 1907; Horatio Kitchener was for several years with the Palestine Exploration Fund; Captain G.B. Gosling and Lieutenant Boyd Alexander, both of the Rifle Brigade, surveyed the area between the Nile and the Niger between 1904 and 1907, and Gosling lost his life; Alexander was killed in 1910 while exploring near Lake Chad. The list of officers and their accomplishments in non-military activities in Asia and Africa is long and impressive.

A sense of fair play marked the British method of waging war, and they seldom resorted to dirty tricks such as poisoning wells. During the Anglo-Boer War, when the Boers were replenishing their ammunition supplies by policing camp sites of British units and picking up what careless soldiers dropped, it was suggested that over-charged cartridges that would explode in the chamber, destroying the rifles and injuring or killing the user, be left on the velt for the Boers to pick up, but this suggestion was rejected with repugnance by British officers. As far as can be determined, the only cases of wholesale deliberate cruelty prior to the First World War occurred during the Indian Mutiny.

The Mutiny saw atrocities committed by both sides. After Delhi was taken, Major William Hodson murdered in cold blood the three sons of the last Moghul emperor who were his prisoners. Captured Indians were tied to the muzzles of guns and blown to bits merely on suspicion of being mutineers. At Cawnpore, where British women and children who had been promised protection were wantonly murdered, captured mutineers were forced to lick up a square foot of the bloodstains before they were hanged. Many prisoners were shot out of hand. Sergeant William Forbes-Mitchell of the 93rd (Sutherland) Highlanders later wrote of how the men 'spoke of putting a wounded Pandy [mutineer] *out of his pain*, just as calmly as if he had been a wild beast; it was even considered an act of mercy. It is horrible to recall it all, but what I state is true'.

Officers were not unaware of the fact that their men killed prisoners. Lieutenant-Colonel Hope Grant described without comment this scene:

Execution at Jellalabad during the Second Afghan War (*Photo: Graham Brandon*)

A prisoner was brought in by two of the men. . . . One of the soldiers put his rifle to the prisoner's head and pulled the trigger, but the piece missed fire; then the other shot him through the body, and his comrade beat out his brains with the butt-end of his rifle. The poor wretch gave one suppressed groan, and his sufferings in this world were finished.

Officers could be incredibly callous. Neville Lyttelton, a brigadier during the re-conquest of the Sudan in 1898, described the following scene, which occurred a day or two after the battle of Omdurman:

I saw two wounded Arabs who had been shot through both thighs and unable to walk. They were propelling themselves along the ground in a sitting posture with short sticks and left a conspicuous track in the sand. A day or two after I came across these two just arriving in our lines, I should say 3 miles from where I had first seen them.

It appears not to have occurred to Lyttelton that he might have helped them.

The use of torture to gain information which will save soldiers' lives is always a temptation in war. Captain John Seely (later Lord Mottistone) seems not to have understood that torture can be mental as well as physical. He himself related that during the Anglo-Boer War he once threatened to shoot a small Boer boy in the presence of his mother unless he told where his father was hiding. The boy steadfastly refused, even when a firing squad was formed. Seely, who had no intention of carrying out his threat, was well pleased with the courage of the boy and, before he rode away, congratulated the terrified mother on the possession of such a son.

In the 'concentration camps' formed by the British army in South Africa in 1900, more Boer children under the age of sixteen died of disease through stupidity and neglect than there were combatants killed by bullet and shell on both sides. To this day, many Afrikaners believe that the British were deliberately practicing genocide. This was not the case, but cruelty, even when unintended, remains cruelty.

WORDS AND MUSIC

Every trade and profession develops its own vocabulary, technical terms for its tools and methods, particular expressions which attach themselves to a line of work, a unique way of speaking. Soldiering is no exception. John Masters once complained that publishers were willing to accept any amount of nautical jargon but required that every military term be explained, a bias he found incomprehensible. In the Victorian–Edwardian army most of the technical words and some slang were used by all ranks, but the gap between officers and men was so wide that two vocabularies developed, both profane.

The Victorian–Edwardian army was not unique in its habitual use of blasphemous and obscene language. Some recruits found the hard swearing 'frantically disgusting and terrible'; one said the oaths 'pained my ear'. Private Stephan Graham in the Scots Guards complained that drill sergeants 'had a way of standing quite close to you and delivering a whispered imprecatory address on adultery, the birth of Jesus, the sins of sodom, and what not'. Due to the delicacy of the Victorians in expressing themselves in print, we have only vague notions of exactly what was said, but we do know that it was different from current expressions. Even as late as the First World War other ranks still said 'Gor blimey'!, and Kipling noted that he first heard 'God damn' from a soldier in France in 1915. Officers, their classical education showing, still frequently swore 'By Jove'!

Kipling commented on the difference in the swearing to be found in Irish regiments:

> The Irish, particularly in their own battalions, have not the relief of swearing as other races do. Their temperament runs to extravagant comparisons and appeals to the Saints, and ordinary foul language . . . is checked by the priests.

Some soldiers learned to swear in several languages. At least one battalion of every regiment of the line served at one time or another in India, which became in a sense the true home of the British army. There soldiers learned what was called 'crab-bat'. This, according to Private Frank Richards of the Royal Welch Fusiliers, was 'all the swear words in the Hindoostani language and a few more from the other Indian dialects'. Some soldiers, said Richards, 'studied it seriously'.

It was not just profanity that Tommy learned. As readers of Kipling know, every soldier acquired a number of Hindustani or Urdu words which became a part of his permanent vocabulary. Some of the most common were:

soors	pig
hitherao	come on, or come here
tamasha	public function, an entertainment, a party
pukka	proper, genuine, thorough
dekko	a look
juldee	hurry

Perhaps the most used, because most useful, of words was 'wallah'. It was applied to anyone who was in charge of something, who excelled at something, or who sold something. Thus, there was the machine gun wallah, the competition wallah (successful in passing examinations), the flower wallah, and so forth. Staff officers who stayed behind the lines were base wallahs. So extensive was the development over the years of an Anglo-Indian argot that *Hobson-Jobson*, a dictionary of colloquial words and phrases, was compiled in 1886; it was immediately popular and was enlarged in 1903. In addition to Urdu and Hindustani words, there were also some words acquired in the course of various wars elsewhere. Every war added its quota. Men with South African ribbons on their chests spoke of a march as a trek, a village as a dorp, a hill as a kop.

Soldiers with common English names found themselves with traditional nicknames. Men named Miller or Rhodes were always called 'Dusty'; there was always a 'Topper' Brown, a 'Nobby' Clark, a 'Timber' Wood, a 'Knocker' White, a 'Dodger' Green, a 'Tug' Wilson, a 'Spot' Fraser, a 'Kidney' Weston, *et al.* Men also acquired communal nicknames by virtue of their regiments or places of origin. A Grenadier Guardsman was a 'Bill Brown', a Life Guardsman a 'Piccadilly cowboy' or, more commonly, a 'donkey walloper', while a soldier in the Royal Horse Guards was a 'tin belly'. Highlanders were always 'Jocks' and Irishmen were 'Micks' or 'Paddys'.

The name of Jesus Christ was incorporated into the favourite blasphemy of other ranks, as in 'Jesus Christ himself couldn't escape punishment in this battalion', or 'Not in Christ's creation could you do that'. The expression 'doing a Jesus' meant doing an inordinate amount of work.

Other ranks exploited the natural rhythms of the English language in rhyming-slang. If a soldier left the God-forbids at home and took the joy of his life to the rub-a-dub and set out a couple of pig's ears (or fusiliers) on the Cain and Abel, he had left the children at home, taken his wife to the pub, and put two pints of beer on the table. During the First World War, French was made easier by rhyming-slang. Thus, *vin blanc* became 'plinketty plonk'.

Officers never used rhyming-slang, but they did swear. During the unsuccessful attack on the redan at Sebastopol during the Crimean War, Evelyn Wood was hit in the elbow by a 5½-ounce musket ball. The pain was excruciating and he fainted. He was revived by a corporal shaking his shattered arm and saying, 'Matey, if you are going in, you'd better go at once or you'll be bagoneted'. Wood gasped out a stream of curses and his rescuer started back with, 'I beg your pardon, sir. I didn't know you was an officer'. A colonel once heard one of his men refer to him as 'that damned ugly old fool'. He promptly rounded on the man and berated him: 'Look here, you blasted young jackanapes, if you live as long as me, and do as much fighting, and drink as much liquor, and do as much fucking, you will be a damned sight uglier old fool than I am'. The men admired a hard-swearing officer and did not in the least feel that his swearing detracted from his quality as a gentleman. A non-commissioned officer in the Gordon Highlanders once said of General Horace Smith-Dorrien: 'The general was a favourite with us. . . . I never knew an officer who could swear like him'!

Officers of all ages mixed sporting terms with their talk of war. Sometimes sport and war did seem to go hand in hand. Captain R.H.L. Collins of the Rifle Brigade told of a group of regimental snipers who 'varied their game with an occasional partridge'. A 'good shoot' was characterized by a pile of corpses in front of the firing line. Brigadier-General F.P. Crozier perhaps carried the hunting analogy too far when he said that 'a stray shell or two, machine gun fire at night and all the rest of it, with a casualty here and there, cannot but do good, for young soldiers are like young dogs, they require careful shooting over before being put into the big business'.

Officers in the Brigade of Guards conformed to a careful speech code. They never said 'cheers' before drinking; never said 'batman', always servant; called their headgear 'bearskin', not 'busby'; always went to London, never 'up to town'; and talked on the telephone, not the phone. Guards officers used 'cart' as a verb; 'to cart' meant to let down someone by not doing one's part. 'To Cossack' was to tell a tall story. Cavalry officers affected an inability to pronounce the letter 'r', using 'w' instead; thus 'wegiment' for regiment, and General Sir Henry Brackenbury called himself 'Bwackenbewy'.

Gentlemen rankers often found it difficult to communicate with their fellows, as Private Stephan Graham discovered:

> If you spoke to them in normal correct English they did not quite understand and you had to re-express yourself in halting working man's English, full of 'you see' and 'it's like this' and expletives and vulgarisms, or the working man would be rather offended at the way you spoke and imitate you in a drawl when your back was turned.

Yes. What an English gentleman regarded as 'normal correct English'.

As for ordinary slang, the officers called all paper work 'bumf'*; playing around with women was 'poodle faking'. Other ranks talked of 'swinging the lead' (shirking duty), 'pokey drill' (practice handling of weapons in barracks), 'working a ticket' (obtaining discharge papers), 'muckers' (pals, mates, buddies). For all ranks, 'having the wind up' was to be frightened, and the dead were said to have 'gone west'.

It is curious that music should be associated with the business of

---

* The word 'bumf' was a contraction of the public school boy's term for toilet paper: 'bum fodder'.

killing, although it seems ever to have been so, even in the days when the Roman legions marched over the downs and dales of Britain. There is no mistaking martial music, of which the march occupies a special place. According to Ralph Townley: 'Bands have an important military use. They impress the natives. A company of infantry, if they have the regimental band marching up and down, can tranquillize better than a whole battalion'. The drum and bugle have always been regarded as particularly martial instruments; indeed they served the purpose of helping soldiers keep in step or of communicating orders above the din of battle, but they also stirred the souls of men. The regulation bugle calls of the British Army were composed, not by an Englishman, but by the great Austrian composer, Franz Joseph Haydn.

Although soldiers quickly acquired a few words of the language of any country in which they found themselves, they never developed a taste for any music but their own. In spite of many years spent by regiments of the line in India, not a single Indian musical instrument was ever added to a British regimental band nor a single Indian tune to its repertoire. The instruments and the tunes played on them were always reminders of home. This was particularly true of the so-called tribal regiments. In Scottish units, of course, the bagpipes played an indispensable part in all regimental activities, from the celebration of Hogmanay to the charge; the pipes (distinguished by having one less drone) were also important in Irish regiments. In Welsh units, where the human voice has always been held to be the best of music makers, the call of 'Singers to the front'! was ever the command when music was required.

British military bands have always had a propensity for the homely or popular rather than more martial airs. When one battery of artillery wanted its own tune, something which could be sung on the march or played by a fife and drum band it had formed, it was decided to leave the selection to the gunners themselves. The sergeants were directed to ascertain the men's choice. Four days' discussion in barracks and canteen produced a near-unanimous decision: an ephemeral music hall ditty beginning with: 'When we are married we'll have sausages for tea, sausages for tea'.

The fine martial music of the French and Germans was never popular with the British, who preferred the songs of the music hall. Even today, gallant soldiers are often presented with their decorations by the

Queen while a band of the Guards Brigade plays selections from 'The Sound of Music' or the theme of 'Butch Cassidy and the Sundance Kid'.

Every regiment had its slow march and its quick march. The Grenadier Guards, of course, had 'The British Grenadier'; other regiments also liked this piece and adopted it. The 11th Hussars had as its quick march an extract from Rossini's 'Moses in Egypt', but most regiments had some homely air, often one related to their own part of Britain. The Lincolnshire Regiment naturally adopted 'The Lincolnshire Poacher'; the Derbyshire Regiment did the same with 'The Derby Ram'; the quick march of the Suffolk Regiment was 'Speed the Plough'. But the Devonshire Regiment stepped out to the un-martial 'We've Lived and Loved Together', and the Liverpool Regiment marched to the tune of a song called 'Here's to the Maiden of Bashful Fifteen'.

All Highland regiments had bagpipes, but they were never issued, and, in fact, the pipers themselves were paid by the officers until 1856, when a pipe-major and five pipers were authorized. (Their pay was 2d. per day plus a penny a day for 'beer money'.) For obscure reasons, fifes were authorized for Highland regiments, but were never drawn. Bag-

The 72nd Highlanders dancing a reel at Kohat (*Photo: Graham Brandon*)

pipes and other special items of equipment for the bands were bought by the officers, and the share of each was added to his mess bill. The pipe-majors and drum-majors of the Scots Guards had a special distinction: they held personal warrants as 'Household Pipers (or Drummers) to the Sovereign'. In the Scots Guards, in addition to regimental marches, each company had its own tune (B Company's was 'The Drunken Piper'), and when a company was detached from the battalion, a piper was always sent with it.

In 1884 the bands of the Foot Guards were authorized twelve oboes. The oboe was soon adopted by others, and most bandmasters came to regard it as the starting point for the creation of a regimental band and the most important instrument in it.

Kipling in one of his stories ('The Rout of the White Hussars') wrote, 'the bandmaster is one degree more important than the Colonel'. Well, not quite; but bandmasters certainly occupied a rather special place in the hierarchy, and they had particular privileges. It was, for example, customary for the bandmaster to be invited to have a drink with the colonel after dinner, at least on guest nights. Sir Arthur Sullivan's fa-ther, Thomas, was an army bandmaster at Sandhurst, and the future composer's first piece was written there when he was eight years old.

Learning to beat a drum or blow a bugle was often the beginning of a military career for a young boy whose prospects in life might otherwise have led him to the gallows. Catherine Gladstone, wife of the great Prime Minister, founded an industrial school for street urchins. There they were taught to read and write, and those who showed some musical aptitude were trained by the bandmaster of the Scots Fusilier Guards and eventually placed in regimental bands. By the end of the century it was said that every regimental band in the army contained at least one bandsman who had been recovered from the streets of London by Mrs Gladstone.

In the late eighteenth century, before bandsmen were officially put on the strength and were, in effect, simply employees of the colonel and his officers, it was popular to enlist blacks, usually from the West Indies, as trumpeters or drummers, and they were often provided with quite elaborate uniforms. The Life Guards sought out exceptionally tall men as trumpeters. The 29th Foot (Worcestershire Regiment) was one of the last to use black drummers. In 1759 they had acquired ten black boys, former slaves, a gift from Admiral Lord Boscawen, who obtained them at the capture of Guadeloupe and presented them to his brother, Colonel George Boscawen, then commanding the 29th. Black drummers remained a feature of the regiment until 1843.

Some soldiers, officers and men, were good amateur musicians. Hugh McCalmont, who became a major-general, was a better than average performer on the piano, and Sir Hope Grant was a virtuoso on the cello, which he even carried with him on his campaigns in India and China. In 1865 young Ensign Algernon Heneage Drummond of the 3rd Rifle Brigade, stationed in Bombay, wrote the Eton Boating Song. Other ranks also composed songs which became popular. During the Crimean War a Corporal John Brown wrote 'The Battle of the Alma', which was often sung around the camp fires before Sebastopol.

Certain songs, popular at the time, attached themselves to particular wars, songs such as 'We Don't Want to Fight, but by Jingo if We Do . . .' and Kipling's 'On the Road to Mandalay'. Most do not now associate 'Annie Laurie' with the Crimean War, but such was once the case. 'The Soldiers of the Queen, My Lads' came from the Anglo-Boer War, and, of course, 'It's a Long Way to Tipperary' will always be identified by Englishmen with the First World War. Still, although English soldiers enjoyed an occasional sing-song around a camp fire and Welsh soldiers liked to sing at any time, a booklet of marching songs issued by the government was not a success. The British (Welsh excepted) did not constitute a 'singing army'.

A PECULIAR RELATIONSHIP: Officers and Men

One day during the final weeks of the Indian Mutiny, Lieutenant-Colonel Alfred Horsford of the Rifle Brigade made a brilliant capture of the last battery of horse artillery the mutineers possessed. That evening, while his officers celebrated their success, he went to his tent to lie down. Outside he heard two of his men talking: 'The colonel, 'e 'as done well today, 'asn't he, Bill?' 'Yes, 'e 'as'. 'What will they do with 'im'? 'Oh, make 'im a general or a K.C.B. or something, and then, please God, we will never see the brute any more'. Horsford was amused.

The attitudes and feelings of officers towards their men and of the led towards their leaders have always varied considerably in all ages and among different nationalities and even within any given army. Because other ranks have always been less inclined to write letters or memoirs or to express their feelings in print, it is more difficult to know how they felt about officers; still, enough can be gleaned to form some idea.

Except on actual service during a campaign, other ranks saw very little of their officers or they of them. Lord Curzon observed some soldiers bathing and remarked: 'I never knew the working class had such white bodies'. Field-Marshal Sir William Robertson, remembering his days in the ranks, said of the British private:

In not a few regiments his officers saw little or nothing of him, except when on parade or at stables; they showed no interest in his personal concerns and sometimes did not even know his name, although he might have been under his command for weeks.

Kitchener was never known to address a man in the ranks except to give him an order. Generals Douglas Haig and Horace Smith-Dorrien were said to have had a 'constitutional inability to communicate with the private soldier'. Some officers were able to identify only two other ranks in their regiment: their sergeant and their servant.

Soldiers in the ranks admired bravery in their officers. Lieutenant-Colonel Thomas Harte commanded the 10th Foot (Lincolnshire Regiment) at the battle of Sobraon. He was a martinet, detested by officers and men alike, and he knew it. He also knew that there was a plot afoot to kill him. Before the battle he addressed his men: 'I understand you mean to shoot me today, but I want you to do me a favour; don't kill me until the battle is well over'. He was spared. Athletic powess was also admired, but for the most part men judged their officers by the treatment they received at their hands. Officers demanded discipline, but it was the non-commissioned officers (NCOs) who enforced it; consequently, it was the sergeant who was the more likely to attract hatred. Officers were distant and different beings; it was the N.C.O.s who were familiar and ever-present with rebukes. It was the sergeant-major who marched the defaulters to the colonel and though it was the colonel who pronounced sentence, it was the sergeant whom Tommy Atkins tended to blame for his punishment.

The company officer who carried out his duties in the normal way, paying little attention to his men, could still be respected; the officer who went out of his way to be cruel was hated; the officer who expressed any form of kindness or made any attempt to be helpful was popular. Soldiers sometimes had great affection for worthy superiors, and the number of illustrations of their devotion is endless. In 1840, when Captain Henry Havelock and his wife lost a child and all their possessions in a fire, the men of his regiment, the 13th Foot (Somerset Light Infantry), knowing him to be relatively poor, offered to contribute a month's pay to make up for his losses. When, during the Indian Mutiny, Lucknow was at last captured and there was a considerable amount of looting, one group of soldiers in the 93rd (2nd Argyll and Sutherland) Highlanders came upon a bejewelled replica of a tomb with a magnificent gem serving as a dome. A private cut off this jewel and presented it to a poor but popular lieutenant who, it was said, regularly sent part of his pay home to support his mother. The gem was sold in London for £80,000, enabling the officer to purchase his captaincy and, presumably, take care of his mother's financial needs for life. When Lieutenant George Brooke of the Irish Guards was fatally wounded by a shell at Soupir, his men refused to let the medical corpsmen touch him, but carried him back themselves to the field hospital and openly wept when they left him. Young Brooke's last words to them were that they should 'play the game'.

Every officer had at least one servant, and these soldiers were, naturally, much closer to their officers than were their colleagues in the ranks. Soldier-servants held coveted positions. They were excused from drills and the more disagreeable fatigues and, in general, led relatively comfortable lives, often with special privileges. Their regular pay was supplemented by 2s. 6d. per week in the cavalry and artillery and by 1s. 6d. in the infantry. Tips often swelled this sum. The old adage that no man is a hero to his valet seems not to have been applicable. There are innumerable examples of the affection of many soldier-servants for their officer-masters, and of masters for their servants. When Captain Charles McDonald of the 93rd Highlanders was killed in battle, his soldier-servant was seen crying over his body, and Sergeant William Forbes-Mitchell sent a lock of the young officer's hair to his sweetheart. General William Butler paid for and erected a headstone over the grave of his soldier-servant when he died. The fortunes of master and servant were often closely linked. Private Christie, servant of Captain James L.G. Burnett of the 2nd Gordons, who won the D.S.O. at First Ypres, found his master badly wounded on the battlefield and carried him to safety at the risk of his own life, a brave act which earned him the Military Medal. Burnett lived to enjoy a successful military career, and when he was Major-General Sir James Burnett, Bt, his faithful servant-soldier was with him as his chauffeur, heroes both.

Men in the ranks often covered the deficiencies of their officers. Privates invariably knew the drill better than their superiors, and frequently young officers depended upon their pivot men for guidance. Many soldiers learned the knack of prompting their officers, signalling the proper commands to give without turning their heads or moving their lips.

One of the most serious charges that could be brought against an officer or an other rank was that of being drunk while on guard duty. Neville Lyttelton of the Rifle Brigade told of a major in his regiment who, as field officer of the day, discovered a subaltern in charge of the guard dead drunk. Before taking action, the major went off to find another officer to be a witness for the serious charge he would have to make. The sergeant of the guard acted promptly, putting a large, dirty thumb down the lieutenant's throat until he vomited. By the time the major returned with his witness, the sergeant had his officer in a state of spurious sobriety.

Forbes Macbean of the 1st Gordons was 'born in the regiment'; his father had commanded a battalion from 1869 until 1873. When in 1903 his own term of command ended, the entire battalion spontaneously turned out to bid him goodbye, and the sergeants carried him on their shoulders to the barracks gate. Macbean, incidently, became a major-general, and his only son, in his turn, joined the regiment. But the family connection ended – as it did for so many pre-Great War 'military families' – with the death of that son, who fell at Festubert in 1915.

During the pre-World War I years the mystique of the British gentleman pervaded the ranks. British soldiers wanted to be led by a 'proper gentleman', a 'real toff'. This was an additional handicap for the officer promoted from the ranks. Kipling, who talked with many soldiers and ex-soldiers while writing a history of the Irish Guards, remarked on how they spoke of their dead officers: 'intimately, lovingly, and humorously as the Irish used to do'.

Officers often had ambivalent feelings about their men. Captain Ivar Campbell of the Argyll and Sutherland Highlanders, writing at the end of the pre-World War I period, said: 'Sometimes, back in billets, I hate the men – their petty crimes, their continual bad language with no variety of expression, their stubborn moods. But in a difficult time they show up splendidly. Laughing in mud, joking in water. . . .'

Lord Wolseley, speaking of the late Victorian era, wrote: 'It was not our custom to trust much in the honour and patriotism of our soldiers during peace, though we were certain they would follow us in action.' He described the British soldier as 'a daring and self-sacrificing fellow', but, he added, 'he must be well led, and as a general rule I believe that leader must be a British gentleman'. Wolseley thought that the differences that existed between officers and other ranks were more than social and economic:

> A senseless panic at times seizes even the bravest soldiers; I know not why but it rarely spreads to the commissioned officer. He is better bred and better educated, and, accustomed to think for others, he acts less on impulse and more upon reason than the private. Taught the habit of command and trained to lead others, he is far less liable to this heart-sinking than the brave fellows who follow him.

The same note of condescension was exhibited in a letter from Gerald Graham, a young engineer officer, to his sister, Joanna:

> You must acknowledge that there is virtue in 'blood' (or, perhaps better expressed in 'breeding') which is not to be found in the mass. . . . Our men are the best fighting troops in the world, will follow their officers through the heaviest fire, to certain destruction if necessary; but supposing the officers do not lead or direct, then the men are helpless. As on the officers lies all the responsibility, so they require not only physical but moral courage and presence of mind, whereas for the men the possession of mere animal courage is sufficient.

This attitude prevailed not only in the Victorian era but for a time beyond it. Lieutenant Goerge Rosworth Parr of the Somerset Light Infantry wrote at the beginning of World War I to his old form master at Wellington:

> The men like you to fuss about. It's extraordinary how they rely on their officers for everything; no N.C.O. will do if they can get hold of an officer, however junior.

Some officers regarded their men almost as pets, and occasionally the distinction between a willing soldier and a faithful dog became blurred. In the early Victorian era Captain Leonard Irby had a soldier-servant whom he trained as a retriever, 'and no matter how deep the water where a duck fell, he quickly brought it to his master'.

Often, however, an officer's respect for and devotion to his men was profound. John Chalmers, regimental sergeant-major of the 2nd Scottish Rifles, was much esteemed by all who knew him, and those who had known him never forgot him. When Captain Malcolm D. Kennedy of the same battalion was severely wounded at Neuve Chapelle and forced to leave the regiment and the army, he carried with him a small oval photograph of Chalmers. Fifty years later this photograph alone graced the desk in his study. Every day for fifty years he had looked at the image of his batallion's old sergeant-major. The pride of officers in the Rifle Brigade in their good relations with their men was reflected by Colonel C.H.B. Norcott, who commanded a battalion of the regiment during the Anglo-Boer War: 'I have many happy recollections of my association with the men, and it was a great treat to me to be invited to tea in one of the Company Rooms . . . we had many a happy evening together'.

At the end of the pre-World War I period, when officers censored mail, they gained new insights into their men's lives. Lieutenant Stephen Hewett, Royal Warwickshires, expressed his surprise in a letter to his mother: 'What a lesson it is to read the thoughts of men, often as refined and sensitive as we have been made by the advantages of birth and education, yet living under conditions much harsher and more disgusting than my own!' Second-Lieutenant A.D. Gillespie, Argyll and Sutherland Highlanders, observed that 'men don't write to their fathers often, but to mothers and sisters a great deal, and also to "dear old pals"'. He also noticed that the men 'send so many kisses, often to three different girls by the same post, and they are fond of quoting poetry copied from cigarette cards, or sometimes their own composition – and there are the usual Scoth phrases, "lang may your lum reek"'. Officers tended to lace their letters with Latin and Greek phrases and quotations from Shakespeare or Milton.

The only things most officers and men had in common were a love of sport and a devotion to their regiment. However, as John Bayne pointed out in his excellent study of morale: 'The interplay between the relative simplicity of mind of officers and the childishness of outlook of many other ranks should be noted'. Bayne estimated that the average mental age of recruits was about ten, and that army training raised this by only two or three years. Whether or not the private was indeed childish and irresponsible, he was always treated as though he was. If two soldiers were needed to empty dustbins, a lance-corporal accompanied them to supervise the work. When a soldier left on furlough, a non-commissioned officer took him to the station. Tommy Atkins was not quite as stupid as his officers believed him to be, but lack of education is easily equated with lack of intelligence, and those who are treated like children behave childishly.

Whether because or in spite of the views which officers and other ranks had of each other, a peculiar relationship developed which, in military terms, worked. Whether this perception was just or imperfect, officers and men, working and fighting together, won battles and wars.

EDUCATION AND TRAINING

British boys of the upper and middle classes were moulded into British gentlemen through a peculiar process carried out in unique private institutions – the public schools. In spite of the antiquity of a few, most of them – and some of the most famous – were not founded until the Victorian era: Cheltenham (1841), Marlborough (1843), Rossall (1844), Radley (1847), Wellington (1856), Haileybury (which began as a training college for the Honourable East India Company) and Clifton (both 1862), and Malvern (1865). Certainly the public school ethos was an early Victorian creation. It was not until after the Crimean War that Prince Albert suggested that perhaps it would be best 'to fit a gentleman with a gentleman's education'. So little boys from the appropriate social classes were packed off to public schools, where they developed that set of attitudes and beliefs which the British define as character, and learned the accents, manners, habits and social behaviour which would enable them to exhibit to their peers and to the world that they possessed the credentials of gentlemen.

Children were sent to these schools less to learn anything useful than to acquire a proper accent and acceptable manners. As Lieutenant-Colonel Frederick FitzWagram, 15th Hussars, said, he left Eton 'without the slightest knowledge of any subject which had been of the smallest use to me in after life'. Boys were expected to have their characters

Public school corps training at Aldershot (*Photo: Mansell Collection*)

formed, and the desired character was what came to be known as 'muscular Christianity'. Skill at games was more highly valued than academic excellence; manliness and godliness were considered more important than knowledge for the leaders of men in the armed forces and for the administrators of Britain's far-flung and increasingly large Empire. Given this concept of education, the public schools of Britain did admirably, turning out fairly uniform products for a known market: young men who, although generally ignorant, were extraordinarily brave, unquestioningly loyal, blindly obedient, and irreproachably well-mannered in their own milieu. The imprint was lasting on most. When Major Amery-Parkes was severely wounded and Brigadier-General E. P. Crozier came over to where he lay dying, Amery-Parkes said in a faint whisper, 'Semper domus floreat', the motto of Wellington, which both men had attended.

The public school system was to place a boy in a primitive environment with bad food and few bodily comforts, allow him to be bullied by older boys, and expect him to keep himself reasonably clean and properly dressed, engage in active sports, eschew sex, and learn Greek and Latin. What the boys were given, and what their fathers expected them to be given and paid handsomely for, was what Sydney Smith characterized as 'the safe and elegant imbecility of classical learning'. Somehow the system worked, and as proof every public school could point to dozens of old boys who had demonstrated their worth on the North-West Frontier, in Ashantiland, China, or elsewhere in the world. Throughout the Victorian era the importance and influence of the public schools steadily increased. It did not really matter that the young men left school with little knowledge of the arts and sciences, or that many lacked even elementary skills. Garnet Wolseley, the cleverest of the Victorian generals, was a fifty-one-year-old major-general and a viscount when he was given some advice by his wife: 'A word about your spelling. *Week* (*semaine* not *faiblesse*) is not spelled *weak*, and development has not got two "p's" or "l's" '.

General Sir William Butler did not attend public school; he had very little formal education, but he possessed one of the brightest intellects in the Victorian army. Looking back in 1911 on his forty-seven years of service, he wrote:

> The thing that astonishes me most is the entire absence of the thinking faculty in nine out of ten of the higher-grade officers with whom I was associated. . . . I knew one very successful leader at Aldershot who regulated the movements of his brigade by the direction which the refreshment carts took at the commencement of the fray.

The Duke of Wellington thought that all military education was nonsense, and this attitude remained with many officers. When John Gaspard Le Marchant, a Channel Islander who became the father of British military education, first put forward his plan for a military school, the Duke of York warned him of the prejudice against professionalism, but Le Marchant persisted, and the Royal Military College was founded in 1802. The scheme for the education of other ranks, included in his original plan, was rejected, for it was thought to be 'inconsistent with the habits of the country to raise private soldiers to so close an equality with their officers'. It was feared that it might even lead to promotion from the ranks.

There were, throughout Victorian and Edwardian days, two military schools for the training of 'gentlemen cadets': those destined for the cavalry and infantry attended the Royal Military College, Sandhurst; those intended for the artillery and the engineers went to the Royal Military Academy, Woolwich (known as 'The Shop'). Until 1861 there was another institution for those who were to enter the Indian army: the Honourable East India Company's school at Addiscombe, near Croydon. Sandhurst and Woolwich did not, as did West Point and St Cyr, attempt to give the equivalent of a university education. Certain public schools were more oriented towards the army than others. Many had cadet corps. In 1891 (as today) Wellington supplied more cadets to Sandhurst than any other school. Perhaps this was only natural, for originally Wellington's express purpose was to provide an education for 'orphan children of indigent and meritorious officers of the army'. Wellington was followed by Eton, Clifton, Marlborough, Harrow, Haileybury, Charterhouse, Cheltenham, and Kipling's school, Westward Ho – all of which helped prepare a boy for a career in the army. Special classes were offered for those who intended to take the examinations for Sandhurst or Woolwich, but those in the 'army class' tended to be, or at least to be regarded as, the idle and the stupid.

Attendance at one of the great public schools did not guarantee acceptance at Woolwich or Sandhurst. In 1849 the Duke of Wellington decreed that no one should be given or allowed to purchase a commission 'unless he could prove by examination to have good abilities and to have received the education of a gentleman'. From this time forward, prospective officers were required to pass examinations. In 1885 entrance examinations were required for Woolwich and shortly after for Sandhurst. By the end of the century examinations had taken hold in the army and were required for every step of promotion from lieutenant to lieutenant-colonel.

Although the army made sincere efforts to gear its entrance examinations for Woolwich and Sandhurst to the subjects taught in the public schools, most public school boys found them difficult. Two were required. The first, known as the preliminary, tested such elementary skills as handwriting, spelling, composition, grammar, geography, elementary mathematics ('algebra and Euclid'), geometrical drawing and languages (Latin was obligatory after 1891). About one-fifth failed geography, one-fourth failed spelling, and nearly half failed in languages. The second examination, called the 'further', usually taken a year or more after the preliminary, was a fairly comprehensive survey of a candidate's knowledge and academic skills, lasting for six hours each day for eight successive days. It included questions or required essays in mathematics, English history, languages (Latin, French and German), English composition and drawing. The first day of the further was taken up with physical examinations, which became more strict over the years. By the end of the Victorian era the eye test appears to have been the most feared, and entrants with imperfect eyesight attempted various impositions. One, who was short-sighted, learning that the examiner customarily asked a candidate to look out of a window and name the most distant object he could see, hired a man with a cart to draw up and feed his horse at the end of the road. When his turn came, he reported seeing the cart and the horse being fed. The doctor had to use field glasses to verify the sighting. 'Well'! he exclaimed. 'You'll do. You have splendid sight'.

Schools which tried to educate boys for the army were naturally anxious that their pupils pass the examinations. One schoolmaster, putatively successful, had his own system; his scholars were required to leave off all study for two days before going up for the ordeal, and during those two days were dosed with salts and castor oil. They were then said to present 'a fresh, healthy appearance when inspected by the medical examiner and afterwards went through their papers with clear intellect'. Lieutenant-General Sir William Bellairs, writing in 1889, recommended that candidates take Lampplough's Pyretic Saline just before breakfast.

Even with such aids, many candidates found the examinations too difficult, and they had to resort to 'crammers'. Henry James has given us a picture of the Victorian crammer in the character of Spencer Coyle in his story 'Owen Wingrave'. They were usually retired officers who were knowledgeable about army examinations and skilled in teaching young men to pass them. Most were located in the London area: Captain Walter James, Captain Lynch, and Colonel Lonsdale Hale, all in Kensington, were among the most famous. Young Winston Churchill, although he had been in the army class at Harrow, twice failed the further and was sent to Captain Lynch to be crammed. Of this establishment Churchill later wrote:

> It was said that no one who was not a congenital idiot could avoid passing thence into the army. The Firm had made a scientific study of the men-

tality of the Civil Service Commissioners. They knew with almost Papal infallibility the sort of questions which that sort of person would be bound on the average to ask on any of the selected subjects. They specialised on these questions and on the answering of them. . . . He [Captain Lynch] was like one of those people who have a sure system for breaking the Bank at Monte Carlo, with the important difference that in a great majority of cases his system produced success. Even the very hardest cases could be handled.

Such experts crammed not only young men for Woolwich and Sandhurst but also officers who aspired to take the entrance examinations for the Staff College.

The report of the Royal Commission on Military Education headed by Lord Dufferin (1870) spoke of 'the irregular system of "cramming" we so earnestly deprecate'. It was felt to be somehow morally reprehensible, not because those who went in for it were educationally suspect, but because, as one officer put it: 'The great fear was that the introduction of such a large proportion of crammed candidates would cause the army to lose its "tone" '. However, the necessity for crammers became apparent almost as soon as examinations were introduced. In the period 1858–63 sixty-five per cent of the candidates for Sandhurst and ninety-seven per cent of those for Woolwich were tutored by them. In 1889, of the successful candidates, 112 out of 251 for Woolwich and 215 out of 307 for Sandhurst had been assisted by crammers.

Examinations were not popular. Fathers complained of the additional expense of paying for crammers, and officers and cadets complained that examinations allowed a few 'not of the right sort' to be admitted to Sandhurst or Woolwich simply because they were clever. Charles à Court, speaking of his colleagues at Sandhurst in 1877, lamented that 'there were some dreadful outsiders among us, as could hardly be prevented in an open examination'. When three or four of these 'outsiders' demeaned themselves by accepting a dinner invitation from the commandant's cook, their classmates threw them into the lake. When Colonel Frederick Dobson, commandant of the college, learned of the assault, he told these young defenders of the gentlemen's code: 'I'm damned glad you did'! Montgomery, at Sandhurst in 1907, set fire to the shirt tail of an unpopular cadet and, as he was not wearing trousers at the time, burned him so badly that he had to be sent to hospital.

There were some who were able to enter Sandhurst without taking competitive examinations. Queen's (or King's) Cadets – the sons of officers who had been killed or had died of wounds while on foreign service and had left families in reduced circumstances – were given not only free tuition (sons of gentlemen had to pay £150 and sons of officers lesser sums) but also an allowance. In addition, pages of honour were exempt from competitive entrance examinations, as was the one cadet admitted each year from a chartered colonial university.

Young men usually entered Sandhurst between the ages of seventeen and twenty. The course of instruction normally lasted from one to two years, after which cadets were commissioned in the cavalry or infantry. When Winston Churchill was at Sandhurst in 1893–4, the course lasted only sixteen weeks. Cadets at the Royal Military Academy, Woolwich, were mostly younger, sixteen to eighteen, when they entered and the course lasted longer, usually two years. The average age of cadets on joining in 1899 was nineteen years and three months at Sandhurst and seventeen years and eight months at Woolwich. Their average height was five feet eight inches and their average weight ten stone. There were usually about 270 on the roll at Woolwich and 330 at Sandhurst.

When a young man arrived at Sandhurst or Woolwich, he found himself surrounded by others with backgrounds similar to his own. Their fathers were usually officers, clergymen, country squires or members of the Indian Civil Service. Officer-instructors and cadets spoke the same language in the same accents, possessed similar vocabularies, had the same manners, and entertained the same set of attitudes and beliefs. Lieutenant-General Brian Horrocks, looking back, wrote:

> We regular army officers of those days might all have come out of the same mould. We had been to identical public schools. . . . We talked the same language and were, I'm afraid, terribly dull.

When a student arrived at Sandhurst or Woolwich his character was assumed to have been formed; what was required was the infusion of some useful knowledge. At Woolwich in the 1870s cadets studied mathematics, French, German, artillery, fortification, military surveying, landscape drawing, chemistry, military history, riding, gymnastics and drill. For the first year all cadets followed the same course; then those in the upper ranks of their class could choose the Corps of Engineers and read engineering subjects during their second year, while the remainder, destined for the Royal Regiment of Artillery, studied gunnery and other subjects peculiar to their arm. After graduating from Woolwich the young officer of engineers had to attend the School of Engineering at Chatham for a further two years, whereupon he was offered his choice of service in Britain, India or the colonies.

The curriculum at Sandhurst varied over the years, but in the late Victorian era it included military engineering, topography, military law, tactics, French or German, mathematics, and, of course, drill and gymnastics. Although fencing and riding were compulsory – even during the First World War cadets had to learn horsemanship and sword drill before being sent off to the trenches – musketry was not a required subject until 1892. The cadets lived like gentlemen and most did little studying. Ian Hamilton spoke of 'my year of idleness at the Royal Military College, Sandhurst'. Although it was said that Sandhurst 'combined the evils of the life of a schoolboy with those of a private soldier', this does not in fact appear to have been the case. Each cadet had a room, sometimes shared, and a servant, usually shared, who would black boots, pipe-clay belts, clean rifles, clear away slops and, for an extra tip, do odd jobs. During the hunting season leave was easily obtained on Saturdays. Permission to visit friends in London could be obtained from last study on Saturday until Sunday night.

It seems curious, given the near-obsessional passion of the British for games, that there was no sport at Sandhurst during the first half-century of its existence; it was said that gymnastics would make the cadets 'too active and nimble and not stiff enough for the ranks'. All this changed, of course, with the acceptance of the public school ethos and the concept of muscular Christianity. The cadets were in any case quite active and nimble; frequently they were riotous. In 1862 they staged a particularly well-organized mutiny. They selected a piece of high ground, made it into a well-stocked fort, and from there set forth their complaints concerning bad food and generally poor living conditions. They held out for three days, using loaves of bread as ammunition to beat back any officer who ventured near. Finally, the commander-in-chief, the Duke of Cambridge himself, came to Sandhurst. He pointed out the heinousness of their actions, delivered a sermon on duty, well punctuated with the many damns for which he was famous, and promised reforms. The cadets surrendered. Henry Hallam Parr, speaking of these periodic outbreaks, remarked that 'the authorities were always touchingly grieved and astonished at the depravity of human nature in general and of gentlemen cadets in particular'.

As the time for the passing out parade approached, cadets applied to the governor of Sandhurst for the regiments of their choice. Provided there were vacancies, those who stood at the top of their class had little difficulty in being placed where they wanted to go. If a cadet had a claim to a particular regiment – that is, if his father or other relative had served in it – he was allowed to wait for a vacancy to occur. Those who passed out lowest frequently had to lose pay and seniority because of a lack of vacancies. Only those nominated by the colonel-in-chief of the regiment could be accepted in the Household Cavalry, and appointments to the Foot Guards, the King's Royal Rifle Corps or the Rifle Brigade had likewise to have the blessing of the commander-in-chief.

For a time it was possible for some to avoid Sandhurst; those who obtained the highest marks in an examination were given direct commissions and sent to regiments without receiving any previous military training. Robert (later Lord) Baden-Powell, who became the hero of Mafeking during the Anglo-Boer War and then founded the Boy Scouts, twice failed his entrance examination for Oxford (where his father was a don) but was gazetted straight into the 13th Hussars for his high marks in the army examination. Some of those who for one reason or another obtained direct commissions never learned some of the elementary skills of their trade. Adrian Carton de Wiart was one. He had been awarded the Victoria Cross and was a lieutenant-colonel in command of a battalion of Gloucesters when one Sunday at church parade the general asked him to move his battalion. He had to confess that he did not know how.

Carton de Wiart obtained his regular commission during the Anglo-Boer War, but most direct commissions were given to militia officers. This was the 'back door' to an army career, and about 150 regular vacancies were filled in this way every year. It was the easiest route to a commission, but also the longest. Applicants had to serve at least fifteen months in the militia and there was limited competition. Such officers tended to be older, but they could not be more than twenty-two unless they went into the West India Regiment.

Graduation from Sandhurst or Woolwich was not the end of an ambitious officer's schooling. Later in his career he might decide to apply for the Staff College at Camberley, founded by Le Marchant four years before the Royal Military College. For a considerable time there was a prejudice against the Staff College, and officers showed little enthusiasm for it. As an officer in the Royal Welch Fusiliers remarked: 'Training and keenness and Staff College were suspect in the Fusiliers'. And in most other regiments. Staff College was thought to be a 'mug's game', a mug being an officer who, although a gentleman, 'neither rode nor shot nor played any games, who drank water at Mess, went to bed early, and "swatted" at algebra, fortification, and French as a recreation'. In the Victorian era keenness was considered bad form. Gradually, however, as graduates proved their worth and more and more were seen to rise to general officer's rank, appointments became much sought after, competition for places became keen, and officers intending to take the examination had again to resort to crammers.

In the Gordon Highlanders, where it was not the custom for officers to volunteer for anything, none, even as late as 1875, had ever attended the Staff College. Prior to 1879, only one officer of the Coldstream Guards had ever applied to go. When Captain (later Field-Marshal) Edmund Allenby, 6th (Inniskilling) Dragoons, went in 1896, he was the first man in his regiment ever to do so. By the end of the nineteenth century, however, all of the Foot Guards and all but six regiments of line infantry boasted at least one officer who had 'p.s.c.' (passed Staff College) in front of his name on the army list. Interestingly, though, none of the Household Cavalry and only seventeen out of twenty-eight other cavalry regiments had officers who had passed through it.

The numbers who went to the Staff College remained small; in fact, few officers studied or even read anything after leaving Woolwich or Sandhurst. Colonel John Bayne made an interesting and probably accurate list of the books (other than school books) which an officer born in 1890 would have read. In early life they would probably have included *Jackanapes* and *The Story of a Short Life*, both by Juliana Horatia Ewing, and perhaps *Teddy's Button* (the button in the story is from the tunic of the boy's father, who died defending his regiment's colours). In his teens a boy would have gone on to G.A. Henty, Sir Walter Scott, Rider Haggard, Arthur Conan Doyle and Kingsley's *Westward Ho!* He might also have read some of Jules Verne, Marryat and H.G. Wells, as well as 'The Boy's Own Paper', which was filled with romantic adventure stories. It was probably Kipling, however, whose writings had the greatest influence on his outlook on life, particularly the early works: the Indian tales and *Barrack-Room Ballads*. When a young man passed out of Sandhurst and was gazetted to his regiment, however, he usually said goodbye to books. There were exceptions, of course, but the subaltern would find very few books to read in the officers' mess; the usual literature was 'Blackwood's Magazine', *The Times*, and some sporting periodicals. Many officers never opened a book unless it was the *Queen's Regulations* or *Hart's Army List*. Bayne overstated the case only slightly when he said that 'the officer had done his reading for life' by the time he joined his regiment.

If one wishes to gauge the viability, strength or prosperity of a nation for, say, two to five decades ahead, perhaps no better yardstick could be found than the current status of its educational establishment. A look at Britain's educational establishment on the eve of the first of the great wars of this century goes far to explain its fall as a great empire. Britain's public schools and universities had served it well until the flowering of the Industrial Revolution, but in an expanding and changing world they neither grew nor changed to any appreciable degree. Schools were backward in comparison with those of many other countries, particularly Germany. By 1913 there were only 9,000 university students in Britain; in Germany there were 60,000. During the Edwardian era, England and Wales were turning out only about 350 university graduates a year in mathematics, technology and all the branches of science; Germany was annually producing some 3,000 engineers alone.

In one respect only was there improvement in British education, but it was an important one. In the last quarter of the nineteenth century there was a dramatic reduction in illiteracy. This was almost entirely due to the efforts of W.E. Forster (1818–86), who in 1870 pushed through Parliament the Compulsory Education Act, which eventually almost rid the army of its illiterates. In 1858 a fifth of all other ranks could neither read nor write and only five per cent enjoyed 'superior education' – that is, could read and write with some ease. In 1861 the number with superior educations was only 7.4%. In the same year, when Ensign Neville Lyttelton joined the Rifle Brigade, he found that twenty men in his company could not sign their names and several others could do so only with difficulty. Just twenty-five years later, however, 85.4% of all other ranks possessed a superior education. It was not until 1913, though, that recruits were required to attend school until they had gained at least a third-class certificate.

Illiteracy had been a problem in the army. Some regiments employed

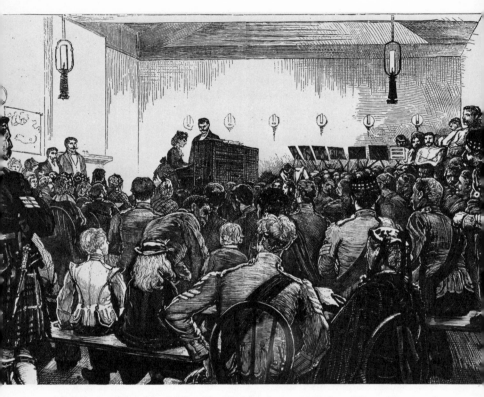

A penny reading class for the 91st Highlanders at Aldershot (*Photo: Illustrated London News Picture Library*)

schoolmasters and excused men from drill if they attended classes. For a time the government itself provided small sums for this purpose, but attendance was never compulsory and few soldiers took advantage of the opportunity. In India classes were offered in Hindustani and Persian and a bounty was given to those who earned a certificate, but there were few indeed who studied original languages seriously. Most were content to learn 'crab-bat'. In 1904 a private was rewarded with a substantial increase in pay if he had no bad marks against him in the regimental conduct sheet for two years, became a first-class shot and earned a third-class education certificate. But in spite of all inducements, it was not until 1933 that an entire battalion – the 1st Gordon Highlanders, 917 strong – was certified entirely literate.

If the young Briton entered the army ignorant, he learned very little during the term of his enlistment – even about his profession. In the 1890s General Evelyn Wood made a surprise inspection of a battalion at Portsmouth and discovered fifty-three young soldiers, none with more than one year's service, engaged in menial work; they had done only two hours' drill in three months. Sir William Butler, speaking of British infantry in 1890, said: 'The "march past" was still the supreme test of tactical fitness for war, just as it had been nearly forty years earlier when I joined the army at Fermoy'. And General Hubert Gough wrote of the cavalry during the same period: 'All this drill was based on that of Frederick the Great's cavalry under Zeithen and Seidlitz – but it bore no relation to modern war'. In 1900 the army still used drill which had been instituted in 1780. The bayonet exercise was, as Evelyn Wood said, 'more suitable for a Music Hall than for training men to fight'.

In 1854 the British army acquired Aldershot and made it the primary training centre. Prior to this, the army had no room for even a brigade to exercise. But 'Aldershot was a strange place', according to Lord Wolseley. 'I can conscientiously assert that I never learnt anything there, nor heard of any regimental officer who did. There was no one there who was capable of teaching us'.

The first large-scale manoeuvres ever held in Britain took place in the autumn of 1871 and then were held annually for a few years before the practice was abandoned. It was not until 1883 that Wolseley managed to persuade the War Office that officers should train with the troops they commanded. In 1892 there was a revived army manoeuvre, so-called, but it was merely a series of tactical exercises carried out from standing camps rather than real manoeuvres. Wolseley described it to the Duke of Cambridge: 'The artillery has been badly handled, generally losing many guns during the action from want of tactical handling. The infantry straggle all over the country in an aimless fashion'. Some of the exercises practised in the days just before the Anglo-Boer War were ludicrous. Attacks were carried out according to strict rules laid down by regulations with prescribed intervals between bodies of troops regardless of the nature or condition of the terrain. In order to stifle any tendency towards initiative, battalions were provided with 'Attack

Cards', giving the precise positions to be held by each company and half company at every stage of the advance.

One might imagine that if a soldier was to receive any instruction and practice at all it would be with his primary weapon, but this was not the case. Prior to 1852 the Guards were allowed only thirty rounds of ammunition per man every three years. Matters did not improve much in the next fifty years. In 1902 army teams competing for a cup fired 1,100 rounds, only five of which hit the target. The experience of the army in the Anglo-Boer War came as a shock to professional officers and civilians alike: a Boer army that never numbered more than 35,000 men in the field at any one time – an army that knew no drill, wore no uniforms and did not even salute – successfully held off the best land forces the Empire could muster for more than two years.

After the Anglo-Boer War a great many officers developed a keenness for their calling which had previously been absent. Their desire for a well-trained professional army did not, however, have any influence on the War Office clerks or the politicians. There was still not enough money provided for practice ammunition. When Lord Dundonald commanded a regiment of the Life Guards he called on past and present officers to subscribe to the purchase of ammunition, the hiring of a range, and the payment of the rail fares of soldiers to and from the range. When Lieutenant-Colonel F.I. Maxse commanded the 2nd Coldstream Guards he contributed his own money and even persuaded his men to give up two days' pay each year in order to buy practice ammunition and to build a firing range at Windsor. Other officers were equally energetic in obtaining funds for musketry practice, and it was as a result of such individual efforts that by the beginning of the First World War British standards of musketry rose from being the worst in Europe to the best. Ironically, however, this skill contributed to the belief that fewer machine guns would be needed.

Ill-educated and badly trained as they were, officers and other ranks possessed the British ability to make do, to muddle through, and to fight against all odds. Yet it is sad when character must be counted on to replace foresight, and bravery to replace brains – when blunders must be paid for in blood.

REFORM

. . . there was very much more in common between the Army of 1661 and that of 1850, than between that of 1850 and that of 1900.

John Fortesque, *The Empire and the Army*

After each major war there were official inquiries into the deficiencies and inadequacies of the army. These were generally followed by some improvements, some trimming of administrative fat or the application of some patches on the old system, but by 1870 this mossy, tradition-laden, antique army, although still capable of fighting 'colonial wars', was badly in need of a thorough overhaul. The briskly efficient Prussian army's swift victory over the French in 1870–71 made some thinking Englishmen acutely aware of Britain's lack of preparedness to fight a major war or to repel an invasion.

Great Britain was fortunate during this period (from 1868 until 1874) to have as Secretary of State for War a remarkable man, Edward Cardwell, who picked up the British army and shook it to its foundations. In fact, he started with its foundations and instituted radical, dramatic reforms. He was followed some thirty years later by another extraordinary man, R.B. (later Lord) Haldane, who, as Secretary of State for War between 1905 and 1912, prepared Britain as best he could for the

153

Lord Cardwell (*Photo: Illustrated London News Picture Library*)

First World War. History has not given these two politicians the credit they deserve, for it could be argued that without them the history of Europe in this century would have been quite different; certainly the years in which they served in the War Office constituted watersheds in the history of the British army.

Edward (later Viscount) Cardwell (1813–86), a man with a particularly strong abhorrence of violence, was in many ways a peculiar choice as Secretary for War. But Gladstone knew what he was doing. Cardwell had already made his mark by the introduction of important legislation affecting the Royal Navy, merchant shipping and the railways. As Secretary for the Colonies he had abolished transportation of criminals and withdrawn from the colonies in times of peace all imperial troops, thus saving the British taxpayer considerable sums and promoting colonial self-defence. He was an unusual combination of able politician and brilliant administrator.

Born the son of a Liverpool merchant, he was educated at Winchester and at Balliol College, Oxford, where he achieved the remarkable distinction of taking first class honours in both classics and mathematics. He was called to the bar in 1838, but four years later he entered the House of Commons as member for Clitheroe and devoted himself to politics. Before becoming Secretary of State for War, Cardwell had exhibited neither interest in nor understanding of the workings of the War Office, but he quickly mastered its intricacies and then undertook the reorganization of the army, particularly the infantry. He did not remain in office long enough to carry through all his reforms, but his immediate successor, Hugh C.E. Childers, continued his work.

Garnet Wolseley, then a colonel, became one of Cardwell's staunchest supporters within the army, but Cardwell himself astonished him:

> The subject [military reform] was not congenial to his tastes, and there was nothing in common between him and the fighting British soldier. The ambitions, the prospects, the feelings and prejudices of our officers were not known to him. He did not himself belong to what I may call a military family.

Nevertheless, Cardwell saw that the army was, as Wolseley put it, 'absolutely behind the age in every way', 'out of date', and 'an anachronism'. In spite of fierce opposition within and without the service, he was able to push through Parliament a series of Acts – the War Office Act and the Army Enlistment Act in 1870, the Regulation of the Forces Act in 1871 and the Military Localisation Act in 1872 – which together transformed the institution.

One of the most important and certainly the most difficult of his reforms was the abolition of the system whereby commissions and ranks in the infantry and cavalry were purchased. In this he was opposed by many members of the House of Commons, who were horrified by the thought of the expense involved, and by most army officers, led by the commander-in-chief himself, the Duke of Cambridge, who regarded all Cardwell's reforms not only as mad folly, but as virtual crimes against the state. In Parliament the greatest opposition was in the House of Lords. When the Regulation of the Forces Bill, which proposed not only to abolish purchase but also to remove control of the militia and volunteers from the lords-lieutenant of the counties, came to them, the Lords threw it out. But when Cardwell persuaded Queen Victoria to abolish purchase by royal warrant, the Lords did an about turn and passed the Bill. With uncharacteristic generosity, government even agreed to pay officers the true market value of their commissions instead of the official rates.

Perhaps more important – certainly for the other ranks – was the Army Enlistment Act, which introduced short service. The previous system of long service enlistments had created two major problems: it was difficult to recruit and it was impossible to build up a trained reserve. The Army Establishment Act provided for a twelve-year military commitment, but, depending upon the type of regiment and where it was serving, the actual time spent 'with the colours' varied from three to seven years; the remaining time was spent in the reserve, subject to recall in case of war. It was Cardwell's notion that, as he said, 'In time of peace the army will feed the reserve and in time of war the reserve will feed the army'. So it worked out. The system was not unique – even Turkey and Russia, the most backward of European nations, possessed similar schemes – but it seemed a radical idea to Englishmen and it had some powerful opponents, Lord Roberts and Rudyard Kipling among them. In 'The Drums of the Fore and Aft' Kipling told a story of a regiment in India that broke and fled in the face of the enemy. The cause: the short service soldiers.

> He has, let us say, been in the service of the Empress for, perhaps, four years. He will leave in another two years. He has no inherited morals, and four years are not sufficient to drive toughness into his fibre, or to teach him how holy a thing is his Regiment. He wants to drink, he wants to enjoy himself . . . and he does not in the least like getting hurt. He has received just sufficient education to make him understand half the purport of the orders he receives, and to speculate on the nature of clean, incised and shattering wounds. Thus, if he is told to deploy under fire preparatory to an attack, he knows that he runs a great risk of being killed while he is deploying. . . . He may either deploy with desperate swiftness, or he may shuffle, or bunch, or break. . . .

Armed with imperfect knowledge, cursed with the rudiments of an imagination, hampered by the intense selfishness of the lower classes, and un-
supported by any regimental associations, this young man is introduced
to an enemy who in eastern lands is always ugly, generally tall and hairy,
and frequently noisy. If he looks to the right and left and sees old
soldiers – men of twelve years service, who, he knows, know what they
are about – taking a charge, rush or demonstration without embarrassment, he is consoled and applies his shoulder to the butt of his rifle with a
stout heart. . . .

But, on the other hand, if he sees only men of his own term of service,
turning white and playing with their triggers and saying: 'What the hell's
up now'? . . . he becomes unhappy; and grows acutely miserable when
he hears a comrade turn over with a rattle of fire irons falling into a ten-
der, and the grunt of a pole-axed ox. . . . If he is not moved about, and
begins to feel cold at the pit of the stomach, and in that crisis is badly
mauled and hears orders that were never given, he will break, and he will
break badly; and of all things under the light of the sun there is nothing
more terrible than a broken British regiment.

In spite of Kipling and other critics, short service, with some varia-
tions, remained in force up to the First World War. One result was to
lower a soldier's average age, even though the minimum age for recruits
was raised from eighteen to nineteen. With short service the army numbered fewer old sweats such as Privates Mulvaney, Ortheris and
Learoyd, Kipling's infamous trio. In 1871 nearly a third of all other
ranks were over the age of thirty; by 1894 less than nine per cent were
over thirty and three-quarters were between twenty and thirty. There
were also fewer middle-aged sergeants, and the youth of the non-commissioned officers worried many, though in 1879, when short service
may be said to have had a fair trial, it was found that seventy-one per
cent of all sergeants who had completed six years service re-enlisted.
In the end, the army accepted the abolition of purchase and it
adopted short service, but what it found hardest to swallow was the
'linked battalion' system. It had no effect on the cavalry. (Indeed, the
cavalry contained too many influential and conservative aristocrats for
Cardwell to make much of an impression.) The linked battalions
scheme affected only part of the infantry, but it caused an uproar
throughout the army. Although not fully implemented until 1881, after
Cardwell had left office, it has always been the reform most closely associated with his name. There were three principal features: each regi-

ment was to have at least two service battalions, most regiments were to be identified with a county or city, and militia battalions were to be tied to regular regiments.

Since 1857 the Guards infantry, the Royal Scots, the King's Royal Rifle Corps, the Rifle Brigade and the first twenty-five regiments of the line had all possessed more than one (usually two) battalions; regiments of the line whose numbers were higher than 25 had only one battalion. It was Cardwell's notion that two-battalion regiments were better, as one full battalion could be sent on foreign service while the other remained at home to recruit and train; every few years the order could be reversed. Cardwell therefore 'linked' all the one-battalion regiments. Thus, the 109th Foot (the highest numbered regiment) was linked to the 100th, the 99th Regiment was linked to the 62nd, the 59th to the 30th, and so forth. The linked regiments were to act as if they were two battalions of the same regiment, but they kept their individual numbers and traditions. In 1881 Childers was able to force the actual amalgamation of the regiments, though many years later many officers and men still stubbornly referred to their battalion by the number it had had as a regiment of the line. When the 71st and 74th Regiments merged to form the Highland Light Infantry, the officers and other ranks continued to refer to themselves by their old numbers, and not for half a century did the officers freely exchange from one battalion to the other. Although the 28th and the 61st Regiments were amalgamated in 1881, to become respectively the 1st and 2nd battalions of The Gloucestershire Regiment, one old soldier, Victor E. Neubury, writing in 1977, referred to his former unit as 'the Gloucestershire Regiment (the 28th Foot, as I like to think of it)'.

The only place in Kipling's writings where he used (or tried to use) the true titles of actual regiments was in the autobiographical *Something of Myself*, and then he made a hash of names and numbers:

> I first got to meet the soldiery of those days in visits to Fort Lahore and, in a less degree at Mian Mir Cantonments. My first and best loved Battalion was the 2nd Fifth Fusiliers [2nd Northumberland Fusiliers] with whom I dined in awed silence a few weeks after I came out [to India]. When they left I took up with their successors, the 30th East Surrey [1st East Surrey Regiment] – a London recruited confederacy of skilful dog-stealers, some of them my good and loyal friends.

Kipling's confusion was understandable, for he was speaking of the early 1880s, when the change from numbers to names had just taken place.

Sometimes the amalgamation of 1881 involved more than just a change of name. The 75th Foot, which had been disbanded in 1783 after fighting in the American Revolution, was reconstituted in 1787 as a Highland regiment. In 1809 it became an ordinary marching regiment and remained so until in 1881 it was amalgamated with the 92nd Highlanders and became the 1st Battalion of the Gordon Highlanders, which meant that they were obliged to wear kilts. The merger was not popular. A Sergeant Sharp of the 75th carved an epitaph on a stone at Floriana Barracks that read:

EPITAPH ON THE 75TH, 30 JUNE 1881

Here lies the poor old Seventy-Fifth,
But under God's protection,
They'll rise again in kilt and hose
A glorious resurrection!
For by the transformation power
Of Parliamentary laws,
We go to bed the Seventy-Fifth
And arise the Ninety-Twas.

Colonel Charles Poole, who had spent his years of service in the 67th Foot (merged after his retirement with the 37th Foot to form the Hampshire Regiment), spoke for many a choleric old soldier when he replied to an invitation to a dinner given by the Hampshire Regiment:

Damned names mean nothing. Since time immemorial regiments have been numbered according to their precedence in the Line. Nothing can alter the rightness of such a plan, and interfering boobies in the War Office can have no effect on my determination to ignore their damned machinery at all costs to myself. I will not come to anything called a Hampshire Regimental Dinner.

My compliments, Sir, and be damned.

A second aspect of this scheme of Cardwell's was the localization of the regiments. The desirability of giving them county or city connections had been recognized half a century earlier by Lord Palmerston, who said:

I believe there is a great disinclination on the part of the lower orders to enlist for general service; they like to know that they are to be in a certain regiment, connected, perhaps, with their own county, and their own friends, and with officers who have established a connection with that district.

Many regiments had borne place names, usually county names, as part of their titles since 1782, but they had been meaningless. It was Cardwell's intention to give most regiments a city or county name to replace its number, to place the regimental depot there, and to restrict recruiting to that area. By 1881, when the actual amalgamation took place, each regiment had been assigned a depot in its eponymous locality. This certainly helped to give them a more distinctive character. By 1893 more than a quarter of all soldiers in the infantry were serving in regiments representing the cities or counties in which they were born. By 1911 the first battalion of the Hampshire Regiment, for example, had 604 Hampshire-born men out of a total strength of 911; and only fifteen were Irish.

It was also part of Cardwell's plan to link the local militia to the county regiments, usually as the 3rd and 4th battalions; Irish regiments were allowed three militia battalions. By 1885 the system was in operation, although not yet complete, for many English regiments lacked their second militia battalion. Typical of the new system (at least as it was supposed to work) was the Essex Regiment, which was a merger of the 44th (East Essex) and the 56th (West Essex) Regiments. Its 3rd and 4th battalions were formed from the Essex Rifles and the West Essex Militia. The 1st battalion of the regiment (formerly the 44th Foot) was at Colchester, having returned from India in November 1884; the 2nd battalion (formerly the 56th Foot) was in Egypt. The regiment's depot (Regimental District No. 44) was at Warley.

In addition to his great reforms, Cardwell managed to make a number of other changes which, although not so earth-shaking, were nevertheless important. It was he who finally pushed through the bill that abolished flogging except under exceptional circumstances. He increased the pay of the private soldier to one shilling per day *in addition to* free meat and bread and made other improvements in Tommy's living conditions. Further, although the Commander-in-Chief at the Horse Guards had always, in theory, been subordinate to the Secretary of State for War, in point of fact he was not. Cardwell changed all that. He brought the Commander-in-Chief to heel and instituted some much needed reforms, organizing all army administration under three heads: military, supply and finance.

Following Cardwell's reforms, Hugh Childers pushed on. In 1881 the term of command of a regiment, which had originally been indeterminate but had been brought down to five years, was further reduced to four; for a time the rank of major-general was so freely offered to colonels commanding regiments or battalions to speed their retirement that the country was flooded with surplus major-generals. In 1881 it was decreed that all captains would be obliged to retire if by the age of forty they had not been promoted, but it was found that there was such an immense number in this category that to avoid the political scandal that would certainly have followed the wholesale discharge of men who were, after all, in the prime of life, something special had to be done. The problem was handled by doubling the number of majors allowed in each infantry battalion and tripling the number in each cavalry regiment. The new infantry majors were not, however, mounted, and they continued to perform the duties of captains. 'Mud majors', they were called.

Between 1868, when Cardwell took office, and 1880 there were no less than eighty-nine official bodies prying into army affairs. Commissions and inquiries continued after Cardwell and Childers had made their mark and departed from the scene. The next great reformer was R.B. Haldane, but in the forty years that separated him from Cardwell there was some progress and some additional reform.

In 1885 Britain established a Colonial Defence Committee, but this committee failed to address itself to broad questions of imperial strategy, and lacked a staff to provide it with the necessary support. What was badly needed, of course, was a general staff, and the creation of such an organization was one of the chief recommendations of the Hartington Commission in 1889–90; another was the abolition of the office of commander-in-chief. Neither was acted upon immediately, but, with other proposals, they constituted the basis for all future administrative and policy-making reforms prior to the First World War.

More than other people, perhaps, the British like not only to study and worry about new ideas but to let them stew for long periods with occasional stirrings. From time to time something actually develops. Because of the personalities involved, as much as politics, the government could not bring itself actually to abolish the commander-in-chief's position, but in 1895 there was a reorganization of the army's high command which greatly reduced his authority, giving him only 'general supervision' of the military departments and limited responsibility for military plannning. When the Duke of Cambridge finally was persuaded to retire, after nearly forty years, the post was given to Lord Wolseley, who had long coveted it. Wolseley was bitterly disappointed to find that although he had inherited the title, he lacked the authority which the Duke had exerted and that he held a position which, in effect, burdened him with responsibility but deprived him of power. Queen Victoria, who always took a keen interest in all military matters, tried to puzzle her way through the complexities of the new command structure and concluded that there was 'something wanting or at all events undefined'. She was right, as she so often was when politicians came up with muddled schemes. In the end the reorganization satisfied no one, neither politicians nor soldiers.

From 1879 until 1885, the period when Lord Hartington was Secretary of State for War and headed the commission bearing his name, his private secretary was Viscount Esher, a man obsessed with the desire for army reform. Esher was the kind of man who likes to make suggestions and recommend actions but has no taste for responsibility. As an adviser to King Edward and his ministers, Esher enjoyed considerable influence, but when Balfour offered him the post of Secretary for War, he declined. More congenial to him was the appointment to the chairmanship of the Prime Minister's Committee on War Office Reform. This committee (known as the Esher Committee) again recommended the abolition of the office of commander-in-chief. It also recommended the setting up of an Army Council and a Committee of Imperial Defence.

The first result, in 1904, was the creation of the Army Council, consisting of the chief of staff and the heads of departments, each responsible not to the commander-in-chief but to the Secretary of State for War. Later in the same year an Inspector General of the Forces was appointed and a Committee of Imperial Defence constituted. Then, in 1906, a general staff was at last set up to handle war organization, operations and training, but responsibility for personnel and discipline remained with the adjutant-general, supplies and transport with the quartermaster-general, and arms and equipment with the master-general of the ordnance. These officers, together with the Secretary of State for War, the Financial Secretary to the War Office and the Permanent Under-Secretary, constituted the Army Council, which was then the supreme authority. The British army still had no one person in command – and has not to this day.

When in December 1905 Campbell-Bannerman formed his cabinet, the appointment of Richard Burdon Haldane (1856–1926) as Secretary of State for War seemed as curious a choice as had that of Cardwell for the same post in Gladstone's first cabinet in 1868, but it was an equally good one. Haldane, a Scot, educated at the universities of Edinburgh and Göttingen, was called to the bar by Lincoln's Inn in 1878 and took silk in 1890. Meanwhile, he had become a Member of Parliament in 1885 and he remained in Parliament for twenty-six years. He never married. He had read philosophy at university and its study remained a life-long passion. Together with a friend, John Kemp, he translated Schopenhauer's *The World as Will and Idea* (3 volumes, 1883–6), but it was Hegel who held a special appeal for him. It was perhaps this philosophic turn of mind which led him to raise a question rarely asked: 'What is the army for'? When he talked of re-fashioning the army, the generals asked him what sort of an army he had in mind. 'Hegelian', he replied. It proved a discussion stopper.

Haldane had no military experience and, before he came to the War Office, had evinced no interest in military affairs, but he applied his legal and philosophical mind to the administrative and military problems he found there and the reforms he was able to carry through during his seven years in office were dramatic.

Although Hartington and Esher had headed commissions recommending the formation of a general staff, it was Haldane who in 1906 was instrumental in its embodiment. In addition, Haldane converted the militia into a Special Reserve which was legally embodied as part of the army's reserves and could in time of war be at once taken into the regular forces. The Yeomanry and Volunteers, constituting historically a haphazard establishment, were formed into Territorials, a home defence force of all arms with a divisional organization. There were other changes. An Officers' Training Corps was set up with branches in the public schools and universities. There were improvements in rationing the army, in the organization of the medical and nursing services, in training for both regulars and reserves, and in transportation arrangements. Haldane's greatest contribution, however, was to form the army into units larger than a regiment, to provide them with staffs, and to prepare them to fight a major war. By 1912, when Haldane left the War Office to become Lord Chancellor, the army had six infantry divisions and one cavalry division ready to fight, and as early as 1905 he sanctioned talks between British and French staff officers.

In addition to all these high-level reforms there was an internal change that was more visible to regimental officers and the rank and file. Instead of the usual eight service companies in an infantry battalion, each battalion was transformed into four 'large companies', each commanded by a major or a senior captain, and each consisting of four platoons under subalterns. There were now six officers to a company with the company commander mounted.

Haldane and the British army had profited greatly from the reforms of Cardwell; Haldane had studied and benefited by the work of the many committees and official inquiries since. Having said this, it must also be said that it is easier to conceive ideas and to put forth recommendations than to execute new policies and to force conservative men to do things differently. Haldane achieved this and more. He correctly surmised who Britain's next enemy would be, and who her allies, where the conflict would take place, and what kind of army would be needed to fight that war, at least in its initial phases. From his position at the War Office he could see how pitifully small were the country's forces in comparison with the huge conscript armies on the continent, but as a politician he could also see the impossibility of trying to persuade the electorate to adopt conscription in time of peace, in spite of the obvious need and in spite of the strong advocacy of such a popular general as Lord Roberts.

In short, Haldane took the army as he found it and, in spite of the fact that he was a member of a Liberal cabinet committed to peace and that a considerable portion of his party was opposed to almost any military expenditure, he shaped it as best he could for the war he foresaw against the Germans on the European continent.

THE REWARDS OF SOLDIERING

No country in the world has found so many different ways in which to honour its soldiers' achievements as has Great Britain. During the Victorian era new honours both for units and for individuals proliferated as at no other time in history.

Battle honours were the most common unit awards. These gave a regiment the privilege of inscribing on its flags (called colours) or on its drums the names of the battles or campaigns in which it had participated. The oldest battle honour, 'Tangier 1662–1680', carried by five regiments, was given to The Queen's in 1909 – more than 225 years after the event. Each regiment of infantry carried (until 1881, actually into battle) two colours: the Queen's (or King's) and the regimental colour. When, even though not exposed to shot and shell, they became thin and frayed, they were laid up at a cathedral or church, and new ones were presented by some distinguished, or at least titled, person.

This reverence for colours was a Victorian phenomenon. In an earlier age regiments were more careless. The guidon of the 19th Light Dragoons (dragoons had guidons instead of standards) was lost for a hundred years. The colours of the 71st Foot (1st Seaforth Highlanders) were left behind and apparently forgotten when the battalion moved from one station to another in Ireland in 1788. They turned up in 1921 in a Limerick pawnshop.

Regiments had reason to be proud of their battle honours, for they were grudgingly and often quite belatedly bestowed. The oldest battle honour of the Royal Berkshire Regiment, for St Lucia (1778), was not conferred until 1909; it took even longer – 150 years, in fact – for the regiment to be given permission to place a naval crown on its colours for its part in the battle of Copenhagen (1801). Not until 1910 was the Scots Guards given battle honours for 'Namur 1695' and for two engagements in the Peninsular War: 'Fuentes d'Onoro' and 'Nive'. Those for the battles of Blenheim, Ramillies, Oudenarde and Malplaquet, earned in the early eighteenth century, were not awarded until 1882.

Regardless of how heroically a regiment behaved, no honours were awarded for defeats – usually. However, the Black Watch and the 8th Bombay Native Infantry were awarded the battle honour 'Mangalore' in spite of the fact that it was a British disaster suffered at the hands of the Maratha in 1783–4.

Sometimes cities honoured regiments by giving them permission to march through their streets with 'bayonets bared, drums beating and colours flying'. The Royal Marines, the Royal Fusiliers, the Grenadier Guards, the Honourable Artillery Company and the Buffs had this privilege of the City of London and, from time to time, with great ceremony, exercised it. Edinburgh granted the same privilege to the King's Own Scottish Borderers.

Regiments could also earn the right to add the word 'Royal' to their title. 'Royal' regiments wore blue facings; the only non-royal regiment to have the same distinction was the 13th Foot (Somerset Light Infantry). It was also an honour to be named as a royal personage's 'own'. After its heroic activities at Jellalabad during the Second Afghan War, the 13th Foot was called 'Prince Albert's Own', and it retained the title even after the prince's death. The 19th Foot was 'The Princess of Wales's Own', the 85th and the 25th Foot were 'The King's Own', the 32nd Foot was 'The Duke of Cornwall's Own', etc.

It was the more particular and peculiar honours that soldiers valued most. There were, for example, the six 'Minden regiments' who on the anniversary of the battle of Minden (1 August 1759) had the privilege of wearing roses in their caps. No one really knows why. Some say that on their way to battle the troops stopped while passing through a rose garden to pluck some blossoms and set them in their caps. The Cheshire Regiment wore acorns and oak leaves on the anniversary of the battle of

Dettingen (27 June 1743), the last battle in which an English king personally led his troops, apparently because George II was driven to take refuge under an oak tree and was stoutly defended by the Cheshires (then the 22nd Foot).

Almost every regiment had some individual distinction based on its history. There are conflicting stories of why the Black Watch was given the privilege of wearing a red vulture feather, the 'red hackle', on its bonnet; according to one version, it was in recognition of the regiment's gallantry at the battle of Guildermalson in 1794. The staff for the colours of the South Wales Borderers was surmounted by a silver wreath of immortelles as a reminder of the near-total destruction of a battalion at Isandhlwana during the Zulu War in 1879. The Scots Guards, on the anniversary of the battles in which the regiment won honours, wreathed its colours with laurel.

In addition to unit awards, Britain had a cornucopia of individual honours to bestow, particularly on its officers. Medals, of course, were the most common, and there were few soldiers who did not garner at least one in the course of their careers, though, of course, not all received the recognition they merited. Lieutenant-Colonel Rowland Feilding once wrote about this to his wife:

> I have known men – good men too – eating their hearts out through want of recognition. How petty this sounds! Yet a ribbon is the only prize in war for the ordinary soldier. It is the outward visible sign – the ocular proof to bring home to his people – that he has done his job well.

Whether soldiers received the decorations they deserved, or any decoration at all, often depended upon the literary abilities of their commanding officer; if he lacked the skill properly to describe a subordinate's gallantry, a brave man might go undecorated.

Medals and ribbons in their present form are a nineteenth-century innovation. In the eighteenth century special medals in gold or silver were sometimes struck to commemorate great victories, but they were often privately minted and given only to senior officers. The Honourable East India Company awarded medals to all those who took part in the battle of Seringapatan (1809), but different metals were used for different ranks: gold for generals, silver for other officers, bronze for noncommissioned officers, and tin for privates. British regulars, however, were not allowed to wear this medal until 1851, by which time there were few veterans alive to do so.

The first campaign medal awarded by the British government to all ranks was the Waterloo Medal, which became the prototype for most of the campaign and general service medals that followed. Suspended by a multi-coloured ribbon, it was in silver for all ranks, 1.4 inches in diameter, with the head of the sovereign on the obverse and an appropriate design on the reverse. The recipient's name, rank and regiment were usually impressed on the rim. Officers who fought at Waterloo were given an additional distinction: on army lists their names were preceded by a gothic letter W; those who served in the Peninsula were given a gothic letter P. Later, those who served in the Indian Mutiny were given a gothic letter M.

The Waterloo Medal proved so popular that medals were subsequently awarded for nearly all major campaigns. They were much valued by officers and other ranks alike. More different kinds were awarded during Queen Victoria's reign than in all the years before and since. General service medals were also issued, to which bars or clasps could be added for specific battles or for minor campaigns – and some not so minor, owing to government parsimony. The first of these was the most peculiar. It came to be called the 'dead man's medal' because it authorized clasps for twenty-nine engagements prior to the battle of Waterloo (1815) but was not issued until 1847. Surprisingly, though, there were two old veterans who received the medal and fifteen clasps.

There was never much method in determining whether a medal or a clasp should be issued. A medal was struck for the defence of Kelat-i-Ghilze by 950 men, but those who took part in the Tirah campaign, where British forces were larger than those sent to the Crimea, had to be content with a mere clasp on the India General Service Medal. Native troops were usually issued the same campaign medals as the European troops – but in bronze, not silver. The medal for the Red River Expedition in Canada, the only one ever awarded for a bloodless campaign, was not struck until thirty years after it ended. No medal or clasp at all was issued for the battle of Ginnis (30 December 1885), a victory by British arms over a force of Dervishes in the Sudan, because, as Sir Henry Campbell-Bannerman explained to the House of Commons, British casualties were so light; only nine men killed and thirty-six wounded.

Queen Victoria presenting medals to the wounded officers from the Crimea
(*Photo: Graham Brandon*)

In 1833 a Long Service and Good Conduct Medal was instituted for soldiers who had managed to survive for eighteen years in the army without falling into serious trouble. Soldiers liked to belittle it, calling it the 'root gong' or 'rooti gong' (a corruption of the Indian expression for a round loaf) because, they said, it came with the bread ration, and was a reward for eighteen years of undetected crime. In fact, it was not easily earned, and many a soldier who confidently expected to receive it was disappointed, caught short by some long forgotten indiscretion of his youth.

In 1845 the Meritorious Service Medal was authorized for sergeants and warrant officers who had performed good service other than in battle. Curiously, there was no recognition of any sort for gallantry in action until in December 1854 a Distinguished Conduct Medal was available to reward sergeants and lower ranks who had served with distinction in the Crimea. Then in 1856 the Victoria Cross was instituted, and the first awards were announced in the *London Gazette* of 24 February 1857 for heroes of the Crimean War. This medal was, and still is, manufactured by Messrs Hancocks and Company, London jewellers, from the metal of Russian guns captured at Sevastopol. Although at first disdained by some, it quickly became the most coveted of all. All ranks in all services, and even civilians, were eligible. Only 522 were awarded prior to the First World War, and of these 348 were won by soldiers; four were given to civilians for service during the Indian Mutiny; two were awarded to foreigners (a Swiss for Rorke's Drift and a German for Balaclava). The youngest recipient ever was fifteen-year-old Hospital Apprentice A. Fitzgibbon for his heroism in China in 1860.

Seven soldiers were required to forfeit their Victoria Crosses for subsequent misconduct. Gunner J. Collis, of the Royal Horse Artillery, who received one for bravery during the battle of Maiwand in the Second Afghan War (1880), was fifteen years later, and more than four years after his discharge from the army, convicted of bigamy, imprisoned, and deprived of his medal. Interestingly, he re-enlisted during the First World War and served in the Suffolk Regiment; perhaps he hoped, vainly, to win it back. Private F. Corbett of the King's Royal Rifle Corps was gazetted for the decoration in 1883 for gallantry in Egypt but was forced to forfeit it just seventeen months later.

There was a tendency not to give the V.C. to senior officers; this was to discourage them from 'unnecessary displays of valour'. Ian Hamilton felt that he was defrauded of the award because he was acting as a general when he was recommended for it. Evelyn Wood, when a midshipman, was one of the first to be cited, for 'the most beautiful courage and conduct, and manners that were exemplary', but not until five years later, as a cavalry officer in India, did he obtain the medal for attacking with only two native soldiers a band of seventy robbers.

No woman has ever won the Victoria Cross, but in 1883 Queen Victoria instituted the Royal Red Cross, which was awarded to women for special attention to sick and wounded soldiers or sailors; it was won by Winston Churchill's Aunt Sarah Wilson during the siege of Mafeking in the Anglo-Boer War.

The Victoria Cross remained the only medal for gallantry until the Distinguished Service Order (for officers only) was instituted in 1886, although the C.B. (Companion of the Bath) was frequently given to field officers for distinguished services. Recipients of all three were ever after entitled to post-nominal letters. A number of foreign decorations were also authorized for wear, but usually only if the awarding country was an ally in a war.

There was a strong feeling (at least among officers) that medals were reward enough and that it was discreditable for a soldier to capitalize on his valour. It was for turning his gallantry into something more substantial than a bronze medal that Piper Findlater, of the Gordon Highlanders, seemed an embarrassment to many officers. During the Tirah campaign on the North-West Frontier (1897–8) the 2nd Gordons made a spectacular charge on the heights of Dargai. Piper Findlater fell in the charge, wounded in both legs, but propped himself against a rock and continued his playing of 'Cock o' the North'. His deed, which won him a Victoria Cross, caught the popular imagination, and he found himself a hero when his battalion returned to Britain. Discharged from the army because of his wounds, he accepted an offer from Mr Dundas Slater, manager of the Alhambra Theatre in London, to play 'Cock o' the North' on the stage for £30 a week – twenty times his army pay. Several officers clubbed together to stop the performances, and on 28 May 1898 General Sir Evelyn Wood, their spokesman, in formal dress uniform and looking his glittering best, went to Slater's office and offered to pay Findlater's salary if Slater would cancel the act. Slater laughed at his soldier's naïveté. He explained that he had already spent £300 in promotion.

Medals were not the only honours available. A man could be 'mentioned in dispatches' – one of the oldest methods of recognizing meritorious service or gallant behaviour. In after action reports, commanding generals would single out those who had been brought to their attention, sometimes merely listing their names but occasionally including a brief description of their services. Before the Sind campaign, only officers were mentioned, but in General Charles Napier's dispatch of 2 March 1843 he named other ranks as well, including even sepoys. This soon became standard practice. In the Victorian-Edwardian army there was no distinctive decoration or even certificate for those so singled out, but the names were published in the *London Gazette*, and in the 'war services' sections of army lists the phrase 'mentioned in dispatches', or perhaps 'twice mentioned in dispatches', was used. It had meaning among those whose opinions counted most: fellow officers. Lord Roberts, perhaps the most decorated and honoured of the military heroes of Mr Kipling's army – and, incidentally, a great personal friend of Kipling, who wrote a poem about him – was said to have been mentioned in dispatches twenty-three times. Curiously, only the Victoria Cross and a mention in dispatches – the highest and lowest of honours – were ever awarded posthumously. Lord Roberts's son was the first such recipient of the Victoria Cross, for gallantry at the battle of Colenso in the Anglo-Boer War.

There were other honours that bestowed neither medals nor postnominal letters but which were nonetheless prized. To have received the 'thanks of Parliament' or the 'thanks of the Government of India' looked good on army lists; such 'thanks' were given only to senior officers. This was also true of the civilian tributes that came to successful generals: honorary degrees from universities, honorary memberships in guilds, presentation swords, and grants of the 'Freedom of the City'. This latter was, in fact, often something tangible in the shape of an ornate silver casket to hold a scroll. Generals could also be made colonels of regiments, and there were a number of other honorary appointments such as Constable or Lieutenant of the Tower of London. The Lieutenant of the Honourable Corps of Gentlemen-at-Arms was normally a distinguished colonel, and the Lieutenant and two Ensigns of the Yeomen of the Guard were usually lieutenant-colonels.

Another honour in the form of a job with no duties was the appointment as an Aide-de-Camp to the Queen. In 1899, besides the Duke of Cambridge, who was Chief Personal Aide-de-Camp, and three other relatives of the Queen who were Personal Aides-de-Camp, fifty colonels were so honoured, of whom seven were Supernumerary Aides-de-Camp and six were Extra Aides-de-Camp. The Aides-de-Camp to the Queen received £200 per year in addition to their pay, but they were also required to buy expensive uniforms trimmed with much gold braid.

In addition to the strictly military honours there was also a full panoply of orders of chivalry, some of which had, and still have, separate civil and military lists. There was not supposed to be any special ranking among the orders, but in fact the prestige scale was something like this for orders that included knighthoods:

Date of Founding	*Order*
1348	Order of the Garter (K.G.)
17th century	Order of the Thistle (K.T.)
1783	Order of St Patrick (K.P.)
1399	Order of the Bath (G.C.B., K.C.B./ D.C.B., C.B.)
1861	Order of the Star of India (G.C.S.I., K.C.S.I., C.S.I.)
1818	Order of St Michael and St George (G.C.M.G., K.C.M.G./ D.C.M.G., C.M.G.)
1886	Order of the Indian Empire (G.C.I.E., K.C.I.E., C.I.E.)
1896	Royal Victorian Order (G.C.V.O., K.C.V.O./D.C.V.O., C.V.O.)

The origins of some of the oldest orders are obscure. No one knows why, for example, the peculiarly-named Order of the Garter was formed. A charming but unlikely story is that Edward III at a ball picked up a garter dropped by the Countess of Salisbury and put it on his own leg, saying, 'Honi soit qui mal y pense' (Evil be to him who evil thinks – the motto of the order). The number of people who could be honoured by most orders was limited. The Most Honourable Order of the Bath could have only 68 appointments as Knight Grand Cross (G.C.B.), 173 as Knights Commander (K.C.B.) or Dames (D.C.B.), and 943 to the military list and 555 to the civil list as Companions (C.B.). However, Grand Crosses were awarded only to the old, who often died a few years afterwards.

Successful generals often obtained knighthoods in several orders and could be raised to the peerage as well. Lord Roberts of Kandahar, who started his career as simply Frederick Sleigh Roberts, was by 1899 a nobleman, holder of the Victoria Cross, a colonel commandant of the

Royal Artillery, and could add the additional post-nominal letters: K.P., G.C.B., G.C.S.I., and G.C.I.E. And this was before his victories in South Africa brought him further honours, inculding a K.B. (which had not been awarded to a victorious general in eighty-five years) and an earldom.

After a popular, spectacular success, honours were usually awarded promptly, but in most cases they were tardy and often seemed rewards rather for the ability to survive into old age than for brave deeds. Neville Bowles Chamberlain was a doughty fighter on India's North-West Frontier who in 1863, after receiving his ninth wound in the Umbeyla campaign, retired and fought no more. A year later he had risen to the rank of colonel, was an Aide-de-Camp to the Queen, and had been given a K.C.B., but that was all. However, he was made a K.C.S.I. in 1866, a G.C.B. in 1875, and in 1899, at the age of eighty, he became a field marshal.

Sometimes honours were accompanied by more substantial rewards. A private who won the Distinguished Conduct Medal for gallantry was given a gratuity – although he was not allowed to spend it, for it had to be placed in the regimental savings bank until he was discharged. The Long Service and Good Conduct Medal also carried a small gratuity, and holders of the Victoria Cross received a pension of £10 per year – unless they were officers. In 1884 holders of the Distinguished Conduct Medal were given an extra 6d. per day pension (but only 3d. per day for 'black soldiers').

There were sometimes curious rules, usually reflecting the desire of the government to save money. In 1855 Staff-Sergeant George Marvin of the Royal Horse Artillery was awarded the Distinguished Conduct Medal with a £20 annuity for service in the Crimea. The following year he was given the Long Service and Good Conduct Medal with a £15 gratuity. However, it was decided that the latter 'cannot be conferred on an individual enjoying an annuity for "Distinguished Conduct in the Field" ', so Marvin had to relinquish his Good Conduct Medal. Glory could be more profitable for generals. Wolseley was given £30,000 after his Egyptian campaign of 1882, and Lord Roberts on his return from South Africa in 1900 even more: an appreciative Parliament voted him £100,000.*

---

* The First World War was profitable for its successful (if that is the right word) generals: Haig received £100,000 to go with his earldom, French and Allenby were given

In addition to money, medals, presents, fine words (and some occasional loot), there were other means of expressing recognition. All who took part in the battle of Waterloo, for example, were given credit for two years' additional service. Promotion to a higher rank was also a frequent reward, and it was possible for sergeants who had demonstrated their bravery to win commissions.

From time to time some unusual favours were shown. During the Anglo-Boer War five khaki scarves crocheted by Queen Victoria, with the initials VRI on one of the knots, were awarded to men of the British and colonial forces who were voted by their comrades to be the best all-round soldiers. Some thought it amusing, others embarrassing, that one scarf went to an American soldier of fortune.

Rewards (deserved, perhaps, but not always properly come by) were sometimes available to Victorian soldiers in the form of loot. When a rich city was captured there was often looting, but the victorious commanders usually tried to put it on an organized basis. An officer was appointed prize agent, the troops were shaken down to disgorge their pickings, and the plunder was auctioned. The resulting cash was then divided according to a system whereby the lion's share went to the commanding general. After his victorious campaign in Sind in 1843, General Charles Napier's share was £70,000; his privates received only a few shillings. Napier's looting was thorough: he even claimed as a prize of war the bed (and the gold hidden in it) of the pregnant wife of a Sindian chief. Most looted when they could, both officers and men. Major Reginald Pole-Carew of the Coldstream Guards, while in Burma in 1886–7, peeled off strips of gold leaf from a temple, and Major Ian Hamilton of the Gordon Highlanders stole a rare and ancient Buddha from a shrine.

The British were incensed when, in the China War of 1860, the French started looting the beautiful and treasure-laden Summer Palace before they arrived, but there was much left over and everyone got something before the British army, in one of its most notorious pieces of vandalism, burned the palace to the ground. Lieutenant George Colley of The Queen's complained in a letter home that because of the French his share of the plunder came to only 'between 40l and 50l'. However, he added, 'I have a pretty good collection of silk embroideries and robes.

£50,000 each, and most army commanders received £30,000 and corps commanders £10,000.

Sale of loot during the Ashanti War, 1874 (*Photo: Mary Evans Picture Library*)

. . . Our mess is taking home a magnificent china vase as a reminis-
cence of the palace. It was presented by Colonel [Thomas] Addison,
who bought it from a soldier for a mere nothing. The amount of valuable property destroyed must have been incalcuable'. The share of the
private soldier was not quite £4. Even the Queen received some loot
from this campaign. In Pekin Captain Hart Dunne of the 99th Foot
(2nd Wiltshire Regiment) acquired a small 'lion dog' which he brought
back to England and gave to her. This, the first Pekinese seen in the
West, was aptly named 'Lootie'.

SICK AND WOUNDED

Evelyn Wood began his remarkable career as a mere boy fighting with the naval brigade in the Crimea; then, taking an army commission, he saw much active service, and rose to the rank of field-marshal. He was both brave and able. He was also the most sickness-prone and accident-prone officer in the British army.

In the Crimea, while skylarking on board H.M.S. *Queen*, he fell overboard. Later he was severely wounded in the left arm; he hurt the same arm twice again and the wound abscessed before it finally healed. Invalided back to England, he slipped and fell down a flight of steps in a barracks. Back in Turkey as a cavalry officer, he soon succumbed to typhoid, pneumonia and dropsy. He recovered and, with only an in-growing toe-nail, joined his regiment in India. There he suffered severe sunstroke, intestinal complaints, indigestion, fever, ague, and acute toothache. For a bet he tried to ride a giraffe, fell off and was stepped on. The giraffe's hooves cut holes in each of his cheeks and made a mash of his nose. He won the Victoria Cross while suffering from a 'face ache'.

Back in England, he fell from a horse and nearly broke his neck; he broke an ankle in another fall from a horse; he was tormented by 'neu-ralgia of the nerves of the stomach' and insomnia. A doctor inadver-tently gave him an overdose of morphia. During the Ashanti War he

Sir Evelyn Wood (*Photo: Mary Evans Picture Library*)

collapsed from exhaustion, and when the stretcher on which he lay was
set down on top of an anthill, he was attacked by ants; shortly thereafter,
a nail fired from a musket pierced his chest. Throughout the Gaika War
of 1878 he endured severe 'neuralgic pain'; during the Zulu War of
1879 he suffered from swollen glands and 'continuous pains in the eyes,
coupled with gastric neuralgia.' During the First Boer War (1881) he
was riding in a spider when it hit an anthill and he was tossed out, striking his spine on the off-horse's head. The 'irritation set up in the spine

was so severe as to make my feet swell to an enormous size,' he reported. He also had 'intestinal complaints for eight days, induced by overwork.' His aide-de-camp complained that it was necessary to 'carry a chemist shop' to treat his many ailments.

In Egypt during the campaign to relieve Gordon, Wood not only had severe diarrhoea, but caught his finger in a folding camp chair as he sat down, 'crushing the top so that it was in jelly-like condition' and the nail had to be removed. While in England in 1897 he tried to learn to ride a bicycle, and in the process thrice collided with hansom-cab horses; one, understandably, bit him and his arm was permanently marked by the horse's teeth. During the Anglo-Boer War, Wood, as adjutant-general, had to stay in Britain, where he was once again assailed by pains in his stomach and distressed by progressive deafness. In 'a heavy fall when riding an impetuous horse with hounds' a gold crucifix and a locket were driven into his ribs. Still, he did not die until 1919 at the ripe age of eighty-one.

They were a tough lot, these Victorian soldiers. At the battle of Agra during the Indian Mutiny, Lieutenant Stowell Jones, 9th Lancers, was shot from his horse and then set upon by rebel sowars armed with sharp-bladed tulwars. He lost an eye and a piece of his skull was sliced from his head; in all, he suffered twenty-three wounds before he was rescued. He recovered, won the Victoria Cross, rose to the rank of lieutenant-colonel, and sired three sons, all of whom became officers.

Although few suffered as many wounds, accidents and illnesses as Wood or Jones, still, such things were common enough in the army. In every campaign illnesses accounted for more casualties than wounds inflicted by enemies. Officers and men had to learn to survive the medical attention they received, for the medical and sanitary standards of the army were incredibly low. It is difficult to account for this. There were few senior officers who did not at one time experience the horrors of military medical attention. Yet few generals concerned themselves with the human debris which was the necessary concomitant of their strategies. Officers and other ranks all seemed to accept the needless pain, the rough handling, the springless ambulances, the crude and insensitive hospital orderlies, and the incompetent doctors as unchangeable aspects of military life.

Proper medical care in all armies depends upon four factors: competent doctors, adequate supplies of proper instruments and medicines, at-

tention to organization and administrative detail, and an acute aware-
ness on the part of commanding officers of medical and sanitary
problems. The Victorian–Edwardian army conspicuously lacked all
four. Although statistical proof does not exist, it would appear that in
general only the worst doctors, those unable to earn their living in
private practice, took employment in the army.

Doctors were professionals – or were supposed to be – living among
men who admired amateurs and scorned professionalism. Perhaps for
this reason officers ignored the problems of medical administration,
where their talents might have been greater than those of the doctors,
who in any case are notoriously bad administrators. However, combatant officers had no interest – medical administration was not a gentlemanly pastime – and their interference would have been strongly resented by the medical officers.

Only the intelligent interest of senior commanding officers could
improve the lot of the sick and wounded soldiers. Wellington, in 1812,
appointed Dr. James McGrigor as his principal medical officer. It was a
wise choice. McGrigor gave the army for the first time an organized
medical service; he introduced a system for the evacuation of the
wounded, had pre-fabricated hospital huts constructed, and required
that casualties be registered so that statistical records could be kept. It
was a giant step forward, but after Waterloo the army took two steps
back, and all that was learned was forgotten. When the army went to
the Crimea, the only medical and surgical aid provided was by the regiments. If the regimental surgeon could not cure a man, he died. The
system (if such it can be called) was such an obvious failure that the War
Office attempted to establish field hospitals and dispatched 300 decrepit
pensioners to constitute a Hospital Conveyance Corps. When this
proved unsatisfactory, a Medical Staff Corps was formed. It was supposed to be composed of 'Men able to read and write, of regular steady
habits and good temper and of a kindly disposition,' but all too many
possessed none of these qualifications.

It is necessary perhaps to mention here the work of Florence Nightingale in Turkey, not because of any impact she had on British army medical history, but because the attention she received at the time and her
subsequent apotheosis have distorted her importance in that history and
have magnified the extent of her accomplishments. Miss Nightingale
was an intelligent, energetic, innovative, courageous woman who es-

Florence Nightingale's hospital at Scutari (*Photo: Illustrated London News Picture Library*)

tablished a clean, well-managed hospital where she provided a superior medical service to a small portion of the sick and wounded during the Crimean War. She did no nursing in the Crimea, and soldiers had to survive for days or weeks before they had an opportunity to reach her hospital. A comparative handful of soldiers were made comfortable and quite possibly were enabled to survive only because of her efforts. But she came to the seat of war for a few months, did her good works, and departed. The medical officers, most of whom vehemently opposed her, were there before her and remained after her. She showed the way to better, cleaner medical service, but the path she marked was not followed. She continued to be keenly interested in sanitary conditions in the army, particularly in India, but she had little or no effect on the practices of the Royal Army Medical Corps. Her influence may have been, in the long run, what is now called counter-productive. Rather than admit their own deficiencies, rather than follow enthusiastically a female and a rank outsider, army doctors simply became hardened in their old ways, more determined than ever to pursue the treatment of wounds and diseases as they had always done; they became even less receptive to new methods, new instruments, new ideas.

Some of the medical beliefs of doctors were quaintly pernicious. Wolsely said that 'doctors starved wounded men to keep down inflammation,' and he described a river boat in Burma on which doctors sat laughing, eating and drinking in the midst of their hungry and thirsty wounded. Even when anaesthetics were known, doctors often neglected to use them. Wolseley received multiple wounds from an exploding shell in the Crimea. He lost the sight of one eye and his left cheek lay down as a flap over the collar of his shell jacket. A jagged piece of rock embedded in his jaw was removed without anaesthetic; one doctor pulled it out with forceps while another held his head between his knees.

Nearly a half century later, in the Anglo-Boer War, the large number of civilian doctors taken into the service were appalled by the medicines, instruments and methods of the Royal Army Medical Corps. A distinguished professor of surgery who went to South Africa noted that the service was 'not up to date,' an understatement surely. Dr Frederick Treves – later to win fame and a baronetcy for removing the appendix of King Edward VII – told a commission after the war that the R.A.M.C. was using 'instruments which I should have thought would only be found in museums'.

The Anglo-Boer War was notable for the number of incompetent British generals who emerged, particularly in the early months. In terms of tactics and strategy, few were worse than General Sir Redvers Buller, who was commander-in-chief in South Africa until superseded by Lord Roberts. Buller was, however, an excellent administrator, and he took a great interest in the health of his troops. He consulted regularly with his medical officers, and his arrangements for the efficient evacuation of the wounded were the best that any British army in the field had ever seen. They even included a corps of Indian stretcher-bearers raised by a man later known as Mahatma Gandhi.

In striking contrast to Buller was the performance of Lord Roberts, who conquered the Orange Free State and the Transvaal. Generals are judged by their ability to bring their troops into action in the proper numbers at the proper time and in the most suitable location. In this respect Lord Roberts was, in 1900, the best general the British had, as proved by his skill in outflanking the Boer army at Magersfontein and making his triumphal march through the Orange Free State. But Roberts's victorious progress was brought to a sudden halt at Bloemfontein, for he had failed to issue the necessary orders to ensure that his troops drank uncontaminated water. They fell in massive numbers of typhoid – enteric, it was called then – and the British suffered more casualties in a four-month period from this one disease than were killed and wounded by the Boers in the entire war.

Water was often drawn from polluted streams into which dead horses or oxen had been thrown, and put in water carts of which Colonel W.D. Richardson, Roberts's chief of supply, said: 'Probably nothing harbours germs and disease more than our present type of wooden barrel water cart'. There was no way in which these barrels could be cleaned. From the carts the soldiers drew water into equally unsatisfactory canteens. As Colonel Richardson said: 'After a few months' use the interior of the service water bottle is often covered with mould, which smells offensively and is very probably a fertile source of disease'. Even when orders were issued that all water must be boiled, they were frequently ignored. It was bothersome to boil water; fuel was often scarce or unavailable; the men complained that boiled water was tasteless and they did not like it. No wonder then that thousands of young men were stricken with typhoid; the wonder is that all did not succumb to the disease.

No cure was known, but by 1896 an inoculation had been developed. Three years later, when the war broke out in South Africa, the army had an opportunity to attack its greatest enemy. Inoculation was offered, but it was not made compulsory. Because it was given in a single injection instead of two or three smaller ones, the recipients became violently ill; consequently, less than five per cent of the troops sent to South Africa volunteered for it. Inadequate records were kept, and the official conclusion was that the value of the inoculation was 'doubtful'.

Typhoid was not the only killer. Serving in far-way places, soldiers were felled by malaria, cholera, yellow fever, smallpox and a host of other diseases. In a cemetery near Agra there still stands a monument to 147 men of the Yorkshire and Lancashire Regiment who died of cholera within a forty-eight-hour period. In 1837 the 3rd King's Own Hussars sailed for India with 420 non-commissioned officers and privates; only forty-seven of them returned with the regiment in 1853. Not all of the missing were dead; many had been sent home because they had secondary syphilis, hepatitis, or some other disease, or because of 'general debility'.

Attending to the sick and wounded after the Battle of Kassassin, 1882 (*Photo: Graham Brandon*)

Even in England soldiers faced greater dangers than civilians. The death rate from tuberculosis in the army was five times that of the civilian population. In the 1850s a convict was allowed 1,000 cubic feet of air in his cell; a soldier in barracks had 400 cubic feet, and sometimes less. In 1858, when the death rate in the civilian population was nine per thousand, it was eleven per thousand in line regiments and, in the crowded barracks of London and Windsor, mortality among the Foot Guards was more than twenty per thousand. Conditions improved however. In the ten-year period beginning in 1882 the average death rate for soldiers was only 5.73 in the United Kingdom. But most were serving abroad, where it remained high: in India during this same period the average was 14.78, and in Egypt it was 23.78.

In the field, officers were felled more often than other ranks by enemy bullets, proportionately, but they were less often sick, and fewer died of disease. But germs had no respect for rank, and in peacetime officers and men were subjected to almost the same hazards from insanitary conditions. In some cases the officers were exposed to greater dangers, for a medical officer in one English military district found that kitchens of the officers' messes were the dirtiest places in barracks, except perhaps the canteens. In one canteen the contractor's agent was found 'sleeping at the back of the grocery bar with his head on a cheese and his feet in a butter bowl'.

Each battalion had its surgeon who, in addition to his medical duties, often ran the mess and performed administrative odd jobs. Not until 1898, after a virtual boycott of the army's medical corps by the graduates of medical schools throughout the United Kingdom, were doctors given army ranks with the same titles as combatant officers. At this time the Royal Army Medical Corps was formed by the amalgamation of the Medical Staff (doctors) and the Medical Staff Corps (other ranks), but this did little to improve the quality either of the doctors or of the system. Army rank did not make the doctors more popular with soldiers or with their civilian colleagues.

In 1900, during the siege of Ladysmith in South Africa, a private in the 2nd Gordon Highlanders suffering from diarrhoea reported to an Irish doctor, who asked, 'Have ye been drinking river water? Have ye been eatin' green peaches?' To each question the soldier replied, 'No, sir'.

'Then to hell out o' this', yelled the doctor. 'You *can't* have diarrhoea!'

Pioneer Sergeant Menzies, also with the 2nd Gordons in Ladysmith, received a more satisfactory response from an army doctor, but then, he was more easily satisfied: he did not ask for a cure. Beards were forbidden, but Sergeant Menzies was allowed to grow one after he was given a certificate stating that shaving was bad for his teeth.

Doctors could be crude and insensitive; it is little wonder that the combatant officers did not always consider them quite gentlemen. Hope Grant in China during the Opium War described in his journal seeing a dead Chinese girl:

> She had the wonderfully small deformed feet common among the women of this country. A surgeon who came to call on us, to my great horror, cut off these tiny feet and preserved them in his private collection.

When Midshipman Wood was wounded in the arm in the Crimea, a doctor cheerily told him to take a seat, and 'I'll have your arm off before you know where you are'. Wood saved his arm by fleeing. Forty-five years later, a civilian doctor who had taken a commission in the R.A.M.C. for the Anglo-Boer War wrote home about the capabilities of regular army doctors:

> Believe everything you hear as to mismanagement and even incapacity and willful neglect. . . . Certainly if I were ill or had been wounded, I would not care to be left to the tender mercies of the majority of men I have come across.

Private Frank Richards said: 'Now it was a common belief among the troops [in 1900s] that as soon as an army doctor rose above the rank of captain he became a little balmy and the higher he rose the more balmy he became'.

After the Anglo-Boer War the standards of sanitation and the quality of medical care improved dramatically, as these figures for the troops in India illustrate:

	1865		1912	
	Number	*Per thousand*	*Number*	*Per thousand*
Deaths	1,761	28.14	342	4.82
Invalided home	2,558	40.90	477	6.70

The British army did not have a dental corps until 1921. Nearly half a million men served in the Anglo-Boer War, but only one dentist went to South Africa – at his own expense.

The dead were handled somewhat more efficiently than the suffering living. Death was common enough in peacetime; on active service it was more common still. It has been said that there are two things which the British army can do to perfection: attempt the impossible and stage a funeral. Certainly a funeral was treated seriously, with suitable ritual and in a practical manner.

A battalion usually paraded in dress uniform for a funeral. Every available officer was present, arms were reversed, and en route to the cemetery the band played a slow march (often the 'Dead March' in *Saul*). In Highland regiments there was the mournful wail of a lament on the bagpipes and 'Lochaber No More' was played over the grave; a service was read by a chaplain, a bugle played 'Last Post', and three volleys (for the trinity, though few knew the significance) were fired over the grave.

The corpse buried, duty done, the mood was swiftly changed as the band struck up a quick march – often the tune of the latest music-hall song – and the battalion was marched briskly back to its quarters. Thursday was normally a holiday for the troops in India, and the men cursed when they were forced to attend a funeral parade on this day. But death does not know the days of the week, and often enough the dead robbed the living of their holiday.

When an officer of any rank died on active service, his horses, uniforms and other possessions were auctioned and the proceeds sent to his widow or mother. This was all any relation received from the army. Whatever the circumstances, each regiment did its best to give its dead, whether officers or other ranks, a proper burial, but this was not always practicable. At Varna, during the Crimean War, wood was scarce and cholera was rife; it was not always possible to make coffins, and many were buried sewn in a blanket and carried to the grave on a stretcher. Once, when two women of the army died, boxes were broken up and coffins were fashioned from them. Lieutenant Frederick Stevenson saw the funeral, 'the coffins carried on men's shoulders covered all over with "Bass's superior Pale Ale". . . . it was impossible not to smile'.

DISCARDS AND
DEPENDANTS

In 1891 Kipling wrote 'The Last of the Light Brigade', a poem in which 'twenty broken troopers', the last of those who charged at Balaclava, shambled into the presence of the 'Master-singer who had crowned them all with his song' (Tennyson); their spokesman says:

No, thank you, we don't want food, sir; but couldn't you take and write
A sort of 'to be continued' and 'see next page' o' the fight?
We think that someone has blundered, an' couldn't you tell 'em how?
You wrote we were heroes once, sir. Please write we are starving now.

Kipling ends his poem with a couplet:

Our children's children are lisping to 'honour the charge they made –'
And we leave to the streets and the workhouse the charge of the Light
    Brigade!

Such indeed was a common fate of those who wore the 'Widow's uniform' – as well as those who wore the khaki of her son and grandson – for the government's treatment of veterans was certainly less than adequate and Kipling was not alone in considering it a disgrace.

Old soldiers received pensions after twenty-one years of service; the

189

amount depended upon the length of service and the damage done them by wounds or diseases, and varied from time to time as the laws changed, but it was always pitiably small.

All too typical was the career of Sergeant Richard Brown, of whom it was said that 'no better man ever drew breath of life'. He appears to have led an exemplary life, for he served twenty-one years in the 11th Hussars, taking part in the charge of the Light Brigade, and was never in the defaulters' book. After he retired – on 1s. 3d. per day – he was fortunate to find a job and worked (often ankle-deep in water at the canal side in Manchester) until age and rheumatism caused him again to retire, this time to the workhouse, where, some time in the 1890s, he died and filled a pauper's unmarked grave.

The army tried in its rough fashion to help its own, the time-expired soldiers, the crippled and sick, the widows and orphans, but its efforts were inadequate. Sometimes regiments would give special banquets or hold ceremonies at which old soldiers were honoured. On 5 November 1877 a banquet, attended by the Prince of Wales, was given in Leicester by the Grenadier Guards for more than 400 Crimean War veterans; the oldest was ninety-three. On the weekend of 14 September 1907, to celebrate the fiftieth anniversary of the storming of the 'Cashmere Gate' at Delhi during the Indian Mutiny, the 2nd Oxfordshire Light Infantry (formerly the 52nd Light Infantry) invited the survivors of the old 52nd who had been at Delhi to a ceremony at Tidworth, all expenses paid. Officers and other ranks contributed, and the affair was attended by five of the eight surviving officers and by twenty-three of the surviving forty-one non-commissioned officers and men. The veterans attended church parade and were critical of the new drill; things were done better back in '57, they agreed.

Such gestures were doubtless appreciated, but they were few and far between. They could not replace regular, systematic care. In the early nineteenth century the old soldier turned beggar was a common sight, dressed in shoddy old clothes with medals pinned on the left breast, their ribbons frayed and faded. Mendicancy was regarded as the normal, almost the only trade of the old soldier. The government's treatment of those who had risked their lives and their health in the army or the navy remained discreditable.

Some pensioners were tough old birds, and long-lived. Having survived a childhood in the slums and then the hardships, diseases and dangers of a military career in many parts of the world, they bid fair to survive such rigours as civilian life offered. Sergeant C. Ellingsworth was in the 93rd (2nd Argyll and Sutherland) Highlanders in the Crimea. As a young man he had been a part of the 'thin red line' that successfully withstood the Russian attack on it. He was the last survivor of that line of heroes, and did not die until 1927 at the age of ninety-six.

The callous treatment of those no longer useful began for the soldier at the moment of his discharge. It was official policy to turn men out of the army with little more than they had possessed when they entered it. In 1902 Sir Evelyn Wood, then a full general, came across a party of invalids at a railway station. They had just been discharged from hospital as cured and from the army as unfit; some had quite a distance to travel. 'They were without greatcoats or rugs of any description,' said Wood, 'the thermometer being at 30°. This was in accordance with regulations. I sent them back, and had coats issued at once. Mr Broderick [the Secretary of State for War] supporting my unauthorized action'.

There were a few places for old soldiers within the establishment. The Yeomen of the Guard, founded by Henry VII in 1485 and still calling itself the sovereign's bodyguard, was (and is) a unit made up of former warrant officers and sergeants, as also the Yeomen Warders of the Tower of London ('Beefeaters'), with whom they are often confused. According to John Fraser, a Yeoman Warder for more than thirty-five years, the job was 'cushy', for 'inclusion in the ranks of the Yeomen Warders of the Tower of London is the Mecca of all old soldiers who do not crave to return to civil life'. The establishment of the Yeomen of the Guard was one hundred, that of the Yeomen Warders forty. A few old soldiers could be accommodated at the Royal Hospital, Chelsea, where, in beautiful buildings designed by Christopher Wren and surrounded by spacious grounds, they could still wear a uniform and their medals and be well looked after. The Royal Hospital, Kilmainham, served a similar purpose in Ireland. But the number of veterans who could be looked after in this fashion was very limited, and for the numbers of veterans of major wars it was inadequate indeed.

A few special jobs around garrisons were reserved for old soldiers. The 'fizzer men', who were allowed to hawk ginger-beer among the troops, were always pensioners. A time-expired soldier in need of assistance was more likely to get help from one of the private charities established for soldiers and sailors. These were supported for the most part by officers, former officers and wealthy military families. Many officers (usually older ones who had seen what feats these hard-drinking, heavy-swearing, disease-infected men could perform) formed societies to aid old soldiers.

The Army and Navy Pensioners and Time-Expired Men's Employment Society, founded in 1855 and supported by voluntary contributions, helped old soldiers find work. Later the Incorporated Soldiers and Sailors Help Society was founded, with the King and Queen as patrons. This organization taught useful trades to veterans, and each applicant was given the name of a 'friend' in his local parish or in the parish to which he retired. Between 1903 and 1913 it found employment for 43,000 discharged soldiers and sailors and gave money or clothing to 85,000 more. The National Association for Employment of Ex-Soldiers also had royalty as patrons; it 'recommended to employers ex-soldiers of the best character only'.

If a man possessed some skill other than in drill or musketry he could perhaps find employment as a clerk, farrier, fitter, plumber or mechanic, but for the most part the kinds of employment these societies found for old soldiers were menial: work as labourers, porters, packers, messengers, coachmen, watchmen, grooms, servants, valets, stokers. The Corps of Commissionaires, an association of pensioned soldiers organized to provide just such work, was originally established in London in 1859 and has proved the most durable and efficacious of these job-finding organizations.

Those old soldiers unable to enter Chelsea or to obtain work found that their only recourse was to charity, the Poor Law, or crime. Some took their discharge in India, where perhaps they had served most of their lives. A few of these managed to find work or even to establish their own businesses. Sergeant William Forbes-Mitchell, who had fought with the 93rd (Sutherland) Highlanders during the Indian Mutiny, became a prosperous industrialist, the largest rope manufacturer in India. Others wandered from one military station to another, wearing their medals and cadging food and drinks; often a collection was taken up for them before they left.

In Britain, too, old soldiers sometimes came around. One day when the 1st Gordons were stationed in Cork (1904–7) a frail old man appeared at the sergeants' mess and announced himself as Sergeant-Major Courtney, late of the battalion. He had indeed, as the records confirmed, been regimental sergeant-major during the Indian Mutiny, nearly a half century earlier. The Gordons welcomed him with all honour. The officers received him at their mess, he inspected the recruits on parade, and throughout the battalion's stay in Ireland he was a welcome guest. When, just before its departure for Aldershot, Courtney died, his funeral was attended by the band, the pipers and all the sergeants.

It was not until after the Anglo-Boer War (1899–1902) that Old Comrades' associations began to be formed in any number, usually on a regimental basis. One of the earliest was the Gordon Association, formed in Glasgow in 1888 to 'keep up the connection with old comrades, assist men of good character to obtain employment when they leave the regiment, and encourage young men of good character to join it'. In addition to raising benevolent funds and providing clothes and work, the Gordon Association had 'an excellent house with garden' which was given rent-free for life to a disabled married ex-Gordon Highlander. One of the reasons Old Comrades' associations became possible, enabling time-expired men to keep in touch with events and friends in their old regiments, was the increased literacy among the other ranks, which gave birth to regimental magazines that served both active and retired officers and men.

As far back as 1820 the Military Widows Fund was formed as a society to which officers in India could subscribe. In the event of the subscriber's death, the fund assured passage back to England and maintenance for six months for the officer's wife and children. The government made no provision whatsoever for widows and orphans. The Royal Cambridge Asylum for Soldiers' Widows was the only Victorian institution which catered in any way for the widows of other ranks. Although it was opened in February 1854 and was under royal patronage, it never grew, and it could not accommodate more than sixty women; in 1877 it provided for only fifty-four widows. In the first sixty years of its existence, only 354 widows were taken in. Each woman was given a small furnished room, an allowance for coal, and seven shillings a week for all other requirements. The Royal Military Benevolent Fund granted annuities of up to forty pounds a year to 'ladies in necessitous circumstances, being exclusively the widows or unmarried daughters of deceased officers of Her Majesty's Army'.

The Soldiers and Sailors Families Association, founded in 1885, provided a variety of services for the families of both officers and other ranks. During the Anglo-Boer War several special funds, national and regimental, were started, the largest and most popular being the Absent-Minded Beggar's Fund, inspired by Kipling's poem. But the Anglo-Boer War was a popular war and Kipling was a popular poet; it was not so easy to raise funds for soldiers' families during less popular wars or in peacetime.

There was a Royal United Service Orphan Home for girls at Devonport, and in 1880 The Soldiers' Daughters' Home in Hampstead reported that 'more than eight hundred girls have been reared within the walls of the Home, and out of these three hundred and fifty have been placed out as gouvernesses and pupil teachers, or else in domestic service'. The institution was proud of its record, but the numbers were small compared to need.

One of the largest and oldest (founded in 1803) of the military charities was Lloyd's Patriotic Fund, which gave support to soldiers, sailors and marines disabled on active service and to the widows and orphans of soldiers killed in action. It also made contributions to a number of schools, homes and orphanages that cared for service men's dependants.

Officers retired to estates, if they had any, or faded into genteel poverty, for rarely could they obtain suitable employment. The age of compulsory retirement and the amount of pay ensuing in the late Victorian era varied according to rank. In 1900 a captain had to retire at forty-eight and his pay was thereafter £200 per annum; a lieutenant-general or a full general had to go at sixty-seven on £850 for the former and £1000 for the latter. There were, however, places for a few. The Honourable Corps of Gentlemen-at-Arms, founded in 1500, contained about forty 'gentlemen pensioners', all of whom had seen active service. The governor and the captains of invalids at Chelsea Hospital were retired officers, as were the lieutenant, ensign and exons of the Yeomen of the Guard. A few could also find places in the military prison system or in the Remount Establishment.

Retirement was a sad time for most, particularly those who had spent the better part of their careers as regimental officers. Colonel Lionel Dunsterville (who, as a boy, had been the real-life Stalky of Kipling's *Stalky and Company*) wrote: 'I think there is possibly nothing so sad in life as this parting from a regiment in which one has spent all the best

The Cambridge Asylum for Destitute Soldiers and Widows, founded at Kingston-upon-Thames in 1852 (*Photo: Illustrated London News Picture Library*)

years of manhood. . . . Soldiers of all ranks are so thrown together in peace and war that they become closely knit by ties which are stronger than any other human ties, the breaking of which is a sad episode in one's life'. (Dunsterville's feelings put in perspective the professional officer's view of the ties binding him to parents, wife and children.)

Colonel Dunsterville's retirement from the army was brief, for he left in January 1914. Before the end of the year he, as nearly every other retired but still fit officer, was happily back in uniform and he considered himself lucky to be able to take part in the Great War. When he retired for a second time it was as a major-general.

16

OFF DUTY

Of the three principal amusements of the British soldier – drink, women and gambling – only gin and prostitutes were cheap, and gave fair value for the money spent. But on board troopships there were neither whores nor spirits, and during the long voyages to India, Australia, China and other distant parts of the Empire there was seldom any organized recreation, so the men spent most of their time gambling. Dice and cards were the principal accessories, but one popular game – the only one to have the approval of the King's Regulations – was 'Housey-housey' or plain 'House', a form of what is today called bingo. Every number had a name: number one was 'Little Jimmy' or 'Kelly's Eye'. Most were expressed in rhyming slang: eleven was 'Legs Eleven'; forty-four was 'Open the Door'; sixty-six was 'Clickety-click'. Some callers, well versed in their army history, gave every number the nickname of the infantry regiment that had carried it – even thirty years after numbers were discontinued as part of regimental names. Thus, number nine was 'Holy Boys' (Norfolk Regiment), twenty-three was 'Old Flash and a Dash' (Royal Welch Fusiliers), fifty-seven was 'Diehards' (Middlesex Regiment).

Equal in popularity to House were Under and Over and Crown and Anchor (often called Bumble and Buck or Diddum Buk); the latter was an old sailors' game which on troopships was usually operated by sailors to relieve soldiers of their cash. The broker sat on deck, legs apart with two caps between them – one for coins and one for banknotes. Before him was a board or sheet with coloured figures in squares. The designs matched the figures on a set of three dice, thrown from a cup. Each figure had a nickname:

Heart transfixed	Puff and Dart
Diamond	Kimberley or The Curse
Club	Shamrock
Spade	Gravedigger or Shovel
Anchor	Mud-Hook
Crown	Sergeant-Major (a crown being the badge of rank of a regimental sergeant-major)

Players put their money on the figure of their choice. Even money was paid for one die of the right figure, double for two dice, and triple for three showing the same.

Under and Over was an even simpler game played with ordinary dice and a sheet with three boxes marked 'under', 'over' and 'seven'. If, when the dice were thrown, the total was under seven, those who had placed their money on 'under' were paid even money; the same for 'over'. If seven was played and that number turned up, the banker paid three to one. Black Jack, which went by many names – Pontoon, Van John, Twenty-One – was also popular.

Of course, all these games favour the banker or dealer. One old sailor confessed that he usually made £500 on the voyages to and from India during the trooping season, and that he made more money on the return trip with the time-expired men than on the voyage out with the recruits.

Card games were also popular. Officers played whist or, after 1900, bridge. Other ranks played kitty-nap (often called simply nap) and brag. In nap each player was dealt five cards and called the number of tricks he expected to take; a player who called five was said to *go* nap. Sometimes, if soldiers were too poor to gamble, they would 'play for noses'; losers would receive smacks on their noses with the five playing cards bunched together. Unlucky men with large noses suffered.

Although there is evidence that in the Peninsula the 18th Hussars played shuttlecock and battledore, and that the 93rd (2nd Argyll and

Sutherland) Highlanders at least once amused themselves chasing a
greased pig, there were few organized games or amusements for other
ranks in the first half of the nineteenth century. In fact, it was not until
the 1870s, with short service and better educated soldiers, that the off-
duty pursuits of the troops were given serious consideration. Sergeant
John Fraser, 2nd Northumberland Fusiliers, said of the 1880s: 'In those
days we did not play outdoor games very much'. Football was introduced into his battalion in 1886, and in the same year the sergeants
took up lawn tennis.

Fear of subversive propaganda led the army in 1825 to ban all books
in barracks except for twenty-eight volumes which had been approved
by a committee of bishops, and even these were only for the benefit of
soldiers who were sick. However, in spite of the fact that few men could
read, reading rooms in barracks were established by Act of Parliament in
1838, and as literacy increased, so did the number of available books.
By 1900 all regiments and garrisons had libraries of varying quality.
Soldiers read Dumas, Dickens, Nat Gould, Paul de Koch and, of
course, Balzac's *Droll Stories*. Private Frank Richards said that 'as for
the *Decameron of Boccaccio*, in my time [1900s] every soldier in the
British Forces in India who could read had read this volume from cover
to cover. It was considered very hot stuff'.

The soldier who wanted the real thing had only to step outside his
lines. The area around the great training base at Aldershot was, according to one appalled observer, 'a perfect network of public houses, dancing saloons and vile houses'. It was here, on 11 February 1863, that that
great humanitarian, the Earl of Shaftesbury, laid the cornerstone for a
Soldiers' Institute, the inspiration and creation of Mrs Daniell, the
widow of an army officer. Although quite deaf and forced to use a hearing trumpet, Mrs Daniell was energetic and, in the days when private
soldiers were regarded as ruffians, she entertained the curious (but correct) belief that at least some would prefer tea to beer, would listen to
Bible lessons and temperance lectures, and would be content with the
diversions offered by deaf old Mrs Daniell rather than a more attractive
baggage to be found in the street.

Mrs Daniell's Soldiers' Institute was not the first soldiers' home.
Thirteen years earlier, Miss Lucy Papillion had established one near
Shorncliffe Camp. It was a modest affair of two rooms for reading and
writing; a few games were spread on tables, and books from a small

library could be borrowed. There were no easy chairs and there was no 'refreshment bar'. The principal attraction offered was a nightly Bible class. Miss Papillion's effort was considered 'an act of marvellous and eccentric benevolence'.

In 1855 the Rev William Carve Wilson opened a small soldiers' home at Portsmouth. It did not last long: Wilson died in 1859 and his establishment did not survive him. That his efforts were valued is touchingly proved by a monument 'erected by non-commissioned officers and privates of the British Army in token of their love and gratitude'.

The most ambitious, energetic and successful founder of soldiers' homes was the remarkable Miss Sarah Robinson. She was a woman of comfortable, independent means, though not wealthy, who, 'having no family claims and few personal wants', devoted her life to the physical and moral improvement of the British soldier in the ranks. She suffered terribly throughout her life from a 'curvature of the spine', and she once wrote: 'I asked God that I might never have the least desire to marry; this request has . . . been granted'.

After serving an apprenticeship under Mrs Daniell, Miss Robinson in 1874 opened her own Soldiers' Institure at Plymouth in a former hotel. She had her problems. The senior chaplain at the local garrison objected to her work, primarily, it seems, because of her insistence on holding Bible classes, a practice he regarded as an infringement on his territory. There was much opposition as well from the local civilians who customarily exploited the soldiers. One local magnate went so far as to ask her: 'If the men like to go to the devil, what business is it of yours'? She received 'disgusting anonymous letters', windows were broken, and for a time she could not go out in a cab without dirt being thrown at her; she was burned in effigy on Southsea Common; one newspaper called her a 'Mars-stricken old maid', and a music-hall song about 'thweet Miss Wobinson' enjoyed a brief popularity.

Miss Robinson also had her troubles with 'ladies' who volunteered to assist her. One, whom she described as 'fat, sentimental and lazy', simply lounged on a sofa and crocheted. She had supposed the Institute to be a good place to find a husband. Another, who claimed to be a nursing sister, was picked up by the police as a 'well-known London thief'. One cannot but feel pity, though, for the fifty-seven-year-old daughter of a general, 'musical and clever', who developed a passion for a twenty-

four-year-old gunner. She purchased his discharge and married him.
Miss Robinson had no sympathy for the affair. It made her Soldiers' Institute 'the laughing stock of the garrison', and that she could not
forgive.

In spite of all her troubles, only two years after her opening, the Duke
of Cambridge paid his first visit and gave his approval to the enterprise.
On a subsequent visit, he brought H.R.H. the Prince of Wales, who
publicly thanked her for her services to the army. This marked the end
of official disfavour and unofficial persecution. Miss Robinson went on
to form other soldiers' homes, and homes for sailors too: the Sailors'
Welcome at Portsea, the Welcome Mission at Landport, and the
Sailors' and Soldiers' Institute in Alexandria, Egypt. In all of these un-
dertakings she was assisted by a former trooper of the Queen's Bays, ex-
private Thomas Tafnell.

Miss Robinson's work was emulated by others. In 1879 two spinsters,
the Misses Jay, opened a Soldiers' Home at 12 Knightsbridge Road in
London. There, for a small charge, a soldier could get tea, coffee,
cakes, bread and butter, or he could play or listen to a harmonium.
There were also readings, recitations, singing, prayer and temperance
meetings. The object was 'teaching the soldier to respect himself by
providing innocent amusement and deterring him from harmful ones'.

One of the first attempts on the part of officers to provide for the off-
duty hours of the other ranks was the formation in 1867 of the Guards
Institute in London, a building which offered a respectable place for
dances, theatricals, concerts, billiards, cards and bowling. Refresh-
ments of all kinds were available; there was a reading room; stationery
was provided free; a library was installed; and, of course, separate por-
tions of the building were allotted for non-commissioned officers and
privates. Monthly subscription rates were low – 6d. for sergeants, 5d.
for corporals and 4d. for privates – so the Institute was heavily sub-
sidized by the officers in the Guards regiments. The War Office was
asked to help, but the Secretary of State for War refused. There were,
he said, no funds at his disposal for such a purpose.

Originally it was hoped that the Guards Institute might be used to
teach soldiers useful trades, but this effort did not succeed, as the second
annual report of the Institute in 1869 records:

> As a place for work or instruction, it has failed; as a place of amusement
> and entertainment, and in developing in the soldier a capacity for self-

control, it has proved in many ways successful, beyond the anticipations of its most sanguine promoters.

Every endeavour has failed in getting the men to work at and learn trades, and the result of these efforts goes far to make it doubtful whether, in a city which offers so many inducements to pleasure as the metropolis, soldiers will be willing, under any circumstances to submit themselves voluntarily to continuous work.

There can be no doubt that the vast majority of soldiers are indisposed to labour, to avoid which many of them have enlisted; but, on the other hand, they are much inclined to spend their time, when off duty, in amusement and recreation.

However comfortable they may now be made in barracks, it is natural for them to go outside for the enjoyment of the society of their friends; and the large majority of non-commissioned officers, and many men, may resort to places known to be respectable. It is, however, notorious, that from considerations of expense, and, still more, from the prejudices of the middle classes, great temptations are put in their way to frequent houses of the lowest description; and it is as the antagonist of these houses that the Guards Institute must stand or fall.

It fell.

In the late Victorian and early Edwardian eras regimental clubs became more common. In 1902 the Gordon Highlanders Memorial Institute was opened in an old mansion in Belmont Street, Aberdeen. The halls and walls were decorated with regimental prints and paintings, pictures of past officers, and trophies of war and of the chase, including heads of ibex and wild sheep that had fallen to the hunter's gun a generation earlier. The Institute was open to all serving soldiers and sailors and to former Gordons.

Left to themselves, soldiers did not organize clubs but turned to other pursuits. Tattooing was always fashionable among other ranks. A young man named Ross Martin was so determined that as soon as he was of age he would enlist in the 92nd (2nd Gordon) Highlanders that he had the number 92 tattooed on his arm before he enlisted in 1867. Hearts, flowers and the regimental crest were always popular, but some soldiers fancied bolder, more imaginative designs. There were those who had 'A Merry Christmas' tattooed on one cheek of their buttocks and 'A Happy New Year' on the other. Still others had their entire backs emblazoned with a scene that depicted a pack of hounds in full cry pursuing a fox which was about to take cover in the anus. During the First World War, when Queen Mary was visiting the wounded in a hospital, she came across a soldier with a portrait of King George V tattooed on his arm. The Queen seemed much interested and asked if he had others. 'Yes Mum', the soldier replied, 'the Kaiser William, but you can't see that, for I'm sittin' on um'.

A few soldiers took up arts and crafts, some of which did not seem very martial. In the Welch Fusiliers around the turn of the century there were two soldiers who were expert knitters, and not solely for pleasure, for they made extra money by selling their sweaters, money belts, scarves, *et al*.

Boxing and wrestling were popular. In India matches were sometimes arranged between soldiers and Indians, but in 1874, after an Indian wrestler defeated the Royal Artillery bombardier who was the champion of the British army, orders were issued forbidding athletic competition with natives. The British took sport seriously, and it was thought too humiliating, perhaps even a threat to the Raj, for them to be beaten at games by those they considered their inferiors.

It was not, however, until the last quarter of the last century that other ranks began to play games. Cross-country running, jumping, tug of war, rugger and other sports gained in popularity. Hockey, usually played on a dry drill square, became a favourite. There were also organized activities from time to time: tent-pitching competitions and events called 'pawnbrokers' races' and, in India, 'chatti competitions' (a chatti was an earthen water jug).

In the eighteenth century officers and men did not engage in athletic competitions together. When, early in the nineteenth century, Lieutenant-Colonel Robert Wilson, commanding the 20th Light Dragoons (20th Hussars) in Cape Colony, in an attempt to encourage sports, urged his officers to play games with their men and played himself, he was sharply reprimanded by his commanding general and ordered to stop. Wilson was ahead of his time, for by the 1870s it was common practice, and sometimes officers and men even boxed with one another.

Cricket is an old pastime, dating back at least to the early seventeenth century, but it did not become popular in the army until the 1860s. By 1880, however, it was being played with enthusiasm by officers and other ranks, separately and together, from end to end of the Empire. Famous scores, like battle honours, were remembered for generations.

In the Rifle Brigade it was well known and discussed by all ranks for more than half a century that Joe Constable of the 3rd Battalion had once made a stand of 500 not out at Dinapore. It was not until the late Victorian era that 'cricket' became synonymous with 'fair play'.

Games of all sorts took on an importance all out of proportion to their value in the general scheme of things. Indeed, General Hugh Gough believed that the games Englishmen played made a 'tremendous contribution to the happiness of mankind'. In what way he did not say.

Some regimental histories contain more information about sporting events than battles. Indeed, one sometimes gains the impression that fighting was simply an interruption. An officer in the Royal Hampshire Regiment wrote in the regimental journal for 1903: 'We mustered a punitive expedition against a sheikh at Kotaibi and returned and played football and cricket, having lost ten'.

Johnson Wilkinson described himself as 'addicted to almost every pursuit in which active, ambitious, and pleasure-loving young men delight, such as hunting, shooting, fishing, racing, running, boxing, even prize-fighting, cock-fighting, and bull-baiting'. He was in the right regiment. While some regiments saw more than their share of fighting, others saw none for more than a generation. Of the 15th Foot (East Yorkshire Regiment) Wilkinson said:

> I am sure that I am not exaggerating when I say that whether at cricket, boating, boxing, hunting, racing, shooting with rifle or gun, we invariably held our own. . . . We suffered under one grievous misfortune . . . we never in my time, excepting in the rebellion in Ceylon, were engaged in any campaign.
>
> We have fought with every kind of wild animals, but never with human beings.

Wilkinson was a major-general when his regiment went off to fight in the Second Afghan War of 1879 and he never did see action.

The passion for sports came to be shared by all ranks, and it brought an almost egalitarian spirit into the army. It was, to be sure, a very particular kind of egalitarianism, for the two castes remained distinct, but at least it gave the gentlemen-officers and the peasant-proletarian other ranks a common interest besides the spirit of the regiment. In time, inter-regimental athletic competitions with both officers and men on each team became commonplace. When the Royal Artillery played the Household Brigade at cricket in 1878 at Lords, the Guards team included a lieutenant-colonel, two captains and several privates, the artillery team a major, a son of a peer, and two musician boys. The gunners won, and the highest scorers were M'Intyre and Simpson, the musician boys.

Scotsmen, who never missed an opportunity to demonstrate their uniqueness, had their own traditional games and Highland Gatherings – even in India. The last Gathering in India before the Great War was held at Lucknow in 1912 with Camerons, Gordons, Black Watch and the Highland Light Infantry taking part.

Another off-duty activity in which officers and men participated jointly was theatricals, which became very popular in the Victorian era. Lieutenant Gilbert de Lacy Lacy of the 63rd Foot (1st Manchester Regiment) took with him to the Crimea a make-up kit and costumes. Many officers not only liked to appear in plays and 'entertainments' but to don disguises. Robert Baden-Powell, who founded the Boy Scout movement, once passed himself off as an Italian count; he was also known as 'the best skirt dancer in the army'. Men often played women's parts, and some enjoyed dressing as women. Lieutenant Lacy not only played women's roles, but once attended a dance given by French officers disguised as a girl and took the attentions he received as a tribute to his acting. His fellow officers thought it a great joke; no one thought of him as a transvestite.

The other ranks were in general more sexually sophisticated – or at least more experienced – than their officers, but some of them, too, delighted in appearing on stage as women, although almost always in comic roles. Rifleman Goodall of the Rifle Brigade – a regiment which took pride in its stage entertainments – liked to dress as an old woman and sing a song called 'I'm Ninety-Five and to Keep Single I'll Contrive'. Goodall and his song were popular and, as ninety-five was the old number of the regiment, the bandmaster converted the air into a march which became the official regimental quick march, replacing the stuffier Huntsmen's Chorus from Weber's *Der Freischütz*.

Other ranks sometimes produced their own stage entertainments. Captain Frederick Stevenson in China wrote to his niece (7 April 1858):

> I witnessed a brilliant performance by some private soldiers the other night which amused me very much, and was creditably performed. The

play was *Douglas*, a first-rate tragedy . . . performed in a Chinese temple upon an altar from which a joss had been recently deposed . . . after which the altar was further desecrated by the laughable farce of *Two in the Morning*.

Half a century later, Lionel Dunsterville, describing his days in India, wrote:

Soldiers are fond of melodrama, and I remember, on one of the hottest nights of the year when the thermometer was over 100 degrees at midnight, a play in which the heroine was dying in a snowstorm. The snow was represented by falling pieces of newspaper which looked most unconvincing, but the freezing heroine looked still more unreal with streams of perspiration pouring down her face.

Typical was the participation of both officers and other ranks in a concert given by the 1st Grenadier Guards at Chelsea Barracks on 8 October 1880. Sergeant Locke sang 'Sad News from Home', Lieutenant-Colonel Viscount Hinchingbrook played 'Zampa' and 'The Devil's March' on the pianoforte, Drill-Sergeant Simpson sang 'The Mulligan Guards', and a trio consisting of Lieutenant F.C. Ricardo, Bandmaster J.A. Smears and Drill-Sergeant Simpson, accompanied by Captain Villiers Hatton, rendered 'The Red-Cross Knight'.

New amusements appeared in later years. In 1908 Corporal William Egbert Seed of the 3rd Hussars stationed in South Africa wrote to his mother (with whom he corresponded faithfully every week for fourteen years) that his chief diversion was roller skating and that he had recently seen a 'marvellous entertainment' that was 'a combination of gramophone & cinematograph' by which he 'saw moving pictures of singers in opera & heard their songs.'

Many more kinds of recreation were available to officers than to other ranks. Officers, but rarely other ranks, played polo, racquets, tennis, badminten, croquet, and billiards; officers indulged in coaching, yachting, racing, steeple-chasing, and riding to hounds; lawn tennis became popular during the 1870s and, during the craze of the 1890s, bicycling. In India, pig-sticking and tent-pegging were frequent pastimes. (Sergeant-Major John Fraser thought that 'polo and pig-sticking . . . have been the salvation of many a young officer who might have ruined himself with drink and betting, because army life had no other outlet to offer him'.) Some regiments specialized in certain sports, and all officers were expected to participate. When Second-Lieutenant G.E. Hawes reported to the adjutant of the Royal Fusiliers, he was informed at once that 'The Royal Fusiliers play polo', and that if he intended to stay in the regiment he had better learn. At the turn of the century the 10th and 11th Hussars and the 9th Lancers were also noted for polo-playing.

Horses played such an important part in the lives of most officers that some tended to think of humans in horsy terms. A Royal Horse Artillery officer, reporting on a subordinate, noted: 'Personally, I would not breed from this officer'.

More and more the distinction between sport and war became blurred in the minds of officers who went from public schools to Sand-hurst to regiments. More and more used the language of games and hunting when speaking of war, which came to be regarded as the great-est game of all. This was evident in dozens of small things: the way officers spoke, the notion that in war one must 'play the game'; officers in the First World War sometimes began an attack by kicking a football at the enemy; Horace Smith-Dorrien, given command of a brigade in South Africa, designed a brigade flag in his racing colours.

It was the rare officer who did not take part in hunting and shooting, always pastimes of British gentlemen, inside and outside the army. Wellington had a pack of hounds with him in winter quarters in south-ern France and he hunted twice a week – until pack and huntsmen were captured by the French. In 1878 there were 16,000 hunting dogs in Britain: 162 packs of English foxhounds (5,280 couples), 68 packs of staghounds (420 couples), and 2,270 couples of harriers, beagles, et al. Some officers and some regiments were more passionately fond of rid-ing to hounds than others. In the 1880s it was possible for cavalry officers to be absent on leave or hunting (often the same thing) for 250 days out of the year. Evelyn Wood said that as a general he normally hunted forty-six days a year and more often when he was younger. Dur-ing his two years at the Staff College it was five days a fortnight, and he cited as indicative of his heavy work load during the Anglo-Boer War that he was able to indulge in the sport on only twelve occasions in one year. Some regiments kept their own packs of hounds. The Green How-ard Hounds, started in Jullunder shortly after the Indian Mutiny, con-tinued in existence in spite of many moves, wars and campaigns for nearly a century. The aristocratic 10th Hussars were passionate sportsmen and had their own pack, the Rock Harriers, which in 1864 was hunted by Captain the Hon Caryl Molyneux with Lord Valentia and Private Bowkett as whips.

Hunting involves dressing in attractive costumes and riding a horse behind dogs who, in fact, do the actual seeking out. Officers loved riding over the countryside, often at speed, leaping over ditches and flying over fences – sometimes leaving the horse on the other side. Cracked heads and broken bones were part of the price willingly paid for the pleasure. They also shot at almost every possible variety of wild creature – pigeons, woodcock, snipe, ducks, quail, partridges, plover, grouse; and hares, stags, and larger, more exotic animals when they could. Occasionally they shot each other – by accident, of course. Quite a number of officers lost their lives or limbs as a result of a mauling by a tiger, panther or wild pig, or through being crushed by elephants. These too were accepted risks.

Many regiments, like country estates, kept gamebooks, which give an indication of the extent of the killing. The gamebook of the 2nd Gordons in India between January 1902 and December 1912 shows that officers shot 674 big game of thirty-six species, including three elephants, six tigers, twelve panthers and eighty-four boars. They also shot 27,293 small game, including 4,256 pigeons, 7,549 ducks and 9,354 snipe. The officer with the 'best bag' killed ninety-nine head of big game of twenty-five species in four and a half years.

Hunting and shooting were officers' pastimes for which other ranks rarely had the opportunity, but in India soldiers would sometimes buy live hares, wild cats and jackals for a coursing match with dogs, usually greyhounds. A more popular activity, however, was to train dogs to fight each other or a jackal.

Although well acquainted with the animal life of the strange lands to which they were posted, few officers or men were interested in the customs and culture of those around them. Lieutenant-General Adrian Carton de Wiart said of Rome: 'I can endure the outsides of buildings, but not the insides, and mural paintings and headless, armless and almost pointless sculptures leave me quite unmoved'. Major A.D. Greenhill Gardyne of the 2nd Gordons was an exception, for he learnt much of the history and culture of India and tried to interest some of the younger officers, urging them at least to see the Taj Mahal. He was pleased when three subalterns finally asked for leave to visit it. When they returned he was eager to have their reactions, but they met his questions with embarrassed silence and then confessed: they had not seen it. Just as they were ready to go, someone had come looking for three guns to join a duck shoot, and they had chucked the Taj and joined the shoot. Gardyne was disappointed, but he himself was a keen sportsman, and when a captain during the Anglo-Boer War had three times asked for leave to go hunting. The requests were, as he knew, 'wholly irregular', yet 'each time the answer was favourable . . . and ended: "Can I do anything to help? Only wish I could come too" '.

The beauty of landscape was lost on most soldiers. Carton de Wiart thought India 'tawdry'. It 'emitted revolting smells and noises and its only attraction in my eyes was that I knew it was a wonderful centre for sport'. Lieutenant-Colonel Charles Head, Royal Artillery, considered that 'the man who said he preferred the scenery of Waterloo station to any other he had seen in the world was not far from an expression of sound good sense'. Other ranks exhibited a similar disregard for the world's wonders. A sergeant in the Gordon Highlanders drilling his men near the pyramids found that their eyes kept wandering towards the monuments. 'What are ye glowerin' at'? he bellowed. 'A great rickle o' auld stanes! Hae ye no seen Ben Nevis'?

So although not much time was spent on musketry training and none at all on learning to throw grenades or dig trenches, it was nevertheless an active, fun-loving army that entered the twentieth century.

DRINK

In their dreary crime-and-drink-sodden homes they had learned to emu-
late the law-breaker, to idolise the criminal, and applaud the football
god. Their philosophy was material – necessarily so: for poverty made
them steal; environment sent them out to seek the heat of the ale house
and the shelter of the jail. Brutes, some people would call them. But they
had never seen these men dying on the sands of Egypt or on the plains of
Hindostan.

Captain R.W. Campbell (1915)

Tommy was a rough article. Wellington once called his soldiers 'the
scum of the earth'; if the French were not frightened of them, he said,
they damn well scared him. Tommy was less likely to be a criminal by
the turn of the century, but, as Kipling noted, 'single men in barracks
don't grow into plaster saints'. Soldiers complained when they did not
get their rum ration and they took their gin and beer as often as they
could get them, which was often enough.

It was considered essential to issue rum or other strong spirits daily.
Wellington believed *all* his soldiers enlisted for drink; it remained a welcome addition to the soldiers' diet in the trenches of Flanders a hundred
years later. The supply of rum was always guarded by the most reliable

men (though even these sometimes succumbed to temptation, for, as General Osborn Wilkinson said: 'the British soldier . . . can be trusted with anything but grog') or by teetotallers (of which there were a few). When it was issued there was a careful supervision to be certain that some did not sell their share to others and that each man drank only the dram to which he was entitled. Drummer boys and recruits had to dilute theirs with water, as did those considered 'notorious drunkards'. When the 19th Foot (Green Howards) were in Ceylon, arrack replaced rum and was issued twice a day: at seven o'clock in the morning and at six o'clock in the evening. It was thought quixotic when in 1884, during his Sudan campaign to relieve General Gordon at Khartoum, Wolseley decided to abolish the rum ration and offer in its place jam and marmalade. The War Office protested, but Queen Victoria thoroughly approved, though many an old sweat must have cursed. It is perhaps coincidental that this was the only campaign in which Wolseley failed.

Keeping the troops sober enough to fight was often a problem. When towns were captured, officers tried, often unsuccessfully, to find the local liquor supplies and post guards over them. At times they resorted – without success – to dumping wine and brandy into the streets. William Butler told how, in spite of every precaution to keep alcohol away from the men during a voyage from Madras to Rangoon, soldiers were found drunk. They had painstakingly hollowed out oranges and filled them with arrack before coming aboard. Before the attack on Tel-el Kebir in 1882 a silent approach across the desert to the Egyptian positions at night was essential, and exceptional care was taken to keep the troops sober; nevertheless, a Gordon Highlander revealed himself to be roaring drunk on the approach march. He was chloroformed on the spot.

Drink was the curse of the army and drunkenness the most common of soldiers' crimes. Spirits were banned from canteens in 1839 and replaced by beer, and beer (known as 'neck oil' or, more commonly, as 'purge') became the staple, traditionally drunk out of pewter mugs. About 1903 these were replaced by glass mugs, a change much resented in this conservative, tradition-loving army, but one which did not diminish the yearly consumption of thousands of gallons.

It should be noted, however, that drunkenness decreased as the nineteenth century wore on and the quality of the recruits rose; before 1880 it had long been the rule rather than the exception for men to return to

V. R.

2nd BATTALION 13th
PRINCE ALBERT'S REGIMENT
OF LIGHT INFANTRY.

REQUIRED
FOR THE ABOVE BATTALION,
A FEW INTELLIGENT YOUNG MEN OF GOOD APPEARANCE & ACTIVE FIGURE.

The history of the 13th Light Infantry is so well known in the annals of our countrys' glory, that it would be needless to describe, at any length, the varied scenes, climes, and countries in which, by its gallantry and devoted bravery, it has added to the stability and welfare of the British Empire, "on which the sun never sets."

Under the burning Sun, and on the sandy deserts of the **Land** of the **Egyptians,** in the tropical climate of the **Carribean Sea,** where the Emerald waves roll o'er the golden sands and glittering coral reefs of the **Isle** or **Martinique**; in the "Indian Hemisphere," that **Koh-i-noor** of England's Crown, in **Ava, Afghanistan, Ghuznee, Jellalabad,** and **Cabul**; in the glorious **CRIMEAN Campaign**; and at a later date serving a second time in India, avenging the fell cruelties of the murderous Sepoys; have waved in victorious triumph the Battle Flags of this Renowned Regiment!!!

HONOURS, PROMOTIONS, REWARDS, & IMMENSE SUMS OF PRIZE MONEY FELL TO THE LOT OF THESE HEROES.

THE SPHINX !!

Emblem of that land where those wonders of all ages, the stupendous Pyramids, raise their undecaying summits to the arch of Heaven.

THE MURAL CROWN!!

Awarded (as in the days of ancient Rome) for deeds of valour, and acts of undying fame, at the heroic defence of the City of **Jellalabad,** a marvel of bravery that sheds a lustre even on the name of Briton!!!

With other motives and Badges of victorious combat, and emblazoned on the Banners of the Regiment, sparkling like jewels in the sun as the breeze gently fans the silken folds.

TO PERPETUATE ITS FAME TO FUTURE GENERATIONS, HER MAJESTY, THE QUEEN HAS BEEN PLEASED TO BESTOW ON THE CORPS THE PROUD TITLE OF

PRINCE ALBERT'S REGIMENT of Lt. Inft.

And in the presence of assembled thousands, His Royal Highness, the **Prince Consort** presented to the **2nd Battalion** the Colours under which they have now the honour to serve, as a mark of the estimation in which the 2nd Battalion 13th Light Infantry is held. Her Majesty, during the past month, has granted a Commission to the Serjeant Major of the Corps.

From the salubrity of the climate and its even temperature, in addition to the advantages of increased allowances, the Isle of France or Mauritius has been selected as the Station for a few years of the Battalion. It will be recollected that this Isle of the Eastern Ocean is celebrated as the scene of the romantic and interesting narrative of the lives of **Paul** and **Virginie,** and their sad and untimely end.

N.B.—It is advisable that Volunteers for this Battalion should present themselves for Enlistment without delay, as the few present vacancies will be rapidly filled, and thus may be lost an opportunity for travel and observation of the striking scenes of foreign life seldom offered to the aspiring Soldier.

Fermoy, March, 1864.

GOD SAVE THE QUEEN.

WILLIAM LINDSEY, ARMY PRINTER, KING STREET, FERMOY.

Recruitment poster, 1864 (*Photo: Somerset County Museum*)

barracks more drunk than sober, and even after the turn of the century
drunkenness was commonplace. Former Company Sergeant-Major
Robert Legget of the Cameronians described a private's life in the Edwardian army:

> You lived between the barracks-room and the wet canteen, without any
> social life at all. . . .
>
> There was a ritual every evening. The men would make themselves abso-
> lutely spotless – uniform pressed, boots polished, hair plastered down,
> bonnet on just so – as if every one of them had a girl-friend waiting at the
> gate. They went straight down to the wet canteen and got drunk. That
> was what they got dressed up for.

In some regiments there were 'boozing schools', in which three or
four men clubbed together for the serious and steady drinking of 'purge'.
One acted as treasurer, and each contributed all his pay except the little
he needed for tobacco and a monthly visit to a brothel. Withholding
money for 'unworthy causes', such as toothpaste or shaving soap, could
get a man expelled. The boozing schools drank as much as they could
afford – and sometimes more. When their financial resources vanished
before payday, they borrowed whatever they could or sold items from
their kit. According to Frank Richards, who was with a battalion of the
Royal Welch Fusiliers in India at the turn of the century, those in his
battalion would only borrow up to 200 rupees; if this was spent, they became teetotallers until payday. Their credit was good, for 'genuine
boozing schools always paid their debts'.

Irish, Scottish and North Country regiments were noted for their
drinking. When the Black Watch returned to Scotland from the
triumph of Waterloo, they were doled out their pay in instalments to
prevent the complete disintegration of the regiment. All their money
went for drink.

In all regiments the heaviest drinking was done at Christmas – and
the most fighting too. Private Richards said: 'Christmas always meant a
damned good tuck-in, with plenty of booze and scraps to follow'.
Sergeants and corporals, particularly those who were unpopular, made
themselves scarce, and the men were allowed to drink and brawl to their
hearts' content. A day or two later they were taken on a fifteen- or
twenty-mile route march 'to sweat Christmas out of them'.

Furlough was also a time for most men to have a glorious drunk. Sergeant John Fraser, speaking of the Northumberland Fusiliers in the 1890s, said:

> I remember many a man returning from a month's furlough and on being asked how he had enjoyed his leave, replying: 'Champion, man. First class. Ah havn't been to bed sober since ah've been away.' Often when a soldier was nearing the end of his enlistment he would 'go on the skin', hardly spending any money on anything and saving as much as he could. The purpose of this exercise in restraint was sometimes to get a start in civilian life, but more often the soldier was simply saving his money so that he could afford a magnificent binge.

It was seldom easy to deal with a drunken soldier. The standing orders of the 52nd Foot (2nd Oxfordshires) gave some wise instructions:

> When officers or non-commissioned officers observe a soldier drunk, they will avoid as much as possible doing or saying anything which may tend to irritate him; as a man who is in many respects a good soldier may by harsh treatment, when in that state, be brought to severe punishment. Should it be necessary to confine or secure a drunken man, a sufficient number of privates must be ordered for that purpose, but officers or non-commissioned officers must not enter into conversation with him, except in places where other military aid cannot be obtained.

From time to time individuals would try to do something about drunkenness in the army. Henry Havelock, a hero of the Indian Mutiny, formed a temperance club in the 13th Foot (Somerset Light Infantry) and its members became known as 'Havelock's Saints'. Both the North and the South Hampshire regiments were full of poteen-bred Irishmen, and drunkenness was a continual problem. In the 1880s a Regimental Temperance Association was formed and medals were issued to men who signed a pledge and managed to keep it. Earlier, in 1862, a larger organization had been formed in India: the Soldiers' Total Abstinence Association, which became the Royal Army Temperance Association. A year later chapters were opened in Britain and the organization received support from the army's leading generals, even though few of them were in fact teetotallers. In 1914 the president was the Duke of Connaught and the chairman of the council was Lord Rob-

The company's favourite (*Photo: Graham Brandon*)

Drink 215

erts. Members who managed to stay sober for six months wore a badge, similar to a regimental badge, which bore the motto: 'Watch and be sober'. Some members of boozing schools who had at one time earned this badge proudly wore it, for it was generally regarded as proof of near-superhuman resolution and endurance. Many soldiers took their temperance vows seriously indeed. One young soldier, lying seriously wounded on the field at Magersfontein, refused a drink from an officer's canteen when he learned it held whisky.

Nevertheless, the army continued to issue grog, and the Temperance Association failed to create an army of teetotallers. In 1915 King George V, on the advice of Lloyd George, gave up alcohol and forbade its use by the royal family or household for the duration of the war in the hope that his subjects would follow his example. But the 'King's Pledge', as it came to be called, seemed to have little or no effect; certainly there was no perceptible decline in drinking in the army.

East of Suez there were other temptations: some men occasionally smoked opium. Sergeant Forbes-Mitchell found opium refreshing and spoke with scorn of 'the ignorant arguments of the Anti-Opium Society'. However, in spite of the army's long association with the Far East, drugs never became a serious problem. Tommy stuck to alcohol.

There were no temperance societies for officers, though they certainly did their share of drinking, usually in the mess. Those who over-indulged were cared for by their brother officers or by servants; they did not cause drunken rows in public houses. Occasionally there were cases of officers too intoxicated to command their units, but in general there were few complaints. It should be noted, perhaps, that differences between officers and men extended not only to their drinking customs but to what they drank. Gin and beer were for the other ranks; officers had wine, brandy and whisky.

GOD
AND THE CHAPLAINS

Soldiers fought for God, Queen and Country. Of course they did. They also, and with more fervour, fought for the credit of their regiments; and, yes, for gin and beer and the camaraderie and, of course, because, quite simply, they were ordered to fight. Patriotism did not mean all that much to the professional soldier in the ranks. What indeed was Britain to an uneducated young man from the slums of London, Glasgow or Manchester who had grown up sharing a cold water tap and a single toilet with seventy other people from a dozen families? The Queen and the royal family were remote indeed.

Officers were loyal to the Crown and for them the monarchy was a living, vital institution. When, on distant stations, they thought of their country, it was of the pleasures of pursuing a fox on a frosty morning, of trout streams, of grouse shoots, of comfortable country houses, of London clubs and the civilized life which the capital of the British Empire offered to those with social position and money; like their men, they were emotionally involved with their regiments, but they were also aware of a larger purpose, of Great Britain's history and glory, of the mighty Empire, growing larger every year, and they were proud.

No one can say for certain just how important religion was in the lives of the officers and men, for there are few statistics; but it is possible to make some educated guesses. Among the officers, many of whom had spent at least five hours every week in church during their boyhood, there was, in general, an unthinking acceptance. If there were atheists, they kept their mouths shut. Most officers considered themselves good Christians, but they did not think too deeply or too often about their religion, and when they did, their thoughts were not likely to be profound. Wolseley once wondered what heaven was like and thought 'surely there must be a United Service Club there where old Army and Navy men may meet to talk over wars by land and sea . . .' Perhaps in a well-ordered heaven there was even something similar for the other ranks.

It is certain that religion was important in the lives of some officers and men, but the evidence seems to indicate that among the other ranks these were ever in the minority. Robert Graves, serving in the Royal Welch Fusiliers, said that 'hardly one soldier in a hundred was inspired by religious feeling of even the crudest kind'. John Bayne thought the numbers higher, but he served in the 2nd Scottish Rifles, a battalion considered to be the most pious in the army. Yet even Bayne wrote:

Sunday-morning service at Balaclava (*Photo: Illustrated London News Picture Library*)

'There is no doubt that there were few believers, but the number of complete unbelievers I would not put much above half the men in the ranks'. Bayne made an interesting and probably accurate guess as to the extent of religious feeling in his battalion at the start of World War I:

	Officers	Other Ranks
An important influence	50%	10%
No importance	15%	50%
Vague and intermittent	35%	40%

A typical breakdown of the professed religious preferences in an average English battalion is illustrated in this table for the Oxfordshire Light Infantry in 1907:

Church of England	1,523
Roman Catholic	91
Wesleyan	86
Baptist or Congregationalists	16
Presbyterians	10
Other Protestants	15
Jews	0

The spiritual needs of the troops were cared for by the army chaplains, and had been since the Army Chaplains' Department was formed in 1796, ranking in precedence immediately behind the Veterinary Department. There were, however, chaplains before there was a Chaplains' Department, for at least two were on the army pay roll in about the year 1300 (one earning a shilling a day and the other sixpence), and there were others at Crécy (1345) and at Agincourt (1414); regimental chaplains were mentioned for the first time in 1621. Prior to 1827 all were Church of England (at least, after Henry VIII), but in that year the first Presbyterian ministers were recognized, and eleven years later Roman Catholics were accepted as equals by their Protestant colleagues. Wesleyans were not officially recognized until 1881, and the first Jewish chaplain to the forces was not appointed until 1892. Although they did not wear military uniforms until 1860, they had been divided into ranks since 1816. The Chaplain General of the Forces ranked as a major-general; below him were four classes of 'chaplains to the forces': 1st class chaplains ranked as colonels, 2nd class as lieu-tenant-colonels, 3rd class as majors, and 4th class as captains.

Even in regiments where the vast majority of the men were Irish Catholics, most of the chaplains were Church of England. In 1898, when Sir Evelyn Wood was adjutant-general, he noted the resentment felt by Irish soldiers when their regimental colours were consecrated by Protestants. Lord Roberts, then commanding the forces in Ireland, sug-gested that the ceremony be performed by a Catholic priest, but the of-ficers, almost all Protestants, objected. Sir Evelyn, whose wife was Catholic, consulted the Secretary of State for War, the Chaplain Gen-eral, and a pair of cardinals, and drafted a ceremony for use in the con-secration of colours that was acceptable to all denominations. It was no mean feat, considering the lack of ecumenical feeling that prevailed at the time.

Some chaplains (always called 'padres') achieved fame in the army. One such was the Rev. J.W. Adams, a handsome and athletic man, known as the 'sporting padre', who won the Victoria Cross for saving the lives of three troopers of the 9th Lancers under fire during the Second Afghan War. For the most part, however, it was the Roman Catholics who won the respect of the troops, whatever their religious affiliation: men such as Father Robert Brindle, who in the 1880s won the D.S.O., was twice mentioned in dispatches, and covered his chest with British and Turkish medals earned in the Sudan and Egypt; he died as Bishop of Nottingham.

Chaplains were often more tolerated than appreciated. There was even suspicion on the part of some commanding officers that their in-fluence was not always for the good of the service. The Rev. A. Robins, chaplain to the household troops at Windsor, was once told: 'Don't try to make the soldiers too good or else you will spoil them'. There was probably little need to worry, for the influence of most chaplains hovered near zero.

Chaplains were expected not only to bring the word of God to the troops and to warn them of the evils of drink and illicit sex, but also (perhaps more importantly) to instil in them the military virtues. Hear the words of the Rev. John Craube in 1833 to soldiers of the Black Watch:

> It is your duty to pay the strictest attention to discipline and due subordi-nation – at all times to pay deference and obey promptly the orders of

your officers and on no occasion infringing the duties required of soldiers – to subject yourselves to punishment. Without subordination in the army confusion must be the inevitable consequence. Nor consider it hard if punishment follows the violation of orders – for you are already aware of it and because the strict impartiality of the laws of the army require it. It is perhaps not saying too much that the government of a regiment is the most perfect species of government. You should enter the army from the *love* of the profession and not from disgust at any other. You should after entering it seek to rest content with your condition. . . .

Some padres were too fond of the bottle; some tried to get close to their men by imitating the slangy, gaudy language of the army; some were enamoured of military discipline and protocol, demanding that men stand at attention when speaking to them and that they always say 'Sir'; and there were some who tried to be conscientious but found themselves troubled and perplexed in attempting to reconcile their religious beliefs with war.

At times church authorities succeeded in interfering with military affairs. In 1908 the 2nd Gordons at Peshawar on the North-West Frontier were ordered to Jullunder and had moved as far as Rawalpindi when they were halted and sent to Calcutta instead. The reason for this change in what the army called 'the route' had nothing to do with military needs but much to do with the vigorous protests of the Church of Scotland: the regiment was, of course, Presbyterian, and at Jullunder there was but one church and that Church of England. Although there was no objection on the part of the Anglicans to the use of the garrison church by the Presbyterians, such an arrangement was unacceptable to the church authorities in Scotland. Calcutta indeed had a Presbyterian church, but it proved to be three miles from the barracks, and a six-mile march on Sundays was not appealing. Quietly the battalion settled into sharing the garrison's Anglican church.

Individuals who insisted on their religious rights were not encouraged. A soldier in the Rifle Brigade objected to attending Church of England services as he was, he said, a 'particular Baptist'. The nearest chapel was six miles away, but his commanding officer had him marched there by an indignant corporal every Sunday. According to Neville Lyttelton, who told the story, 'He promptly conformed to a more conventional denomination'.

Although most other ranks in Highland regiments were Protestants, there were the ubiquitous Irish soldiers, almost to a man Roman Catholic. Sometimes the differences between the sects were exaggerated. One Sunday morning in 1880 when the adjutant of the 2nd Gordons had finished telling off the parties for the different services and was about to report to the colonel 'All ready to march off', the sergeant-major interrupted with: 'Halt a minute, please, sir. There's a Roman Catholic fallen in with the Christians'. It was fairly common practice among dissenters to arrogate to themselves the title of 'Christians' – Roman Catholics and Anglicans being, it seems, beyond the pale. Henry Havelock, hero of the Indian Mutiny and the most ardent Baptist ever to swing a sword or hang a mutineer, once wrote of his desire to prove the worth of Baptists:

> It was the great object of my ambition to be surpassed by none in zeal and determination in the path of my duty, because I was resolved to put down the vile calumny that a Christian could not be a meritorious soldier.

He did indeed prove that Christians could be good killers, and Lord Hardinge said to Havelock that he was 'every inch a soldier, and every inch a Christian'.

Havelock was one of a handful of general officers in the Victorian era known for their piety. Hope Grant and, most notably, Charles ('Chinese') Gordon were among them. Havelock, even as a subaltern, did missionary work among the troops in his own regiment, the 13th Foot (Somerset Light Infantry). He gave Bible readings, and when his regiment was stationed at Agra he began the building of a chapel. His principal assistant in this enterprise was a sergeant, George Godfrey. Havelock managed to get some convict labour and Sergeant Godfrey raised money, but Havelock complained that his work was carried on 'in the very teeth of ridicule and opposition'. His fellow officers thought he was making himself ridiculous; that he consorted with other ranks was considered demeaning and bad for discipline; that he should himself actually conduct religious services appeared unseemly. But the chapel was built and stands to this day, the property of the Baptist Missionary Society. Havelock took pride in the fact that 'the frequenters of this chapel are reckoned the best behaved men in the regiment'. 'Havelock's Saints', they were called. His commanding officer, Lieutenant-Colonel

Robert ('Fighting Bob') Sale, shocked his juniors by exclaiming, 'I wish the whole regiment were Baptist. Their names are never in the defaulters roll and they are never in the congee-house [cells].'

Among the nonconformist Protestant sects were many do-it-yourself religious organizations. In lieu of chaplains, the Army Scripture-Readers' Society provided civilian laymen to form Bible classes. These scripture-readers were assigned to posts and stations instead of to regiments or battalions, so that as units moved from garrison to garrison, their Bible classes disintegrated, and little of any permanence was accomplished.

In the 1860s there was a strong body of 'Christian teetotallers' in the 69th Foot (2nd Welsh Regiment). Its cricket team was famous for refusing to play if liquor or bad language or betting were allowed on the grounds. In 1864 the regiment returned to England from India, and on 13 October it gave a large temperance tea at Gosport; but the attractions of Portsmouth proved too powerful, and Miss Sarah Robinson sadly reported that 'before the 69th left Portsmouth, five hundred stripes and good conduct badges, and £6,000 of Indian savings were lost – all through drink and bad company'.

General Hope Grant was never known to read any book other than the Bible, but this he read faithfully, and he held a prayer service every morning after breakfast, even on active service, which his staff and European servants were required to attend. Some young officers also took a personal interest in religion. Lieutenant (later General) Frederick Stevenson wrote in 1859 to ask his brother to send him some books: 'I would like a volume or two of good sermons, and a good work upon the communion – Bishop Wilson or Wilberforce'. And Lieutenant (later General) Gerald Graham wrote to his sister from the Crimea: 'I have most to thank you for that thoughtful, powerful essay of Froude on the Book of Job. It is indeed a glorious piece of writing. . .' Such officers were, however, the exception.

Other ranks who were deeply religious were known as 'blue lights', and they too were exceptions. Usually some strong character was needed to retain enthusiasm or it tended to wilt. In the early 1860s, when religious fervour in the army reached its height, there was a large and popular Bible class in the 35th Foot (1st Royal Sussex), but by 1868 it had almost completely disappeared.

Conversion to a nonconformist sect was usually allied with a determination to give up alcohol. Miss Sarah Robinson said that 'in nearly every instance of conversion to God, the first step was total abstinence and separation from drinking companions', and that 'a Christian soldier is an abstainer; were he otherwise, none of his comrades would believe in his religion'.

Very occasionally a soldier, such as Francis Yeats-Brown, was attracted to one of the oriental religions of India. Occasionally, too, a soldier would be drawn to one of the obscure Christian sects. The theosophy of Annie Besant and Madame Elena Blavatsky (the latter, according to Kipling's father, 'one of the most interesting and unscrupulous impostors' he had ever known) found some converts. Private James White (1840–85) of the 16th Foot (Bedfordshire Regiment) founded a sect called the Jezreelites and actually directed its activities from a barracks in India.

By 1900, many, perhaps most, officers and senior non-commissioned officers were Freemasons. Freemasonry grew rapidly in the Victorian – Edwardian era. In 1844 there were 500 lodges in Britain; by 1880, when the Prince of Wales was Most Worshipful Grand Master, there were 1,900. Certainly it was popular with royalty, the Protestant aristocracy and the senior ranks of the army. The Duke of Connaught served as Senior Grand Warden, and General Lord Methuen was for twenty-five years Provincial Grand Master of Wiltshire. Freemasonry as practiced in the army made no pretence of being democratic. Private Frank Richards said that in the 1900s it was impossible for anyone under the rank of sergeant to become a Mason, but that immediately a man who wanted to make the army his career reached that rank, he looked for someone to sponsor him. In Kipling's story, 'The Man Who Would Be King', the prestige of Freemasonry is equated with that of royalty in the minds of Privates Daniel Dravot and Peachy Carnehan. Dravot became not only king but 'Grand-Master of all Freemasonry in Kafiristan' with Carnehan as 'Senior Warden'.

Privates and corporals often joined the Antediluvian Order of the Buffaloes, which was known as the 'poor man's Free Masonry'. This organization, although it made some pretence at promoting ethical and religious principles, appears to have been, as Private Richards characterized it, 'a simple boozing benevolent club'.

THE COLONEL'S LADY
AND JUDY O'GRADY

Some men craved strong drink and some salvation, but all – or nearly all – felt the need for sex. Although there was reputed to be a brothel in London that catered to officers, it would appear that before the First World War most gratified their appetites elsewhere. The young Prince of Wales lost his virginity while doing a brief stint as a soldier at the great army camp (founded in 1646) on The Curragh in Ireland. Guards officers persuaded Nellie Clifden, a young actress described by Christopher Hibbert as 'a vivacious, cheerfully promiscuous and amusing girl', to climb into his bed one night. The Prince was pleased as punch.

In India during the early days of the Raj it was a common and generally accepted custom for officers to take native mistresses; it helped them to learn the language. By the middle of the Victorian era, however, there were a considerable number of British women in India, and Indian mistresses were kept out of sight; it would also appear that there were fewer of them.

'As for the men – the other ranks – it is a fact that prostitutes and loose women always follow the drum'. So said one officer; and it was true enough. Army chaplains railed against illicit sex. The Rev. John Craube, chaplain of the Black Watch, cautioned the troops in a sermon to 'guard against indulging in *forbidden pleasures*, which the Apostle calls the *lusts of the flesh*. Drinking and the sin to which I allude are too frequently practised by young men who have no regard for the proprieties of life'. So much for sex education. One wonders if the lads from the Highlands knew what he was talking about. The officers were not much concerned with the sexual proclivities of their men except as it affected their ability to do their duty.

Even after Florence Nightingale had proved the worth of female nurses, their numbers were restricted. In 1899 there were but fifty-six nursing sisters and one 'lady superintendent' in the entire army. It was thought unseemly for young women to nurse men with venereal diseases, and a disproportionate number of soldiers were in hospital because they had 'caught a packet', as they said. Venereal diseases were certainly endemic among the rank and file, and plagued the army in all lands and times; commanders were forever attempting, without much success, to keep their men clean. In 1905, when Lord Kitchener was in India, he tried terrifying his troops. In a long memorandum on the subject, the commander-in-chief, who, as far as is known, never had sexual relations with a woman and had no interest in having any, wrote:

> Syphilis contracted by Europeans from Asiatic women is much more severe than that contracted in England. It assumes a horrible, loathsome, and often fatal form through which in time, as years pass by, the sufferer finds his hair falling off, his skin and the flesh of his body rot, and are eaten away by slow kankerous and stinking ulcerations, his nose falls in at the bridge, and then rots and falls off; his sight gradually fails, and he eventually becomes blind; his voice first becomes husky and then fades to a hoarse whisper as his throat is eaten away by foetid ulcerations which cause his breath to stink. In the hospitals, and among suicides, many such examples are to be found.

There were always prostitutes who made their homes near permanent army barracks, and in Britain they were always ready to welcome regiments returning from foreign service, for, as Colour-Sergeant George Calladine said, 'it is then their harvest'. There was not much commanding officers could do to control venereal disease in Britain, for soldiers even found ways to smuggle prostitutes into their barracks, but in India, unhampered by the constraints of democracy, steps could be taken to increase the chances that the women were free of disease. It was impossible to prohibit prostitution, and many officers would have agreed with Regimental Sergeant-Major John Fraser of the Northumberland Fusiliers, who thought that 'an army – especially an army in a hot, tropical country – without prostitutes available, is likely in a very short time to become a menace rather than a safeguard'. So in a number of locations there were army-supervised brothels – called 'rags' by the men. Their trade was restricted to the European troops in the area, and the girls were inspected by medical officers two or three times each week. A set of brothels at Agra in the 1900s housed about forty girls ranging in age from twelve to thirty who accommodated the 1,500 British troops normally stationed there. Each was required to have several towels, vaseline, Condy's fluid and soap, and she was fined a rupee if found short.

In 1904 the 1st Royal Welch Fusiliers were in Burma and Lieutenant-Colonel Patrick Mantell, commanding the battalion, was determined to do something about his losses from venereal diseases. He pulled down the huts of the Chinese and Burmese girls around his camp and drove them away. He then built new huts and imported a dozen clean Japanese prostitutes from Mandalay. These measures proved effective. A private in the battalion said: 'During the fifteen months I served in Burmah there was never a case known of a man contracting venereal with the Japs in the rag'.

The 'memsahibs' who arrived in India in increasing numbers during the Victorian era doubtless raised the cultural and ethical tone of the British Raj, but in sexual matters their influence had a baneful effect. The moral indignation of what some soldiers called 'the Shrieking Sisterhood' must have contributed to the closing of these registered and supervised brothels in 1885. Only Kipling had the courage to complain publicly: 'It was counted impious that bazaar prostitutes should be inspected; or that men should be taught elementary precautions in their dealings with them. This official virtue cost our Army in India nine thousand expensive white men a year laid up from venereal disease'. He was probably right.

Battalions were inspected once or twice each year by a general officer, and when Kitchener was commander-in-chief in India he offered an Efficiency Prize for the best. In 1904 the 2nd Gordons had every hope of winning, but unfortunately they were rated on 'physical efficiency', among other things, and this included the venereal disease rate: they lost the prize because they had too many men in hospital 'for acts under their own control'.

When regiments were stationed for long periods east of Suez, soldiers often formed more or less permanent alliances with local women. A battalion of the Green Howards was stationed in Ceylon for twenty-five years, in the course of which many soldiers acquired mistresses. There always existed, of course, the possibility that the battalion would be sent elsewhere, but the women, and doubtless most of their men, did not wish to think about it. As the years passed and children were born, it must have seemed more and more a remote threat; but these families were living on the slope of a domestic Vesuvius, and when the order finally came for the Green Howards to move on, it spelt tragedy. The women were not on the strength, and neither they nor their soldier lovers possessed, or were likely ever to possess, the money necessary to be re-united. It was goodbye forever. None of these poor women has left a memoir of this catastrophe in her life, and no private soldier has recorded his feelings, but Kipling could imagine them, and wrote of them in 'Mandalay'.

Although Kipling knew that 'the Colonel's Lady an' Judy O'Grady are sisters under their skins', it was not generally recognized. The difference was officially expressed in the phrase: 'Officers' ladies and wives of other ranks'. Moreover the perceived distinction was not confined to those connected with the army. In the 1860s Lieutenant-Colonel Thomas Crawley, commanding the 6th Inniskilling Dragoons, became angry with his regimental sergeant-major, J. Lilley, and had him confined to his quarters with a guard placed over him. Although the sergeant-major's wife was ill in bed, the guard was so posted that he could see her every movement. This offended the sense of decency of some who heard of it, but *The Times* sneered at such 'false delicacy':

> Privacy is a relative term; a sergeant's wife is not accustomed to the same sort of privacy as a fine lady, and to say that Mrs Lilley's modesty was wantonly insulted because a sentry might have seen her lying in bed if he chose to look . . . appears to us absurd.

Other ranks needed permission from their commanding officers to marry, and only a certain number were allowed to do so, depending upon branch of service (more cavalrymen than infantrymen), rank (more non-commissioned officers than privates), and, at different times, other factors, such as possession of good conduct badges and savings in the army or post office savings bank. Commanding officers did all in their power to discourage marriages by other ranks, as the Standing Orders of the 52nd Light Infantry in the 1860s make clear:

> To prevent the inconveniences that arise from the incumbrance of too many women and children, officers commanding companies must, at all times, make every reasonable exertion to prevent their men from contracting imprudent marriages, as well for the interests of the regiment as of the men themselves.
>
> The regiment cannot furnish employment for more than a few women, consequently any increase of numbers diminishes the means of existence of those already belonging to the regiment. The small quantity of accommodation in barracks, the difficulty of procuring lodgings, the frequency of moving, and inconveniences attending marches and embarkations, are to be urged as dissuasives against imprudent marriages.

A man who married without permission had a hard time indeed, for his wife and children were denied quarters of any sort and were given no extra rations; the wife had to work or starve.

Women on the strength had (to use the official language) 'the privilege of washing for their respective companies'. They might thereby earn a halfpenny per day per customer. Some worked as cooks or did needlework; the more respectable were selected to be maids or nursemaids in officers' homes. Until the last half of the Victorian era, they usually lived in the barracks with the men, their home a corner screened off with blankets or canvas sheets. It was a hard life, and many of the women were rough. Certainly they needed to be tough.

One woman with the privilege of working for her company made a name for herself in the Crimea. Mrs Smith, wife of the soldier-servant of Assistant Surgeon William Sinclair of the 93rd (Sutherland) Highlanders, had just spread her washing out to dry when Turkish soldiers stampeded across it in flight from a Russian attack. But the fury of the Russians was as nothing to the fury of Mrs Smith, who seized a stout stick and lay about her, screaming, 'Ye cowardly misbelievers'. The Turkish soldiers, fending her off, appealed to her as 'kokona' (roughly, 'lady'), but she would have none of it. 'Kokona, indeed! I'll kokona ye'! Her defence of her wash brought her considerable fame; for the rest of her life she was known as Kokona Smith.

Some felt that the presence of women in the army was 'unnecessary

Off to war (*Photo: Graham Brandon*)

and objectionable', but the Duke of Newcastle, when Secretary of State for War, refused to listen to such carping; he declared that the men would be disgruntled if the women did not accompany them to do the cooking, washing, sewing, and to serve 'other purposes for which women naturally go with the army'. Not all the women, even those on the strength, were taken to war, though all were eager to go rather than be left to fend for themselves. Who would go and who must stay was usually determined by lots, and the drawing was attended by all, the men groaning when a Xanthippe drew a 'to go' slip and cheering when a popular wife drew one. Whether they went or stayed, the women's fate was unenviable, their hardships often exceeding those of the men.

Some who had drawn 'not to go' slips tried to stow away on board the troopships, but they were always detected. When the Rifle Brigade embarked at Plymouth for the Crimea, one young wife, her hair cut short and drilled by her husband, managed to march to the dock, file up the gangway, and was on board before she was discovered and put ashore. On the same ship, Colour-Sergeant John Wagner, disconsolate at leaving his wife behind, cut his throat.

These women of the army were illiterate. They did not write memoirs. So we possess no accurate record of their adventures and their feelings. But we get glimpses of them as they appear here and there on the outer fringes of history: Margaret Kewin, wife of a soldier in the Green Howards, striding along the dusty road to Sevastopol with her regiment, carrying a haversack and a water bottle, on her head a small wash tub filled with cooking utensils; the unknown woman, a babe in her arms, who found her husband dead on the field at Badajos; the wife of the 91st Highlander who gave birth beside the road on the retreat from Corunna; Mrs Langley, wife of a sergeant in the 17th Lancers, who went into the Valley of Death at Balaclava to retrieve her husband's corpse and was herself wounded; Nell Butler, age twenty-two and married to a soldier in the Rifle Brigade, who in the Crimea tore her petticoat to make bandages, collected biscuit bags to make poultices, and scarcely raised her head when a shell burst only ten yards from her.

Elizabeth Evans, whose husband was in the 4th Foot (King's Own Royal Lancaster Regiment), was at the Alma and stood watching as the regiments advanced in long thin lines toward the Russian position on the heights. A staff officer saw her and called out: 'Look well at that, Mrs Evans, for the Queen of England would give her eyes to see it'. What Mrs Evans thought is unrecorded, but she was the first woman on the battlefield after the engagement, tending the wounded. She later accompanied her husband to India, and during the Mutiny was among the besieged at Lucknow. When her husband died in 1900 she was given permission to wear his campaign medals, which she did –

together with the Royal Red Cross given her by Queen Victoria for her gallant nursing of soldiers.

In the days when flogging was common, women of the regiments were also flogged. The following order was once posted at Gibraltar: 'No woman to beat a soldier; the first that doth shall be whipped and turned out of town'. They were also put in the stocks or tumbled in a 'whirligig' – a revolving cage. Sometimes, when a regiment was stationed abroad, women were punished by being shipped home. When the Black Watch was stationed in Ceylon, a group of its women were sent back to Britain for 'bad behaviour'. By the middle of the Victorian era other punishments had disappeared, but a woman could still be struck off the strength.

Women whose husbands died usually stayed with the regiment and often quickly re-married. Miss Sarah Robinson knew of a girl of twenty-two who was living with her third husband. Neville Chamberlain told of one soldier's widow who was proposed to by a colour-sergeant the moment she returned from her husband's burial. She burst into tears, not, as the colour-sergeant supposed, because he had been too hasty, but because on the way back from the cemetery she had accepted the corporal of the firing party, thereby acquiring a mere corporal when she could have had a colour-sergeant.

A good woman on the strength had no trouble finding a new husband. Men were plentiful and women few, and for the woman, marriage was a solution to survival. Some widows chose prostitution, particularly if, as sometimes happened, they had been promiscuous wives. Whoring brought in more money than doing the captain's laundry.

Many officers and some men thought that no solider, whatever his rank, should marry. Ian Hamilton once wrote to his wife: 'The fact is a soldier has no business to be married. He is no longer whole-hearted in his pursuit of glory'. Mrs Hamilton must have been delighted to hear this. Frederick Stevenson was even more emphatic; in a letter to his sister from the Crimea he wrote: 'I have seen by far too much of the folly and misery of a married officer in Service ever to make me marry as long as I wear a red coat. . . . It is sad to see . . . the sad depression of spirits I have witnessed in more than one married officer – first rate officers spoilt'. And to his mother: 'I have seen quite enough of married life in this campaign to prove to me that marriage and soldiering are totally incompatible'. Stevenson was a young officer when he wrote these letters, but he never changed his opinion. He died a general and a bachelor.

Kipling understood the feeling, and he put some of the reasons in his poem 'The Married Man':

> The bachelor 'e fights for one
>   As joyful as can be;
> But the married man don't call it fun
>   Because 'e fights for three –
> For 'Im and 'Er an' It
>   (An' Two and One make Three)
> 'E wants to finish 'is bit,
>   An' 'e wants to go 'ome to 'is tea!

Kipling makes a similar point in 'Gadsbys', a story of a good officer forced to leave his regiment because he has married a girl without means. He concludes his story with a poem; its refrain is: 'He travels fastest who travels alone'.

Many of those who most strongly objected to marriage, did not object to sex. A conversation overheard in the mess of the 2nd Scottish Rifles concerned an officer who had recently taken a wife. Said one: 'Another good officer lost. Well, they won't catch us – we'll whore it out to the end'.

There were usually more children than women in the barracks, in spite of the high rate of infant mortality. (Colour-Sergeant George Calladine and his wife had thirteen children, of whom only two survived infancy.) In 1885 the 1st Connaught Rangers had 134 wives and 142 children on the strength. The 13th Dragoons had 74 wives and 117 children. The boys dressed in cast-off bits of uniforms and quickly learned to swear, drink gin and beer, smoke the vile-smelling, short-stemmed clay pipes (the 'nose warmers' commonly smoked by other ranks), and to cause no end of mischief. Barracks, garrisons and cantonments did not provide the most healthful or civilized environments, though many regiments hired schoolmasters and maintained schools. But in a quite real sense the regiment gave security and, unattractive as the children's future was, it did prepare them for it. As early as 1803 the Duke of York opened 'an Asylum for educating one thousand children, the legal offspring of British soldiers', but usually the regiment or battalion functioned as an extended family and, in its rough fashion, took care of its own. Even orphans stayed with the regiment, petted and abused by the soldiers and the women. Girls grew up to marry soldiers (non-commissioned officers if they were lucky) – Kipling told of one such in 'The Daughter of the Regiment' – and boys became drummers or buglers at an early age and then soldiers themselves. It is not much to say, perhaps, but the soldier's child had a better chance to survive than did the children born in the city slums of Victorian Britain.

In 1852 some officers of the Foot Guards raised £9,000 (£1,500 of which was contributed by that great benefactor of the age, Baroness Burdett-Coutts) to build the Victoria Lodging-House for married privates. The War Office stirred uneasily, grumbled that officers ought not to be the landlords of their men, and eventually bought out the promoters for £8,000. It was the first step towards providing proper housing for married soldiers, and from this time on conditions slowly but steadily improved.

Officers had their own courting and mating customs. Unless a young officer had substantial independent means, marriage to a girl without money was impossible. It was believed that an officer 'ought not to take a wife until he knew what to do with her'. A soldier's life was lived so largely among men that many seemed to find women baffling creatures. General Dunsterville confessed: 'I am no use at all with women. If one of them looks as if she were going to cry, I'm done for, and I have suffered much at their hands owing to this deplorable weakness'.

Lieutenant-General William Bellairs, writing in 1889, urged young officers to 'benefit from mixing in ladies' society'. He said that if officers 'will but make the attempt . . . their timidity and reluctance to mix in ladies' company will soon disappear, when they will scarcely fail to congratulate themselves on the change wrought and the purer moral means opened to them for passing their idle hours'. But General Bellairs did not recommend that young officers fall in love. A subaltern, he said, 'should not think of marrying before he is about thirty-five years old'. The rule of thumb was that subalterns may not marry, captains might marry, majors should marry, and lieutenant-colonels must marry.

When Second-Lieutenant Malcolm D. Kennedy reported for the first time to the 2nd Scottish Rifles in Malta in January, 1914, he was required to sign a document promising to pay a fine of £50 if he married before attaining the rank of captain. Such promises were contrary to

King's Regulations, but they were not uncommon. Kennedy noted that his battalion comprised twenty-eight officers of whom only two had wives. Thus, custom, economics, and peer pressure combined to postpone marriage until quite late in life.

Care was taken to see that an early marriage which would prove disastrous to an officer's career did not take place. Ian Hamilton related that as a subaltern in the Gordon Highlanders in the 1870s he and the other young officers were told before a ball not to dance with unmarried girls, who were to be left to the captains and majors. It was all rather cold-blooded. Wòlseley, speaking of his tour of duty in Montreal, said:

> Altogether it was an elysium of bliss for young officers, the only trouble being to keep single. Several impressionable young captains and subalterns had to be sent home hurriedly to save them from imprudent marriages. Although these Canadian ladies were very charming they were not richly endowed with worldly goods.

Two other future generals who served in Canada at about the same time agreed with Wolseley. Frederick Stevenson in a letter home spoke admiringly of the skating of the young women and of the graceful manner in which they contrived to fall so that 'not even an ankle was visible'. Lieutenant Neville Lyttelton wrote: 'These young ladies of attractive looks and manners seldom had much in the way of dowries . . . but I knew several of them as excellent wives and mothers'.

Sometimes there were considerations other than financial which made it imperative that an officer control his romantic impulses. Colonel Charles à Court of the Rifle Brigade, one of the best, cleverest, and most literate of the Victorian officers, fell in love with the wife of a 'well-known diplomat'. Two of his brother officers persuaded him to abandon the affair and to promise in writing that he would never see the lady again. It was a promise he was unable to keep, and Major (later Field Marshal) Henry Wilson reported him to the Army Council. À Court was forced to resign. He took the name of Repington and distinguished himself as a military writer for *The Times* and as the author of numerous military books.

Johnson Wilkinson was a twenty-year-old subaltern in the 15th Foot (East Yorkshire Regiment) stationed on the Isle of Man when he fell in love with a young girl 'rich in everything except coppers'. His colonel, learning of the situation, solicitously posted young Wilkinson else-where. Late in life Wilkinson wrote sadly that an 'alliance for life of that dear young thing with me, an ensign in a marching regiment, however delicious, was not a promising nor a prudent speculation'. Neverthe-less, it was a bitter blow to him when soon after his departure the 'dear young thing' married a wealthy officer of the Sutherland Highlanders – 'a fellow with bare legs who had come to relieve me (relief, indeed!)'. Johnson Wilkinson never married, but lived, as he put it, 'in the cold embrace of celibacy', a fate he regretted 'most bitterly'. Not all bache-lors shared his chagrin. One old general was fond of saying: 'When I was young I fell in love with every pretty girl I met, but providentially none of them would have me'.

Sometimes when an officer reached a suitable age (perhaps forty) and rank (say, major), he concluded that it really was time to marry and that he should set about finding a suitable mate. Some, more business-like than others, actually fixed limits to the amount they would expend on the wooing of any one woman. If, say, £100 was spent without results, they would cut their losses and begin anew.

Neville Lyttelton in 1883 decided that as he was thirty-eight years old and had reached the rank of major in his regiment and lieutenant-colonel in the army, it was clearly time for him to marry, so he took leave from his post in Gibraltar, returned to England, engaged himself, and soon after married Miss Katherine Stuart-Wortley, daughter of a former Solicitor-General. He later concluded that, even though he had had to leave the Eton and Harrow cricket match at a critical moment 'to settle the business', it was 'well worth it'.

Ian Hamilton was thirty-three years old and a brevet major when he fell in love with Miss Jean Muir in India. Although he was of an age and rank to marry, and Miss Muir had money, Lord and Lady Roberts opposed the match, and Roberts, his commanding general, sent him off on a mission to the North-West Frontier. But Hamilton returned, Miss Muir had waited, and they were married. The union had a disconcert-ing beginning – at least for Major Hamilton: his mother-in-law accom-panied them on their honeymoon.

William Butler barely mentioned in his autobiography that in 1877, at the age of thirty-nine, he married; he appears to have been at the time more keenly interested in the Russian advance on Constantinople. Hu-bert Gough was equally casual about his wedding in 1898 at the comparatively early age of twenty-nine: 'During this spell of leave I got some grouse shooting, hunting and more attacks of malaria, and was married to Miss [Louisa Nora] Lewes in December'.

Most officers seem to have regarded their women much as they did their troops, with affection and condescension. Lieutenant George Colley wrote home from South Africa to say that he had not read Madame de Staël's book on the French revolution: 'I should have thought it was not a subject adapted to a woman's mind. Such a subject requires the most powerful, far-seeing, and reasoning mind'. Wolseley, who married at forty-four, once told his wife: 'I have not always patience to bear with women's conversation'.

Given a choice between women and war, officers usually chose war. The women had to understand this – and many did. Ian Hamilton's highest praise for his wife was that she never tried to keep him from going on active service. 'She never said one word to hold me back – not one', he said. Evelyn Wood fell in love with Pauline Southwell, sister of Viscount Southwell, but Wood was Church of England and the Southwells were Catholic; her brother, the head of the family, refused to sanction the marriage. The lovers parted and for four years did not see each other or exchange a single letter. Then Wood wrote and proposed, 'on the distinct understanding that she would never by a word, or even a look, check my volunteering for War Service'. She accepted.

Quite naturally, not all soldiers' marriages were happy. Lord Dundonald, on his way to the Anglo-Boer War, described his shipboard companions:

> There were one or two on board . . . who wished to forget lack of success in obtaining some woman's love, but certaintly more of this category who having obtained it found it quite different to what they had imagined and had wanted to get away from it! . . . What I could not understand then and now is how the soft pud of a female kitten can later develop such sharp talons, or why it is that the female of our species become so malicious against its male partner.

Once in the middle of a battle in South Africa, an officer turned to Dundonald and exclaimed: 'How much happier I feel here than in London with all those women and late hours'. Not all men felt this way and not all turned their backs on romantic love, but certainly war made its enjoyment difficult and often impossible.

There were some officers for whom marriage, even sex, was never a problem. They remained bachelors not for lack of funds or opportunity but because they had no sexual interest in women. 'Chinese' Gordon certainly preferred boys; Kitchener, who would have no married officers on his staff, liked young men. There is no evidence that either Gordon or Kitchener ever made indecent advances or that they were ever other than chaste, but their sexual preferences were unmistakable. Hector Macdonald, who rose from the ranks to become a major-general, was a brave and brilliant officer whose skilful handling of troops at the battle of Omdurman saved Kitchener's army from destruction. He was in command of the British troops in Ceylon when in 1903 he was accused of overt homosexual activities. He went to London to answer the charge but was told he would have to face a board of inquiry in Ceylon. He began the long journey back, but his courage failed. He shot himself in a Paris hotel room.

Many married officers seemed too involved in their own all-male world even to think about their wives. During the Gordon Relief Expedition Lady Wolseley wrote to her husband: 'You have no time for God or me. I don't say that unkindly, but it is a fact – is it not?' Indeed the life of an officer's wife was often a lonely one. In one seven-year period of his career Evelyn Wood spent only fourteen and a half months at home – and much of that time was taken up with riding to hounds. Some officers' wives followed their husbands to war. During the Crimean War a few went as far as Constantinople, and at least three actually went to the Crimea. Eliza Amelia, Lady Errol, wife of William Henry, 18th Earl of Errol, a captain in the Rifle Brigade, accompanied her husband to the seat of war and shared his tent. In later years, when asked by a grandchild if the bed had been comfortable, she replied: 'I don't know, my dear. His lordship had the bed and I slept on the ground'.

The most famous – some unkindly said notorious – of the women in the Crimea was Fanny Duberley, wife of Captain Henry Duberley, the paymaster of the 8th Light Dragoons (8th Hussars). She was the only officer's wife to stay the entire campaign. Fanny was vivacious, gregarious, pretty, and ever eager for excitement; her husband was, in her words, 'kind and patient and good, indolent, complaining, uninterested and bored'. That she was bored by her husband did not much matter, for she was well entertained by the senior officers of the army and by the captains of ships in the harbour. She was a witness to the charge of the Light Brigade; Roger Fenton, the photographer sent out by Prince Albert to record the war, took her picture; the troops called her 'Mrs Jubilee' and often cheered her. A few years later she followed her husband to India and took part in a cavalry charge against the troops of the Rani of Jhansi. It was her last romantic fling. In 1864 she settled down to a quiet life in England, and thirty-two years later complained to a nephew: 'I cannot stand dullness for long and life gets duller and duller as one gets older'. She died in 1903 at the age of seventy-three.

Ladies appear to have been attracted only to the popular major wars, for there are few references to their presence in the countless small campaigns in the forty years between the Mutiny and the Anglo-Boer War, and they seem to have prefered a safe and reasonably civilized base. During the war in South Africa (1899–1902) so many women flocked to Cape Colony – not all of them officers' wives – that in April 1900 Queen Victoria was led to express her disapproval of 'the large number of ladies now visiting and remaining in South Africa' and to deplore 'the hysterical spirit which seems to have influenced some of them to go where they are not wanted'. Most of these 'ladies' stayed in Cape Town where, according to General John Maxwell, 'every hole and corner is crammed with ladies who alternate squabbling among themselves with the washing of officers' faces'. There were no complaints from the sick and wounded officers whose faces were being washed. Lady Edward Cecil, the young daughter-in-law of the Prime Minister, was among the women in South Africa; her husband was besieged at Mafeking. In her memoirs she wrote: 'Nobody in those free and spacious days objected to women who came out to see their husbands or brothers, but there were plenty of others, some of whom were even mischievous'.

A few of the more adventurous left Cape Town and went closer to the action. Among these was Winston Churchill's aunt Sarah Wilson, who managed to get herself captured by the Boers through a clumsy attempt at spying and later to join the besieged at Mafeking. Lady Edward Cecil, together with Lady Charles Bentinck, went to Bloemfontein when it was the headquarters of Lord Roberts's army. There were few women and thousands of men. Of their day of arrival Lady Edward Cecil wrote: 'Every man you ever heard of is in Bloemfontein and they nearly all came to see us that afternoon'. The ladies had a glorious time.

After a war, if officers stayed on as part of the occupation forces, many wives hastened to join them, however remote the location. Quite a number of those who went to Afghanistan in the 1840s found themselves prisoners of the Afghans when the fighting was resumed. Those who went to China following the Boxer Rebellion were more fortunate. Lionel Dunsterville complained that many of them demanded 'impossible things', but his own wife joined him there and in 1902 gave birth to a son in Tientsin.

Women of the upper classes were not mere sex objects or means for producing heirs. Although few were renowned for their intelligence, many were valued for something much more important as far as officers were concerned: influence. None ever possessed the influence of the Duke of York's mistress, who sold it to those who wanted commissions or promotions, but the words of some carried great weight. Students of Churchill's life are sometimes struck by the frequency with which he called on his mother to help him get on in his military career, but there was nothing unusual about this: young men often appealed with success to their mothers, aunts and female friends of the family. When young Dundonald (then Lord Cochrane) wanted to take part in the Gordon Relief Expedition, he called on Lord Wolseley, who was to command it, but received scant encouragement. He then tried Baroness Burdett-Coutts, a distant relative and a friend of the family. The baroness was one of the most remarkable women of the age: she was, for most of her life, the richest unmarried woman in England and a noted philanthropist. She knew everyone of importance and everyone knew her. Dundonald did take part in the campaign, and it was to her intercession that he credited his luck.

Women such as Lady Randolph Churchill and Baroness Burdett-Coutts were listened to and the favours they asked were, if possible, granted, but many others with less illustrious names, not so well known in London society, had less success. Wolseley, in South Africa following the Zulu War of 1879, wrote to his wife:

> In the mail just received I have a letter from a good lady, asking me to give a cousin of hers an appointment in some colonial corps here. He is at present captain in one of the regiments, has a pretty wife, etc. etc. and all the other requisites for the wished for position. Dear me, what curious people are in the world, to think I could, or would, give away appointments to men because they had married pretty girls without fortunes!

All generals were subjected to requests of this sort. Evelyn Wood, adjutant-general during the Anglo-Boer War, later wrote:

> Some of the requests made to me by importunate ladies were peculiar; one was angry with me because the War Office would not send out an establishment for curing . . . horses. Another lady said she did not want her son to go to war, because he was only twenty-one. A third wanted her son, who had just joined the army, transferred to a depôt and kept in England, or allowed to exchange to a regiment at home. I explained to her that if her craven request was granted, none of his associates would speak to him.

Except for the Guards (who were seldom in peacetime stationed outside Britain), all regiments spent time in one of the far-flung posts of the growing British Empire. In 1868, out of 110 regiments of the line, only 47 were at home. In the first 173 years of its existence, the Somerset Light Infantry spent 111 years outside England. The 3rd Battalion of the Rifle Brigade was in India from 1879 until 1905 – the longest stay of any battalion abroad in the Victorian–Edwardian era. Long separations were commonplace. William, son of Private James Reid of the 95th Foot (2nd Sherwood Foresters), was seven years old when in 1838 his mother drew a slip of paper that said 'not to go' and her husband sailed with his regiment to Ceylon. Somehow, William managed to accompany his father. Agnes Reid never saw either of them again. William Reid subsequently enlisted in the 95th, fought in the Crimean War and the Indian Mutiny, and rose to be regimental quarter-master with the honorary rank of captain. Noel Irwin was born in Mirpore in the state of Bihar, India, on Christmas Eve, 1892. When he was six years old he was sent to England to be educated, and he did not see his father until thirty years later, when, an officer in the 2nd Sussex, he met him in the dark at a wayside station in India. 'Is that you, Noel'? asked his father.

The moving of troops great distances around the world meant that most soldiers, their wives and children spent months of their lives on troopships. That living conditions on board were execrable, all agree. James Hope Grant, on board a troopship bound for China in 1841, wrote in his journal:

> No one can picture the indescribable misery of the women and children . . . owing to the high sea, the port below could not be opened. Dirty,

haggard, and wretchedly dressed, they looked like slaves let loose, and yet they had considered themselves fortunate in the miserable privilege of being included in the percentage of six women to every hundred men. Had they been left at home, they and their children would probably have been in a state of starvation. Of course numbers were excluded; and the very night we sailed, we discovered an unfortunate creature who, with her two children, had smuggled herself on board in concealment, hoping to escape detection among numbers until too late for return. She was, however, sent ashore.

Over the years, conditions did not improve significantly. Even officers complained. Lieutenant George P. Colley of The Queen's travelled from South Africa to China on a 'horrible old tub' in 1860 and said that 'in bad weather – or, indeed, unless it is very fine – we have to live entirely by lamplight, which in hot weather is most oppressive'. Subalterns were put in the hold with no fresh air, 'and in the Red Sea the heat in those lower regions was like nothing else on earth. Moreover, it was against naval and military discipline for subalterns to sleep elsewhere than in this inferno. One still remembers the awful and appalling headaches'. So wrote George Younghusband of his experience in a troopship in 1878.

For the other ranks and the women and children conditions were even worse. Ernest Swinton, a Royal Engineer subaltern in 1890, had to inspect the troop decks as orderly officer during a voyage to India:

> It was always hot and in rough weather the stench was appalling. It was bad enough to pay a short visit to the troop decks. To stay down there every night and all night must have been hell. I pitied the rank and file, but men were tough in those days.

In this same year Lieutenant Hubert Gough, 16th Lancers, also travelled to India on a troopship:

> The women on board had no privacy – all sleeping in a sort of long room or cabin in bunks in two tiers. . . . Many of the men slept in hammocks, as did some of us young officers, with no conveniences for washing or shaving. We kept what clothes we wanted for the voyage in our boxes under the hammock. . . .
>
> There were very few bathrooms, all of them on the upper deck, and these had to be shared by all the officers and their wives. To reach the

bathrooms we had to walk through two or three inches of very dirty water, as that deck – on which some horses were stalled – was also being swabbed down.

Gough notes, however, that in spite of the primitive living conditions, officers had to dress for dinner.

Before the opening of the Suez Canal, the voyage to India meant going around the Cape of Good Hope, and the ships always stopped at Simonstown or Cape Town. This would have been an opportunity for soldiers, wives and children to have a respite on shore, but in practice only the officers were allowed to disembark: fear of desertions made the authorities unwilling to permit anyone else to land.

William Butler described the drinking water served during a 124-day voyage to India as 'the colour of tea and with a taste that was nauseating. It had first rotted in the barrels, then fermented, and after it had gone through that cleansing process it was declared to be wholesome'. It is not surprising that many died of disease. The 2nd Battalion of the Black Watch once lost 121 men of 'fever and scurvy' on a voyage to India.

Soldiers were shipped either in troopships of the Royal Navy or in hired transports. Wolseley once called the former 'the acme of discomfort'; troops much preferred the hired transports as less uncomfortable and moreover free of the regulations of the Royal Navy. The voyage to and from India was made only during the 'trooping season', from October to March. If a man completed his years of service at the very end of the trooping season, he had to continue to serve in his battalion until the beginning of the next.

One of the peculiarities of life abroad a troopship was that familiar bugle calls carried different meanings from those on land. 'Retire' was sounded for men to turn out and clean the upper deck; 'charge' signalled permission to smoke; while 'commence firing' and 'cease firing' called respectively for manning the pumps and ceasing to man them.

The danger of shipwreck was all too common. In 1857 the troopship *Transit* (Soldiers called her *Chance It*) sailed from England for China, by way of the Cape of Good Hope. She encountered a heavy storm in the Bay of Biscay, sprang a leak, and had to be pumped constantly; later she broke her main mast, and finally foundered on a rock off the coast of Malaya. The surviving passengers lived for two days on a half ration of biscuit before they were rescued and carried to Singapore. From here

Military life on board a troopship, 1880 (*Photo: BBC Hulton Picture Library*)

Captain Frederick Stevenson wrote exultingly to his nephew, Rivers Wilson:

> I don't think I have ever been happier in my life than during the whole of our voyage out here. It has been one incessant flow of excitement the whole time.

The most famous marine disaster in British military history was the wreck of the *Birkenhead* in February 1852. When the troopship struck a rock off the coast of South Africa, there were 630 on board, including seven women and thirteen children, but only three lifeboats (two cutters and a gig). It was at once apparent that most must drown. The officers drew up their men on deck. The women and children (the youngest, three) were put into the boats. As they pulled away, the men stood still in their ranks as their officers explained that if they swam to the boats, they would swamp them; that the best course was simply to go down with the ship. And that is what they did. Even after the ship's captain called 'Every man for himself'! and disappeared over the side, the troops stood firm – and 438 drowned. All the women and children were saved.

No finer example could be found of the cool bravery, chivalry and discipline of the Victorian army. They were qualities which the British possessed at Waterloo and on the Somme – and at almost every engagement in between. Kipling wrote: 'to stand and be still to the Birkenhead drill is a damn tough bullet to chew'. Yes, indeed. It must not be forgotten that in this quixotic, eccentric, peculiar army these qualities existed to a very high degree and that these were the men who built the British Empire.

INDEX